GUIDANCE AND COUNSELLING

GUIDANCE AND COUNSELLING

PROF. RAMESH CHANDRA

KALPAZ PUBLICATIONS
DELHI-110052

GUIDANCE AND COUNSELLING
(Management counselling, education)

ISBN: 81-7835-143-9

Published in 2007 in India by
Kalpaz Publications
C-30, Satyawati Nagar
Delhi-110052
E-mail: kalpaz@hotmail.com

Laser Typesetting at: A.S. Printers
Printed at: Mehra Offset Printers, New Delhi

Contents

Preface

As the world changes and diversifies, the technology emerges at faster pace, concept and knowledge develop that greatly change society and counsellors. Global conditions such as constraints on individual freedom, overchoice, urbanisation and career markets, are already expressing beneficial and harmful effects. Awareness of these conditions is a must for the careful planning and growth of the ever-expanding field of Guidance and counselling. Well-organised guidance and counselling programmes have became a must in every fields of life to give proper guidance to people for the welfare of the society. The methods used for the programmes should be based on a thorough knowledge of the characteristics of the stages of human development and growth.

The chapters included in this volume of *Guidance and Counselling* complies, succinct and authoritative information in the field, which provides the readers a detailed understanding of the guidance and counselling and acquaint them with the various ways to make their living worthwhile. This book organised into seven chapters, each focusing on different fields of guidance and counselling such as educational guidance vocational guidance, career counselling and so on. The chapters on school counselling and collage counselling provides all the aspects of educational guidance, which helps the individual in utilising his efforts and arriving at wise decisions regarding his educational programmes. It is of great help to those who are engaged in guidance and counselling. Chapters on vocational guidance and career counselling helps the individual in selection of an occupation or vocational profession.

This book includes systematic formulation of theories and practices helping in the process of guidance and counselling. It provides an authoritative account of counselling psychology and will be beneficial to psychologists, psychoanalysts, professional counsellors and students.

Editor

1

Introduction

Competitive examinations for entry into institutions and services have become a normal phenomena in our country as elsewhere. Expert help is required by the students in making wise choices and be successful in competitive examinations. Expert assistance is also required for enabling the students in making proper adjustment in relation to general academic life at college or university to effect maximum intellectual, emotional and physical development.

Pre-admission guidance needs to be imparted to help the students make educational plans consistent with their abilities, interests and goals and to select appropriate courses and co-curricular activities which will enable them to join careers of their choice.

Post-admission guidance needs to be imparted to enable the students to succeed in their educational plans. They need to be guided for developing good study habits, prepare for examinations properly and face examinations with confidence. The students need to be guided in selecting subjects for specialisation and additional courses of studies. They also need to be made familiar with various fellowships, scholarships, competitive examinations, and so on so that their journey ahead becomes smooth and profitable. Special facility of guidance is needed at crisis points *e.g.*, student finds difficulty in following certain subjects; he lacks concentration; he gets poor grades; he is indecisive about a change of subject. He has to be guided as to how he could overcome these difficulties and what special efforts he has to make in that direction.

The students from backward classes need more attention so that they progress smoothly. Special efforts need to be made to help "first generation learners"—those students whose parents may never have gone to college or university may have many special academic problems because of the deficiencies in their own home—background and the inability of their parents to give them much guidance to do well in college and university. The student also needs to be helped in rejecting the attitude of blind acceptance of facts; instead he should be helped to develop an attitude of interrogation, dependence on evidence, and reasonable explanation of facts.

Efforts need to be made to ensure that his intellectual pursuits and interests which have so far been manifold become focalised, few but stable.

There are vocations as there are persons, and certainly all persons are not suitable for all vocations. Every vocation needs a certain educational and professional background and preparation and only those having them can succeed. Hence the need for guidance to the students for a right choice of a vocation.

Arrangements has to be made to assist the students to have a reasonable estimate of their abilities and limitations, strike a balance between their aspirations and those of their parents, between their interests and the availability of opportunities. They have to be assisted in making decisions and choices involved in planning a future and building a career. They have also to be helped in developing an integrated and adequate picture of themselves and of their role in the world of work. Occupational world is also changing very rapidly.

Fresh and new occupational outlets undreamt of before are emerging. Students are helped to acquire clearer perspective of the changes that are taking place in the job world. Thus, for efficient use of manpower and greater economy in the execution of work in industry, business and government offices and so on, guidance for vocations needs to be given to the students.

This guidance should be flexible—it should help the students to be able to respond to their changing needs as they grow more mature and as the circumstances and experiences of life pose unpredictable problems, requiring new information, fresh thinking, revised plans, compromise, and for the acceptance of socioeconomic conditions and personal limitations that cannot be changed. As such, the process of vocational guidance will consist of the following factors:

(a) Enabling the students to discover information about themselves—their abilities, interests, needs, ambitions, limitations and their causes;

(b) Providing them information about their environment, the advantages and disadvantages of different occupations and educational courses, the qualifications necessary for entry into them, and the range of opportunities available to them;

(c) Providing them with *a frame of reference* in which to see themselves in relation to these educational and vocational opportunities; to orient them to the helping agencies available to them, and to alert them to future decision-making points in their careers;

(d) Disabusing the minds of students of any romantic or vague notions about certain jobs;

(e) Providing *counselling* in order to promote self-understanding and to develop educational and occupational plans;

(f) Providing *placement service* to help them to implement those plans;

(g) Providing a follow-up *service* to help them, if necessary, when faced with future decision-making situations.

As the working life of an individual cannot be separated from his non-working life, the total life of an individual has to be taken into consideration, Our effort has to be on developing the individual's self-concept, his occupational self-concept and his extra-occupational self-concept.

The real intellectual life of a body of undergraduates, if there be any, manifests itself, not in the classroom, but in what they do and talk of, and set before themselves, as their favourite objects between classes and lectures. If that be so, responsibility of any college or university does not end with the syllabus and the teacher's performance. We must be keenly concerned with the nature of that day-long learning aside from books or lectures. We need to remember that the student spends only 5 or 6 hours of a 24 hour day in classes.

What goes on the rest of the time is the area of student services—the intellectual efforts outside of class, physical activities, social interaction, emotional experiences, cultural programmes and so on. There is hardly any doubt about this fact that avocational pursuits in which the students engage themselves are no less important in giving a direction to their lives.

This is all the more important as our college and university students get so many holidays—spring break, autumn break, long summer vacations, and so many scheduled and unscheduled holidays in between. Students in Arts subjects particularly have got much spare time.

How to ensure that vacant hours are profitably utilised is one of the problems which we have to face boldly. Avocational needs of the students need to be met before they grow to troublesome proportion rather than being left to drift on a sea of confusion, doubt, anxiety, aimlessness, get exploited by others, or indulge in destructive acts or in unwholesome activities.

The students need to be properly guided for effective participation in varied types of avocational pursuits so that they are able to shape their interpersonal behaviour in desirable direction and widen their outlook. It is common knowledge that hardly 10 per cent of our students take active part in co-curricular activities. Ninety per cent students are onlookers.

The participation of even the ten per cent is only at a superficial level. The counselling officer can ensure larger participation through sustained encouragement and manage through concerned personnel systematic coaching and training arrangements. There may be guidance and counselling arrangement for guiding the students to take part in team games, in intellectual contests, learning of productive hobbies, organisation of small interest groups having healthy aims, and so on.

Social

Most of the students come from a school which served a particular linguistic or socioeconomic group. Friendships had been formed casually and spontaneously. In a city college/university, student body is heterogeneous and drawn from, many linguistic and socioeconomic groups. It consists of adolescents who are self-conscious and tend to formalise their relationships; they seem to need a structured situation within which to socialise, be it the classroom or the college gymkhana, an extracurricular interest or a class picnic.

Some shy students find themselves friendless even after an entire term at college or university. Others do not know what to seek in a friend or try to develop a relationship with persons who have nothing in common. There are others who want to be effective as individuals in their groups. Very often, they have to work with people they dislike.

All such situations necessitate that students are guided to live as socially well-adjusted individuals. They need to be helped in making friends, improving their style of conversation and to know how to become leaders in their own groups. They can be guided in developing constructive expression of their emotions, an objective interpretation of situations. The students are helped in acquiring the feeling of security and being accepted by the group; in developing a social poise; in becoming tolerant towards the behaviour of others; in achieving individuality and freedom from the slavish imitation of the, adults or 'heroes'.

Health

Society has a special stake in the health and physical wellbeing of the college and university students who are or should be the elect of the rising generation and in whom it has to invest large resources and to whom it looks for the advancement of national interest. Total health of the student should be our goal; both the preventive and restorative measures are needed to ensure the achievement of the objective. The basic responsibility for the health programme must rest with the health officer in charge of student health centre. The physician should set a tone of acceptance for student problems.

This climate of acceptance is particularly important in the case of early detection of disorders, since students may be afraid to reveal symptoms like those of venereal diseases, tuberculosis, and so on. It will be desirable to have a medical check up of all the students in the beginning of the academic session and reports may be sent to the parents or guardians and a written report of the action taken may be insisted. For promoting preventive and environmental health, these measures may be adopted:

(i) Supervision of college/university facilities such as hostels and canteens to see that healthful conditions are maintained;
(ii) Specific protection through immunisation against diseases such as smallpox, typhoid, cholera and so on may be enforced; and
(iii) Health education through formal classes and informal propaganda may be started.

For early diagnosis and treatment of illness these measures may be taken up:

(i) An adequate physical examination of every student upon entrance to the college or university;
(ii) Follow-up treatment of detected disorders;
(iii) Reference of students to other medical resources when necessary; and

(iv) Maintenance of confidential files and health records to keep track of mind and body's harmonious functioning.

There are some disabled students; efforts have to be made for their rehabilitation in collaboration with psychologists, educators and social workers. Remedial measures have to be taken for students suffering from speech and hearing defects.

Moral

Students face so many awkward situations at home, college/university or in their peer groups. They find it difficult to get out of them. They tell lies; try to dodge and indulge in so many undesirable practices. Some guidance needs to be provided to such students to keep them on the track and lead noble lives.

Personal

Students face many personal problems related to themselves, their parents and family, their friends and teachers, their educational achievement and social adjustment. Some students are nostalgic which create feelings of disappointment in them. Their parents may be expecting too much of them which leaves them with a feeling of incompetence and insecurity when they fail to live up to their expectations. Many parents nag their children, thus creating an unfavourable atmosphere at home for studies.

At times, due to strained and unhappy home relationships, progress in study is hampered. There may be jealousy among siblings, domination of elders, maltreatment of children, lack of a sense of being wanted, lack of a sense of belongingness—all these disturb the mental equilibrium of the young students resulting in low achievement.

Expert guidance has to be provided to these students to face the situations boldly and with confidence. Students at times find difficulty in understanding the materials of the lectures; they may find the lectures lousy and the educational institution a dump; they may not be liking the teacher and his/her methods of teaching, thus landing in poor achievement.

Guidance needs to be provided to such students to enable them to adjust to the situation which they cannot change. Some students are obsessed with problems such as lack of friends; loneliness; feelings of inadequacy; inferiority etc. They feel a sense of chaos and despair around them. They need counsel to overcome their difficulties.

Students also at times see a danger to their self-concept. Help needs to be given to such students to emerge successful out of this crisis of identity, by perceiving more accurately their self with all its assets and liabilities and identification of this self with the more achievable goals.

Students at times find difficulty in concentration, learning and recall. They feel tense, anxious and depressed. They need to be guided to get relief from all these.

Some students also find adjustment to heterosexual relations difficult. They are not well-equipped regarding knowledge about sex. Parents generally do not make a good job of it. The lack of proper sex knowledge creates social and emotional conflicts. This is particularly so in co-educational colleges and universities.

Most of the students come from unisex schools and

colleges. They feel utterly confused in meeting the members of the opposite sex. Much effort is needed in making these adolescents understand the normal interaction with the opposite sex and casual acceptance of the sexual growth.

This information needs to be given to the students in a scientific manner, rather than treat it as a taboo and secretively learnt from undesirable places.

The students enter colleges and universities at an age when biological sex impulses are new and strong but the consummation of sex has to be delayed till one is able to earn and marry. Sex guidance has to be given to the students; they have to be educated regarding masturbation, nocturnal emissions, and so on, and the educational programme has to be so planned that sex urge of the students finds healthy outlets.

The youth need to be helped in clearing away some of the psychological underbrush which litters their pathways into the world.

Some students are hard-pressed for finances. They need to be guided regarding the freeships, fee concessions, scholarships, stipends and so on, available in the institution or offered by other welfare agencies and how and when to apply. The provision of financial assistance has to be ensured so that no meritorious student is denied education for lack of financial assistance.

In most educational institutions, the resident students form only 30 per cent or less of the students body. That means 70 per cent of the students are faced with problems of both boarding and lodging. Thus, off-campus -dwellers need to be assisted in obtaining proper accommodation and food services so that the search for these necessities does not interfere with the learning process. This is particularly necessary in the case of foreign students.

2

Theories of Counselling

In all our activities, people work from some model of the world, some understanding of How Things Are and how they interact. This working model guides our choices of what to do next, so the more accurate it is, the more effective our actions are likely to be. Most professional fields have a body of theory, the condensed wisdom of the ancestors, that guides the work, and the further exploration, of contemporary practitioners. This cumulative heritage of knowledge is what allows each profession to develop. Without it, each generation would have to start again from scratch.

Counseling - like all psychology - is a relatively new field. There are many ideas about how people thrive and about how things go wrong for people, and many models, competing paradigms, for how to work with people for their healing and growth. Each of these theories of human development generates a set of techniques, a way of working that is consistent with that particular perspective.

You will be happiest working from a theoretical base that is congruent with your own personal values and with your own personal talent and temperament. So, it's best to "shop around" a bit before settling. For a good overview, We used it twenty years ago in graduate school, and it's still in use in a new edition.

The process of developing your own comfortable style of counseling involves becoming familiar with several of these theories, and finding the one - or, far more likely, the synthesis of several - that fits you best. As you work through this exploration, you should, of course, also pay careful attention to what seems to work best with different sorts of clients or different sort of issues. The object of the exercise is to support their growth, not to amuse yourself.

Cognitive theories address themselves to the models that clients use in their daily lives. Does the client hold irrational beliefs, perhaps things s/he was taught as a small child, that lead to unrealistic expectations or maladaptive behavior? The goal of cognitive therapies is to make such beliefs conscious so the client may choose whether to change them.

Psychodynamic theories hold that we invest a tremendous amount of psychic energy defending ourselves against old, painful memories. Some people have so many traumatic memories, and such ugly ones, that little energy is left for living their lives well here and now. So the object of therapy is to make these old hurts conscious and work through the grieving process, thus freeing the client to get on with life. This approach is, of course, rooted in the work of Sigmund Freud. His basic insight is still important, despite his reductionism, his sexism, his obsession with early childhood sexuality and other serious limitations.

Archetypal theories hold that there are certain basic issues, or themes, or energy patterns with which all humans must eventually deal in the course of their growth. Different cultures, even different individuals, will express these in different ways, but the core issues remain the same. Archetypal therapists are generally the most comfortable with spiritual issues, and have written many useful books about mythology, divination, etc.

The intellectual father of archetypal therapy was Carl Jung. The leading contemporary proponent is James Hillman, author of Facing the Gods. More fine resources from this direction include Personal Mythology by David Feinstein and Stanley Krippner, Jung and Tarot by Sallie Nichols, or Working with Dreams by Montague Ullman and Nan Zimmerman.

Body theories postulate that old traumatic memories become stored or anchored in the body. So, sore spots or stiff spots that don't stem from some specific physical injury may in fact hold old tensions. Body therapists will often combine massage or other touch with talk, and will certainly guide their clients to tune in to posture, breathing patterns, etc. If you've ever calmed yourself by deliberately breathing slowly and deeply, you share the basic insight of bodywork. Wilhelm Reich was one of the early thinkers along these lines. Alexander Lowen is more contemporary. Another good resource is Focusing by Eugene Gendlin.

Watch out! Some conditions result from serious and correctable imbalances in brain chemistry. These are not counseling issues, but psychiatric ones. Bi-polar disorder, for example, is best managed with medication; traditional "talk" therapies do no good and may do harm. Conditions like these are beyond the scope even of professionally trained counselors. For a priest/ess doing ancillary pastoral counseling to tackle such situations is beyond irresponsible.

Behaviorism is another aspect of the North. This theory holds that meaningful change begins with changes in behavior, and is sustained by the different responses (the reinforcement) we receive from those around us when our behavior changes for the better. A slogan that well expresses behavioral therapy is "you don't think yourself into a new way of acting, you act yourself into a new way of thinking." The truth in behaviorism is that once a person has understood their situation and decided how they want to change, the way to change is to change. So behaviorism tells us a lot about how a person can maintain and extend a change for the better, but little about how they get ready to take that critical first step. The best known proponent of behaviorism is B.F. Skinner.

Center - choice - balance - integration

At Center we balance the functions, make our choices, and take responsibility for our own lives.

Rogerians believe that each person has within themselves the full capacity to make and implement appropriate choices about their own life. Counselors provide a safe and supportive environment in which people can work through their own issues; we don't do it for them. For me, this is just another expression of the Wiccan teaching that we will find what we seek within ourselves or nowhere. One good introduction is Rogers' book On Becoming a Person. The definitive classic is his Client-Centered Therapy.

Second are the many theories that describe each person as a nexus in a web of relationships: family, community, workplace and many others, obviously including our covens. A lot of the thinking about what it means to come from a dysfunctional family, for example, is rooted in such theories. This approach, in contemporary counseling, is rooted in the work of Alfred Adler. Another important writer about interpersonal therapy is Harry Stack Sullivan.

Deepening Your Understanding

Some of us are drawn, by talent and temperament, to the practice of counseling. If you find yourself spending increasing amounts of time this way, and it seems to you like counseling is going to be one of your major contributions to the Pagan community, you'll probably eventually want to take some classes or workshops to deepen your understanding and build your skills. Somewhere along the line, you'll also want to figure out what your own personal theory of counseling is, the model that works best for you and for those who seek your help. To that end, Dr. Richard E. Watts has suggested a practical and systematic approach for graduate students in counseling.

1. Explore your personal values and convictions about human beings and life in general. How are these values informed by the teachings of our religion? Do not be afraid to test your personal values and beliefs. Any value or belief worth having is one that can withstand close scrutiny.

2. Explore the major theories of counseling and psychotherapy. Choose the one that most closely

resembles your own personal values and beliefs. That's your first approximation, your base.

3. Study your chosen theory in depth. Read all you can by its founder and by those who have developed it further. Take any available workshops to get supervised practice with associated techniques. Identify what draws you to this theory, and why. Identify also your areas of disagreement, and the reasons for them. If you find that disagreement outweighs agreement, begin the process again from the beginning.
4. Apply what you've learned in your work with coveners and clients. Observe how well this approach works for you. If you feel uncomfortable or ineffective working this way, it might mean you need to study the theory and its applications more thoroughly. Or you might simply be discovering your limits, identifying those situations where this theory doesn't seem to work well for you. If, on balance, this way of working doesn't suit you after all, begin the process again from the beginning.
5. When you are feeling well grounded and comfortable working with your theory of choice, re-examine some of the other theories that you considered. Do they seem offer any technique that fit well with your chosen theoretical base? If you can explain these techniques in terms of the theory you are working from, try them and see how they work in practice.

Do any of these other theories offer any explanatory concepts that are philosophically consistent with your base theory, and perhaps cover situations in which your base theory seems weak to you? Do these concepts also blend well with your own personal values and beliefs and those of our religion? Be mindful of philosophical and theoretical consistency, and of consistency of theory and practice.

6. Keep learning about ways of understanding and working with people. Keep checking theory against your own lived experience. Keep cycling through these steps. Gradually, through them, you will discover your own personal working style.

The most important thing to remember is that it never stops. As your mind and heart stay open, you will keep learning from your experiences of working with people, in and out of the Craft. Others will be learning too, and publishing their own new insights and theories. You will be weighing each new contribution to the field against your own experiences and perceptions.

So, as the Gods grant us young and agile minds, our understanding of How Things Are and how they interact will never be set in concrete. A working model - a model that works - is one that is constantly being refined as our understanding grows. The dynamic interaction of theory and practice continues throughout our working lives.

The Counseling Workshop was first taught as a series of five weekly classes by Judy and Marjorie, later as a series of two-day retreats by Judy and/or Gwyneth. Really learning to counsel takes much more than just a weekend, but even in the short time available for our workshops, we can work on acquiring some of the basic counseling 'survival skills.' The Counseling Workshop continues to evolve—we invite you to let us know what we could do to improve it.

You will not become a counselor by reading these notes, or any other book. Real training in counseling is experiential, in-person and in-depth. On the other hand, most working priest/esses have learned a lot about counseling from the hard school of experience. Reading can help you put your experiences in context and integrate the skills and understandings you have developed through your work.

Opinions expressed here are solely those of the authors, and must not be construed as being the opinions, practices or precepts of any Tradition or organization. May these words and the manner of their sharing bring harm to none, good to many, and honor to the Ancient Gods.

A definition of counseling

Counseling is the art of helping basically healthy people work through the normal developmental issues, decisions, problems and even crises that come to all of us in life. Some examples: choosing a career, losing a parent, divorce. Sometimes it just helps to have somebody to talk to, somebody whose compassion we trust and whose wisdom we respect.

Clergy of all religions are often seen as such persons. People particularly turn to their clergy when they are working through religious issues. Since most Wiccans are actively working on their own spiritual development, and since our smaller "congregations" give us far better access to our clergy than the mainstream groups. So when secular issues come up, it's easy and natural to turn to the one who's been helpful in the past.

There are many philosophies and theories of counseling. Carl Rogers was an American counseling psychologist of the mid-twentieth century who advocated "client-centered" counseling. He believed that all of us have within ourselves the capacity to make and implement good decisions in our lives, and that the role of the counselor was simply to provide the client with a safe and supportive space in which to examine the pending issues and make decisions. To me, this is entirely compatible with the Lady's teaching us that we will find what we seek within ourselves or nowhere.

Counselors don't do what psychotherapists do, but they do more than what any sympathetic friend might do. Training and experience do make a difference. There are techniques for helping the client feel safe and supported. More important than filling in the few gaps is helping our working clergy and clergy-in-training to feel more confident in what they already know.

The central purpose of counseling is to facilitate wise choices and decisions. Counseling is initiated when the person faces a problem that s/he feels inadequate to handle without the assistance from a professional or helping person.

Counselors must have a genuine sincere interest in each client—as s/he is now. The client must feel received—make it clear that you are interested, you care, and that this person has your undivided attention. Turn on the answering machine. Turn off the phone. Make eye contact.

Make the client feel safe and respected—confident in you. There is no simple way for winning confidence. This is an ongoing process, by demonstrating that you can be trusted. Don't express your views as you would in conversation with a friend. Be mindful of transference.

We should always remember our limits: we cannot help everyone who comes to us. Some people need help from psychologists, surgeons or other clinicians—pastoral counseling is for them at best an adjunct to the help they really need, and at worst it may do them harm.

Common False Impressions about Counseling:

1) Objectivity - the assumption is that anyone is capable of total objectivity

   (impersonal, free of bias, free of judgement, not influenced by personal history or feelings)

2) Truth - assumption is that we can see truths about the other person that s/he can't see him/herself assumes we have abilities above and beyond those of others—more knowledge

3) Power to Change Others - assumption is that we can change others, that this is desirable—assumes we have the right to change others

The critical dimensions of counseling

Counseling is the process of helping a person who has come to you with a problem to sort out what's happening and how they feel about it, to look at their options, to choose a course of action that fits their values, resources and lifestyles (not yours), to implement their decisions, and to evaluate the practical and emotional results. Counseling is not about mental illness, except rare cases of emergency "first aid" and referral. It is about helping normal, functional people handle the usual problems, opportunities and choices that come up in any life. We do this primarily by providing them with a safe time and place in which to figure out their own situation, and secondarily by sharing our specialized knowledge and resources with them when asked.

There are five "critical dimensions" of counseling, developed by researchers in the field, and also described in other words by workshop members. We think of these as the five points of the counselor's pentacle. Here are some short definitions of the critical dimensions:

Empathy is our ability to perceive the client's feelings, and to demonstrate accurate perception to the client. When the client feels understood, a sense of trust ("rapport") and safety develop. As rapport grows, we may begin to perceive feelings of which the client is not yet conscious. By cautiously and tentatively communicating that perception, we may enable the client to understand and accept ("to own") more of his or her complexity of feelings ("additive empathy"). Additive empathy is not adding feelings the counselor might feel; it is adding conscious understanding of feelings the client is already feeling. The counselor's open acceptance of all feelings permits the client to own feelings that are not conventionally respectable. Knowing how one feels as fully as possible is essential for making proper decisions.

Warmth is also called "unconditional positive regard." It involves accepting and caring about the client as a person, regardless of any evaluation of her or his behaviors or thoughts. It is most often communicated through our non-verbal behavior.

Respect is our belief in the client's ability to make appropriate decisions and deal appropriately with his or her life situation, when given a safe and supportive environment in which to do so. Often, we show respect best by what we do not do, as when we avoid facile advice giving or cheap comfort. Our ability to sit in silence during a session while the client works out a solution is a manifestation of respect, and so is our willingness to provide information and resources for which the client has asked. A more familiar term might be "empowerment." By respectful behavior, the counselor demonstrates that s/he values the integrity of the client.

Congruence (or genuineness) is being honest and authentic in our dealings with our clients. The minimum it requires is that we only work with clients for whom we can have real empathy, warmth and respect, rather than role-playing or "techniquing" those qualities. It also involves know our limits in terms of skills, time and energy and not committing ourselves beyond those limits. Another important component of genuineness is to be aware of how engaging in counseling (or coven leadership) fills our own old and unmet needs and how our own emotional agendas from other times and places can color our reactions to our present relationships with clients and coven members.

Confidentiality normally means that anything discussed during a counseling session is held as absolutely private and not discussed elsewhere. This is essential to the client feeling safe in speaking about intimate and painful matters. Secular counselors have a legal duty to break confidentiality when there is danger that the client will harm self or others. Legally, religious counselors may be exempt from this requirement, especially in those states which have major Catholic political power.

Our religious tradition forbids revealing that anyone else is a Pagan or Witch, and normally requires that we avoid discussing whatever happens within a cast Circle with those who were not there. So, we would have a thealogical basis for invoking the absolute protection of religious confidentiality, but may not have the resources for the major test case that might follow. Beyond that, we may not in conscience want to stand back and allow harm to be done. Perhaps the Wiccan Rede mandates limited whistle-blowing? Although the basic question must remain with the individual priest/ess counselor's conscience, the counseling dimension of genuineness requires an open discussion with the client, before receiving their confidences, of the counselor's position regarding confidentiality.

The spirituality of counseling

Counselors help clients make and implement life decisions. There's always an emotional dimension to decision making. The better we can understand our own inner reactions, our memories, hopes, fears, dreams, the better "insight" we have, the better the decisions we can make. This interior realm is often called the person's "inscape." Empathy is intimate participation in the inscape of another.

The word "empathy" is actually a poor and misleading translation of the German word "einfuhlung." A more direct and correct translation would be "in feeling" or "feeling into something." So, empathy is not something we have, not just passive receptivity to the client's inscape, but something we do. Empathy is the active practice of feeling into the inscape of another. By the classic definition, this is an act of magic. The counseling session is another kind of set-apart time, devoted to the client, during which, by the client's permission, and by our own focused will, we change our consciousness. For that time, as best we can, we set aside our own inscape to enter theirs, hoping to help them explore it more fully.

Allowing another into our inscape is an act of great trust. Entering the inscape of another is an awesome privilege and responsibility. No one is ever perfectly "ready" for such deep contact. Still, if you are serving as a priest/ess, someday, somebody will nervously ask you if you have a few minutes to talk. Then, ready or not, you are acting as a counselor. The work itself will be your best teacher.

This is the Goddess' on-the-job training program: You do the best you can. You keep working on your own growth in insight. You stretch your skills, but do not go beyond them. You keep track of how your clients do, You find an elder to talk things over with. And, above all, you acknowledge your mistakes so you may learn from them.

When you sit with a client, the first challenge is to listen as openly as possible, without expectation or judgment. Always remember: this person is not you. No matter how similar they may seem, they came through a substantially different set of formative experiences. Race, class, gender, culture, region, specific family history, specific personal history, all have their influences. You will hear them better, and they will feel safer to speak, if you can set your theories aside and just listen.

You may be uncomfortable in the presence of grief, pain, anger or confusion. Bear with it. Don't rush to shut them up with slick answers or cheap comfort. That only cuts off their process. The client needs somebody to just be there, listen, and accept what they are saying. They haven't always had that. Being free to speak even the most hurtful things, feeling heard, understood and accepted, this is what it means to feel safe. All their experience, from earliest childhood to the way you respond to them today, builds or destroys that sense of safety.

Some of the client's message is verbal, some is non-verbal (tone of voice, facial expression, posture, and very much more). Some of the client's message is consciously chosen, some comes from their unconscious. You will receive some of it consciously, some of it subliminally. What you have received subliminally will also shape your reactions. If you really listen, and really care, you will inevitably have emotional responses to what you hear.

The second challenge is to listen as openly as possible to yourself. This will allow you to distinguish emotions you are picking up from the client, and likely sharing with them, from those that are entirely your own. For example, confronted with a very angry client, an empathic counselor would feel into the client's anger. But, if the counselor had previous painful experiences with anger, s/he might also be feeling some fear. It's important to be clear about where each feeling comes from.

So, the client shared as much as s/he could in this moment. Don't press or pry. The client knows how much s/he can face right now, and how safe s/he feels far better than you can. You opened yourself as far as you could, to both the verbal and the non-verbal parts of the message. Since non-verbal communication is often also unconsciously sent, you may be aware of some things that are still not consciously available the client. The third challenge is responding with acceptance and encouragement, so the client may feel safe to explore further.

Most often, you'll simply reflect back to the client what you have heard. This is called reflective, or passive, or "resonant" empathy,. A model commonly given to counseling students is "________, I hear you saying you are feeling _______ about ________." (Don't worry, you'll find more natural wordings.) Such easy and comforting responses belong in the early phases of the exploration, while the client is getting used to working with you, and possibly to the whole idea of exploring their inscape. You'll also use reflective responses whenever the client is assimilating some new inner discovery, or if you sense that the client is getting stressed or upset. Gentle pacing helps maintain the client's sense of safety, without which no real work can take place.

As the client becomes more comfortable with you and with the exploration process, you may occasionally want to use a more active form of empathy, sometimes called "additive" or "imaginative" empathy. In these responses, you will be describing your perceptions of the client's non-verbal communication. The model is "________, I hear you saying you are feeling _______ about ________. I am also sensing _____." Additive empathy does not mean adding to the client's feelings; it means adding to their conscious knowledge of feelings they were already having inside.

Always remember that you might be mistaken. You are still likely to be viewing their inscape through the lens of your own, and that might dull or distort the client's message. No one can perfectly distinguish perceptions from inferences from projections. Be sure to present any additive empathy responses very, very tentatively, If you insist that you know better about their life than they do, you will erode their sense of safety.

They may shut down. Worse yet, they may start telling you what you want to hear. Worst of all, especially if they have come to see their priest/ess as an authority figure, they might believe that you know better than they do about their own experiences, perceptions and feelings. If things deteriorate that far, their inscape becomes less accessible not only to you, but to them. Then you haven't just failed to help, you've actively done harm. Instead, realize that, for this work, you are a helper, not a leader. Make your suggestions, but let them control the process.

Please, as you do this, have reasonable expectations of yourself. It's important to understand that empathy is not an inborn talent but a trained skill. It's also an ideal, a model, a goal we work toward but never completely achieve. For one thing, our capacity varies with what's happening in our own lives. It's harder to open to the other when you are tired, scared, hurting. Also, even at our best moments, our own inscapes still shape and color our perceptions.

The practice of empathy, then, requires us to explore our own inscapes, develop our own insights, create the inner clarity that makes real listening possible, This deep self-exploration will bring us to our own hard, frightening, and painful moments. Sometimes we will recall ugly memories, or face, name and integrate the parts of our own hearts and minds that we were taught by example to reject. Neither is it easy to identify and take responsibility for our strengths.

Be careful not to push yourself too hard too fast. Be as gentle and respectful - and as thorough - with yourself as you would be with one of your coveners, Remember, this process is not altogether new to you, and you already have some good tools. Much of Wiccan practice supports self-exploration. Awareness meditation helps, as does journal work. And you may want to get some individual help from someone you trust who has preceded you on this Path.

Empathy is an intellectual, emotional, and, ultimately, a spiritual discipline. Like all others, it requires consistent and patient practice. Practice helps us to listen openly at the times when it isn't easy. Insight helps us distinguish our "stuff" from theirs. Be patient with yourself. Give yourself room and time to grow.

Spirituality is the fundamental part of all of our religious and philosophical systems. It is the core of Christianity, Judaism, Islam, Hinduism, Buddhism and all other religions. It is also at the core of every thought system that we as humans have ever created: modern physics, communism, atheism, humanitarianism, and all the others too! This is because we, as humans, all have the same basic needs and wants. Like it or not, we all wear trousers or skirts, and eat a meal or two (if we're really lucky) each day. So, spirituality is concerned with our deepest and most important desires for happiness, peace, and a bit of fun.

The spiritual part of our nature is subtle and ordinarily quite difficult to fully experience. It is usually so deep down inside of the heart that, most of the time, one can barely hear it. The many experiences and sensations of mind, body, and the external world also tend to drown it out. Thus, spiritual practice is all about learning to get in touch with our most precious part, our spiritual nature.Spirituality builds upon personal psychology and well-being. But it is not the same thing.

Spiritual Healing

Any technique that uses subtle energies for healing.
Such energies are only now starting to be recognised by western medicine. Most eastern medical systems have acknowledged and used such forces for hundreds to thousands of years. "Chi" and "prana" are two of the better known names for these energies. They are related to, and can be directed by, a person's consciousness. Because of this, one can receive such healing forces either in the presence of, or at a distance from, the healer being worked with.

Sometimes, if we are not completely swamped under, problems can indirectly bring about a deepening of our own wisdom and compassion for others. This can occur if we remember that life is a mixture of both good and bad circumstance, and that there are many others who have very similar—or worse—problems with just the same issues that we do. One thing that you can do is to offer up your own pain for the benefit of others. A good technique derived from Tibetan Buddhist practices is as follows:

1) Acknowledge the problem and your pain; open to being with it; you don't have to approve of pain, but to best handle it, you need to experience it fully so that you are in a position to let go of it.
2) Realize that pain—along with pleasure—is a fundamental aspect of this world that we live in: it's a package deal—they come together.

3) Understand that lots and lots of folks have it as bad, if not much worse, than you do with exactly the same problem.

4) Muster up a little (or as much as you can) empathy for all those other folks; wish that somehow you could help them too.

5) Develop the wish to take on their sufferings with this problem through a kind of transference. Imagine that your very real pain now somehow includes a portion (if even only a tiny one) of their sufferings and thereby relieves them of some of their pain.

6) Visualize that, as well as taking on some of their suffering, you also give them some of your happiness to help them as well. You can imagine their problems coming into your heart as thick black smoke, and your goodwill streaming out to them as pleasant white light.

7) You should feel that the black smoke also helps to utterly destroy your own confusion and unhealthy relationships with your problem. This should lead to a feeling of joy.

8) If you would like, you can coordinate this visualisation and imagination with your breath. Breathe in their problems and breathe out your happiness. Breathe naturally throughout.

9) Continue with this for a while until you feel a sense of completion.

It is a wonderful practice and can help balance out the personality. And don't worry, it won't bite! It may seem practically ludicrous to go asking for more trouble on top of all that one already has, but due to the interconnected nature of the world at physical and metaphysical levels, this practice helps to open the heart and can literally contribute to physical and emotional recovery.

Typically spiritual healing is used to shift subtle energy patterns that may be obstructing the healthy functioning of life in the ordinary world of mind, heart and body. Healing is usually directed to an individual but it can also be helpfully sent to practically any collection of beings or situations. In general the more specific the target for healing is, the more energy that is available to promote recovery and well-being.

Healing is not counselling! It can be used as an aid but most practitioners do not have access to sufficient power or good merit to literally shift the mental state of a client. The most practical approach for emotional and mental work is to supplement counselling with spiritual healing. The counselling helps slowly shift a person's thoughts and feelings, and the healing shifts energy patterns so that the overall change process is facilitated and quickened in a gentle way.

Methods that are commonly used for spiritual healing work include:

- Prayer
- Visualisation (understanding, caring, healing, protecting)
- Channelling of spiritual energy (for instance: qi, prana, reiki)
- Devices that transmit healing forces (for example: radionics)
- Channeling of Spiritual Helpers and Guides
- Personal spiritual realisation
- Advanced levels of concentration

- Psychic abilities
- Bodhicitta (Universal Compassion)

There are some very good sites on the Internet that will help you to find the resources that are appropriate for you. For prayer support and metaphysical healing some phrases to search on include: "absent healing", "distant healing", "psychic healing", "prayer", "healing prayer", "reiki", "spiritual healing", "alternative medicine" and "complementary medicine".

Spiritual Counselling

What is Spiritual Counselling?

Advice and support for a person to more fully experience her or his spiritual nature. This counselling usually only lightly touches upon areas that are normally dealt with in personal psychology (such as relations, self-image, self-worth, habits and behaviours). The major focus is upon aspects such as: faith, devotion, wisdom, compassion, spiritual techniques (eg. prayer and meditation), and spiritual experiences.

In general, counselling works best through respect. The person giving advice is at heart, really not that much different than the person asking for it! Only, the counsellor usually has had more experience about the topic being discussed. When that topic is spirituality, the aim is to empower a basically well-adjusted person to further his or her growth towards recognising and becoming part of the larger experience that we call life (or Life, depending on our way of thinking).

The Spiritual Path threads its way through our lives from beginning to end—whether we realise it or not. Because of this, it encompasses all levels of our gradually awakening consciousness. At first, spiritual issues revolve more around the personal level. But gradually we begin to address areas that become transpersonal and universal in scope. This is just the nature of the journey. The following link, Taking the Spiritual Path, provides some tips and ideas for working with the challenges that we occasionally encounter along our road to wholeness and well-being.

One way to ask a question or request counselling is through working with your own inner resources. Parts of your being "inside" are wise, capable and do believe in you fully and whole-heartedly. The guided colour meditation available on the following page, Counselling Meditation, will help you to honour this inner spirit and find a way to make space and quiet for it to share with you. You can actively meet with your inner heart and discover what all parts of your being have to share. Through this, both your whole and your hurt inner voices can have expression to cooperate and discover a fair solution for your entire self.

For spiritual guidance and support, some phrases to search on include: "spiritual counselling", "mental health", "spiritual teachers", "self-help", "psychotherapy", "humanistic", "transpersonal", "positive thinking", "psychosynthesis", "power of mind", "psychology" and "guidance". You will find there are many sites related to spiritual counselling, mental health, and guidance.

The polarity of counseling

Some say that magic is any process not yet sufficiently understood. Others - most of us - say that magic is the art of changing consciousness in accordance with will. By both of these definitions, counseling is magic. We don't completely understand how it works. What we do know is that it works best when the counselor can maintain certain attitudes while working with a client.

Empathy is the extraordinary ability and responsibility to explore the inscape of another person, to see their world through their eyes. Empathy is so contrary to the way most people usually think or act in this culture that we even had to make up a new word for it.

By contrast, warmth and respect are everyday words, used to mean something very close to their common-sense meanings. Warmth means acceptance of and caring about the client. Respect means believing and expecting that they can do what is needful to make their life work. These exist in dynamic tension with one another. Either can be overdone. Each balances and complements the other. Together, they form a polarity that can be described in metaphors that come right out of our own traditions: between mercy and severity, people change, heal and grow.

Warmth is caring about a person without any desire or attempt to own, judge or control them. It is prizing them exactly as they are here and now, even if they are "stuck" or seem to be deteriorating. That's why some of the older counseling literature refers to warmth as "unconditional positive regard." There are no conditions to warmth; warmth is not earned. In reality, most counselors and priest/esses are naturally warm, nurturers by instinct and nature, and drawn to work as helpers by our own strong inclinations.

We express warmth best when our non-verbal behavior shows focus on and concern about the client.

This is called "attending behavior." Although some of these techniques can be practiced and learned, it far more important just to let yourself be free and spontaneous in expressing your naturally warm feelings. Warm feelings are a pleasure both to give and to receive.

The paradox is that this open and unconditional acceptance is just what best creates a safe environment for the client's self exploration. So by not demanding or requiring that they grow, we allow them to grow at their own safe and comfortable pace.

Self-exploration is an inner activity, primarily about feelings. Feelings cannot be forced and should not be judged. All feelings are acceptable, even if they are unpleasant and uncomfortable. Only by facing these feelings, understanding and owning them, can the client know enough to make proper decisions about their own life.

Here's the catch: all feelings are acceptable, but not all behavior. Unconditional positive regard can sometimes give people the mistaken idea that what they do doesn't really matter. Behavior does matter. Some actions are harmful to ourselves, other people, or the Earth. Should we, as counselors, accept behavior that is manipulative, malicious, coercive, destructive? Sometimes we need to draw some lines, even if saying no is uncomfortable for us. Some other human behavior is particularly generous or creative or brave. We want to honor and reinforce such actions. If we treat people as though the way they act doesn't matter to us, we disempower those that are acting well while giving covert permission to those that are acting poorly.

Warmth is appropriately unconditional because it is primarily about feelings. Respect, in contrast, is about behavior. Setting and maintaining appropriate standards is respectful of the client's ability to do well: to make and implement wise decisions concerning their own life. Respect includes the faith that the client can, and should, learn, grow and overcome obstacles, even if they are not doing so right now.

This is even more obvious in our role as priest/ esses. The ethical limits that we set don't just help our coveners feel safer, they actually increase their safety. When we set goals and standards - even challenges - for a student, the achievement adds to their sense of personal competence. But - and this is hard for us - the only real test is one that is failable. When they don't quite make the mark, we will have to give them honest and specific feedback, which is stressful for both sides. If they persevere, the end result is their empowerment. People take more pride in passing a tough course than an easy one.

The practice of respect can demand self-restraint, holding ourselves back to give the client room to grow, instead of facile advice or cheap comfort. Sometimes we sit with them in silence, allowing them to work through a problem and develop a solution. Sometimes we back off to give them room to try their wings. Sometimes, as every parent whose child has learned to skate or ride a bicycle knows, a person's growth is facilitated by allowing them to take risks, and even to take the occasional fall. Respect is tough love.

So, warmth to support and nurture, respect to challenge. Held in balance within the mind and heart of the counselor, these create an important part of the necessary and sufficient conditions for growth.

Congruence: getting real about counseling

Carl Rogers taught us that the real heart of the counseling process is a special kind of relationship between counselor and client. This relationship is focused on the client's feelings and needs, while the counselor offers consistent empathy, warmth and respect. Given these "core conditions," people seem able to explore their inscape and their issues; not just the easy ones but those that go deep, perhaps hurt bad, and potentially release real change.

Now, fifty years later, the very latest research still shows no correlation between any particular therapeutic method or theory and successful results. What really counts, as always, is the relationship in which two people meet to engage on a deep level with the issues of one.

As Witches and as counselors, we know that spiritual, magical or psychological growth comes from the client, from the client's own motivation, courage, and wisdom. All of us have within ourselves the capacity to make and implement good decisions about our own lives, to grow. All a counselor, or priest/ess can do is offer conditions that support our use of this natural capacity for healing and growth.

These core conditions can't be faked or techniqued. They only work if they are real. So, the next critical counseling dimension is often called "congruence," a fancy word derived from the Latin congruere, meaning to meet together or to agree. Other writers simply call it "genuineness." We'd call it walking our talk.

Here's a bitter little joke:

Question: "Do you know how a New Ager says 'screw you'?"

Answer: "No. How?"

Punchline: place hand gently on their forearm, look deep into their eyes, make your voice soft and intense and say: "Trust me."

Although there are techniques you can use to let people know you are listening to them, no amount of "I statements" or eye contact or any other stereotyped patterns of words or gestures will convince people that you care if you don't really. No one can fake empathy, warmth or respect.

People who have had emotionally rough lives usually have excellent phoniness filters, filters that they may have been developing since early childhood. In dysfunctional and abusive situations, good phoniness filters are nothing less than a survival skill. They aren't going to open up, they shouldn't open up, unless their own gut is telling them that this space is safe, that this person is genuine.

We can't fake it, but as Witches, we can create it. We can generate within ourselves real (that is unfaked) and accurate (that is undistorted by our own projections) empathy, warmth and respect. We can shape our own consciousness in accordance with will—that's a classic definition of magic—but, like any other technology, this magic has limits.

These limits are different for different people. so it's important to understand and respect your own limits, whatever they are. Know, for example, how much training, experience and skill you have. Don't take on situations you can't handle with confidence. Know what situations may hit on your particular sore spots—if you come from an abusive, alcoholic household, you may not be able to work supportively with an alcoholic. Know how much time and energy you have, while still honoring all your other life commitments. Don't commit yourself to anything you can't realistically follow through on. Of course, all of this applies equally well to your coven work.

And, unfashionable and embarrassing though they may be, know your prejudices. If you have an irrational aversion to gay people, or fat people, or older people or any arbitrarily defined group of people, seek counseling of your own to help you work towards resolving this handicap. But until it is resolved, don't try to push yourself through it on your client's time. At best you are exploiting the client. Think about how many Witches you've heard complaining about having to spend the first several hours of therapy educating the therapist about Wicca—and, often as not, paying for the privilege of doing so. Worse, if it doesn't work, the client may sense your prejudice—and that may actually do them harm.

Another thing to watch for is to what extent you may be unconsciously using your role as a priest/ess or counselor to fill your own long-unmet needs or desires. A common example is the person who needs to feel needed, and so fosters dependency in client or covener instead of helping them grow toward autonomy.

Empathy, warmth and respect are the essential conditions of the counseling relationship. We can nurture these ways of being within ourselves, develop them over time, but we cannot fake them or force them. We might hurt ourselves or our clients if we try faking or forcing them. So it's best to be honest about our limits and only attempt to enter into counseling relationships where genuine empathy, warmth and respect are really possible.

Where theory and practice can meet together and agree, there is congruence.

Confidentiality: drawing the circle

Counseling is another "art of changing consciousness in accordance with will," like magic in many ways. Counselors help our clients change their consciousness and their lives by offering them a "safe space," a time set apart in which they can examine their lives and reconsider their choices. The change may begin with consciousness, but it never stops there. When consciousness changes, behavior changes, and different behavior calls forth different responses.

A coven Circle is another kind of safe space, of set-apart time, in which we can work toward many kinds of change: healing, and job magic, and closer conscious contact with the Ancient Ones. The style of the work may be very different, but both the goals and many of the underlying processes are much the same. Our work as counselors is consistent and mutually reinforcing with our work as priest/esses.

Willed change can come hard. Old hurts and old habits block the way. The work may involve facing painful memories, long buried. It may require the sacrifice of major components of the client's self image, and significant behavioral risk-taking. Those who experiment with themselves are vulnerable. They need privacy, especially in a community as small as ours. Pagans live in a fishbowl. Few would risk such deep self-exploration if their work seems likely to become common gossip. So a counseling session is like a cast Circle:

whatever is said or done within should normally not be discussed with anyone who was not present. Safe space is private space.

By tradition, Witches keep secrets. Our commitment to silence arose as a response to persecution, an effort to protect each other and our Craft from harm, an implementation of the Wiccan Rede. Confidentiality is still a survival issue in some places, and part of our community's social contract everywhere. We are trained to it, bone deep. And we are vowed to it, bound to keep our secrets by strong spells voluntarily and co-operatively worked between initiate and initiator.

Nothing in nature is so very pure. Although confidentiality is a way of life for us, we need to understand both the practical risks and the ethical limits. Sometimes life presents us with hard and tragic choices.

The risks are legal. We'd like to think that as priest/esses, as clergy, our communications with those who seek our aid are legally protected, "privileged" communication. We'd like to believe that our religious status safeguards us, at least, from the threat of jail. It's not that simple.

In 1994, the members of Iron Oak Coven in Florida faced a different freedom of religion issue. They fought and won their case - yes - but had to take a second mortgage on their house to pay their lawyer. What about those of us who have no house to mortgage? Our legal rights are only made real when we have the resources and the determination to defend them.

Beyond that, the legal right of any clergy to remain silent varies from state to state, and with the type of case. Many states, for example, mandate the reporting of child abuse. In 1984, also in Florida, a fundamentalist Christian minister, Rev. John Mellish, counseled a child abuser in his congregation. The man subsequently confessed, pled guilty, and still the court demanded the pastor's testimony. Pastor Mellish refused on principle, and went to jail for contempt of court, setting an honorable example for all clergy of all religions. Understand, where the law denies the privilege of confidential communication to all clergy, a Witch cannot claim religious discrimination.

Each of us needs to research what the law actually is where we live, in order to assess our risks and protect ourselves as best we can. No protection is perfect. Living by our values is not always comfortable or profitable or even safe, but it is the meaning of the word "religion."

The risks are legal and practical, but the limits are ethical. There are a very few, heartbreaking circumstances in which the Wiccan Rede itself, the heartspring of our religion, might require us to break silence.

The secular counseling profession has its own strong tradition of confidentiality. But professional counselors acknowledge clear limits to that confidentiality, and good reasons for those limits. Witches can learn from this example. In the early '70's, Tatiana Tarasoff was a student at the University of California. Another student, obsessed with thoughts of murdering her, sought help at the University counseling center. The counselor kept silence. Tatiana, unwarned, was later murdered. Her parents won a wrongful death suit. The California Supreme Court upheld the decision on appeal and so established a legal "duty to warn" in situations of serious danger to self or others.

Very rarely, a crisis may arise which is truly beyond our ability to handle within the community. At such times, secular law commands us to get whatever outside help is needed: a doctor, a fire-fighter, a cop. Silence then could leave us legally liable, but that alone is not a good enough reason to break oath.

Ground Rules

If you're acting as priest/ess of a coven or grove, teaching classes on Goddess spirituality, facilitating open rituals or workshops, whatever you may be doing to serve the Old Gods or Their people, you've probably already been doing some counseling.

Know your limits. Counseling is not psychotherapy

You'll feel better, and be more effective, if you acknowledge and honor the limits of your training and experience. Some people do have serious emotional impairments arising from terrible personal history or even from organic and physical malfunction. Their need for healing services is very real, sometimes tragically real. You'll want to help, but this is one case where "fake it till you make it" just doesn't do it. The very best thing you can do for them is to help find someone Pagan-friendly who is also thoroughly clinically trained. Pagan-friendly therapists aren't always easily found in all areas, sad but true. In cases of serious mental illness, clinical competence is the priority.

3

School Counselling

Secondary school counselling and guidance began in the early 1900s when its primary emphasis was on guidance activities that would help build better citizens. Frank Parsons influenced the early growth of the profession, although John Brewer really pushed for the establishment of secondary school guidance in the 1930s. Brewer believed that both guidance and education meant assisting young people in living. The growth of secondary school counselling was particularly dramatic during the 1960s.

Counsellor employment in this speciality more than tripled, from about 12,000 in 1958-1959 to more than 40,000 in 1969-1970. According to the Occupational Outlook Handbook, an estimated 63,000 people worked as public school counsellors during 1986, with a ratio of 3 to 1 in favour of secondary school counsellors over elementary school counsellors. Several thousand more counsellors worked in private schools. Furthermore, the number of employment opportunities for school counsellors began increasing in the late 1980s as many counsellors who had trained in the NDEA institutes began to retire and more states mandated better counselling services in the schools at all levels.

Counsellors in high school environments concentrate on the following four tasks:

— Organising and presenting classroom curricula that focus on developmental concerns of adolescents

— Organising and making available to students comprehensive information Systems necessary for educational and vocational planning and decision making

— Helping students assess their personal characteristics

— Providing remedial interventions for students needing special help

A real conflict exists for secondary school counsellors, who are faced with two needs: (1) engaging in student counselling and (2) doing academic and administrative tasks, such as scheduling, which school administrative personnel often require. School counsellors, especially on the high school level, frequently get bogged down in nonprofessional activities. Dysfunctional counsellors are frequently misunder-stood or misdirected be their principals, are poorly educated, lack a plan of action, are not engaged in public relations, and violate ethical standards.

To combat attempts to cast them into inappropriate roles, secondary school counsellors need to develop and publicise what they do and how they do it—not only to students but to teachers, principals and administrators as well. This task can be accomplished by "writing monthly newsletters, posting the counsellor's schedule, distributing the American School Counsellor Association (ASCA) role statement, developing a guidance service handbook, making presentations at faculty meetings" and pointing out to others the cost efficiency of allowing counsellors to do their jobs correctly.

Peer elicited the opinions of state directors of guidance and counselling and others in regard to views about the role of secondary school counsellor. He found mixed opinions. Those who held secondary school programs in highest regard were principals, superintendents, students, college and university personnel, other secondary school counsellors, and counsellor educators.

Teachers, parents community leaders, and business leaders were less positive. State directors overwhelmingly reported that secondary school counsellors are "probably" or "definitely" heavily involved in nonprofessional activities. If this is true, it is understandable why secondary school counsellors have come under heavy criticism from people outside the school environment. The Peer survey also discovered that secondary school counsellors are not seen as being actively involved in group counselling or group guidance, are not serving as consultants, and are not making an impact on the majority of students. Overall, programs at this level are not viewed as favourably as those in elementary schools in the same district.

On a positive note, however, respondents perceived secondary counsellors as avoiding disciplinarian roles, well qualified, and helpful to individual students, especially those bound for college. Significantly, respondents thought counsellors could affect changes in counselling programs.

Ways of improving the perception of the secondary school counsellor include an emphasis on roles that meet real needs. Jones, for instance, stresses that school counsellors must be facilitators of healthy learning environments. He thinks the primary functions of secondary school counsellors should include facilitating problem solving within the regular classroom, developing professional growth groups, and improving staff communications. All these roles give counsellors maximum exposure among groups who have traditionally held them in low esteem. By functioning as facilitators in student-adult interactions and adult-adult transactions, counsellors provide the means for a productive exchange between divergent and often isolated groups of people. An important function for any school counsellor is the constant remodelling of the counselling program. A systematic plan is crucial to this process. It includes not only implementation of services but evaluation of these activities as well. Some stress can be expected in setting up and restructuring guidance and counselling activities within the school, but a great, deal of satisfaction also results. Secondary school counsellors must be in constant touch with their constituents if they are to keep their services and roles appropriate and current.

The activities of secondary school counsellors can be divided into several areas. In addition to evaluating their own activities, they are involved in prevention, remediation and intervention, and cooperation and facilitation. These categories are not mutually exclusive, and there are a multitude of concerns under each heading.

Secondary school counsellors, like elementary and middle school counsellors, stress preventive services. Sprinthall notes that primary prevention is important in the secondary school because this approach creates classroom educative experiences that affect student's intellectual and personal development simultaneously.

Through a primary preventive approach, students become more self-reliant and less dominated by their peer group. They also become less egocentric, more attuned to principles as guidelines in making decisions, and more empathic. Relationships between teacher and counsellor and student and counsellor are enhanced in this positive process. Many of the common aims of school counselling can be addressed in the classroom through prevention-based curriculum offerings prepared by counsellors. Anxieties about school and tests, study skills, interpersonal relationships, self-control, and career planning may be dealt with in this way.

There are two major advantages to such an approach: less time needs to be devoted to remediation and intervention activities, and the counsellor maintains a positive high profile with teachers and students. Clark and Frith describe procedures for designing an effective counselling curriculum guide for meeting the needs of students from kindergarten through 12th grade.Three examples of problem areas where prevention can make a major difference are substance abuse, adolescent suicide, and prevention of HIV infection/AIDS. Programs for preventing substance abuse work best when they are started early in students' lives, based on social influence models, tailored to the age and stage of different student groups, and involve students, parents, teachers, and community, members in the planning process.

A specific effective model is "Here's Looking at You Two" where counsellors work with potentially susceptible at risk students in a multidimensional curriculum approach that is systematically evaluated. In general, multidimensional approaches increase self esteem, reduce negative peer influence, and provide drug information.

Student assistance programs (SAPs) set up by counsellors in schools are effective also. SAP teams are composed of school personnel from a variety of backgrounds and function in ways similar to multidisciplinary special education teams in schools.

Suicide prevention programs follow broad-based approaches that stress the seriousness of such action. Suicide is the fastest-growing cause of death among adolescents in American society.

There is a suicide attempt by an adolescent almost every minute, making approximately 500,000 attempts annually. Some ways to prevent suicides are to help students, parents, and school personnel become aware of its signs and alert counsellors and other mental health helpers to the professional and legal standards that deal with breaking confidentiality.

Involving school peers, families, and significant others in the community also vital. It is important that suicide prevention programs in schools be proactive rather than reactive as well as systematically designed. A common factor among suicidal youth is depression.

Therefore, preventive programs, such as support or psychoeducational groups, that deal with improving esteem and coping with loss are important. Likewise, individual identification of youth at risk is crucial.

When working to prevent HIV/AIDS, counsellors may or may not persuade students to change their sexual activity. But they can help them avoid contracting AIDS and other sexually transmitted diseases by employing both an informational and skills-based intervention system.

For instance, the school counsellor can make sure students know how HIV is spread and what behaviours, such as sharing intravenous needles and unprotected casual sex, put them into greatest danger.

In addition, counsellors can offer students opportunities for interpersonal skill building by simulating situations that are potentially hazardous.

They can also support teenagers who decide to try new and positive behaviours such as changing their habits or their environments. Support groups, workshops for parents and administrators, and peer education programs can also be used. Peer education is one of the strongest means of dissuading adolescents from engaging in destructive behaviours and helping them focus on productive action.

Secondary school counsellors initiate remediation and intervention programs to help students with specific problems that are not amenable to prevention techniques. Examples of such problems are depression, parental divorce, and teenage parenting.

Depression is related in adolescence to negative life stress. Forrest states that about 15 percent of all school children may be depressed because of external stressors and inadequate individual response abilities. He lists common emotional, physical, intellectual, and behavioural indicators of depression. Further, he emphasises the need for school counsellors to use a variety of approaches in dealing with the problem.

Among the most prominent include using Lazarus's multimodal model; teaching the student how to develop self-esteem; helping the student become aware of depression and the stress factors that influence it; and teaching relaxation procedures, new coping skills, and ways of modifying negative self-messages. All these approaches require a significant investment of time and energy.

Approximately one million children experience parental divorces each year. Cook and McBride point out that secondary school counsellors can help children, parents, and teachers adjust to divorce through both direct and indirect services. Interventions that directly address the problems of divorce are individual and group counselling services within the school for the children. Structured, short-term group work can make a positive impact in helping secondary school students sort out and resolve their feelings about the divorce experience. Cook and McBride also recommend that more indirect services be implemented, such as consulting with teachers and parents about the children's feelings.

Teachers and parents need information about what to expect from children of divorce and what useful interventions they might employ in the process of helping, such as reading and discussing books on the subject. Teenage parenting is filled with emotional issues for both society and teens, When parenting results from an out-of-wedlock pregnancy, feelings run high. The challenge for school counsellors is to develop out reach strategies for working with members of this population.

Cooperation and facilitation involve the counsellor in a variety of community and school activities beyond that of caregiver. Bradley emphasises that counsellors who are not aware of or involved in community and school groups are not as effective as they could otherwise be. Jones believes that part of a counsellor's responsibility is becoming involved with others. Thus, secondary school counsellors often have to take the initiative in working with teachers and other school personnel. By becoming more involved with teachers, administrators, and sponsors of extracurricular activities, counsellors integrate their views into the total life of schools and help create the kind of school environments that stimulate growth and learning.

In a very practical article on the role of the school counsellor as service coordinator, DeVoe and McClam stress the importance of counsellors' being accountable for performing three roles. The first role is information retriever. Here, the counsellor either collects information or works with other professionals to collect information about particularly complex situations, such as the abused and drug-dependent pregnant teenager. The second role is related to service coordination. The counsellor determines if he or she has the expertise to meet the needs of particular students.

If the counsellor does not have the expertise, an appropriate referral is made. The third role is information administrator. The counsellor coordinates a plan in which individuals or agencies in nonschool counselling settings deliver student services. This activity involves planning and implementing continuous communication among service providers. A less involved but important way in which counsellors can cooperate with others in the school and community is through participation in individualised education programs that is, educational programs tailored to the specialised needs of certain children.

Importance of Guidance to Pupils

The provision of diversified courses of instruction imposes on teachers and school administrators the additional responsibility of giving proper guidance to pupils in their choice of courses and careers. The secret of good education consists in enabling the student to realise what are his talents and aptitudes and in what manner and to what extent he can best develop them so as to achieve proper social adjustment and seek right types of employment. The subject of guidance has gained great importance in many countries in recent years particularly in America. In many schools well planned efforts are made to provide assistance to individual boys and girls in deciding upon their future careers and education, and other personal problems. In our country. unfortunately not even a beginning has been made in this direction, except in a few States.

Educational and vocational guidance is not to be regarded as a mechanical process whereby the advisers and teachers sort out boys and girls as a grading machine sorts out apples ! It is not a question of just deciding that one boy should stay on the farm, another work in an aeroplane factory, a third become a teacher and a fourth take to the management of a garage. Guidance involves the difficult art of helping boys and girls to plan their own future wisely in the full light of all the factors that can be mastered about themselves and about the world in which they are to live and work. Naturally therefore, it is not the work of a few specialists but rather a service in which the entire school staff must cooperate under the guidance of some person with special knowledge and skill in this particular field. Guidance in this sense is not confined to the vocational field only. It covers the whole gamut of youth problems and should be provided in an appropriate form at all stages of education through the co-operative endeavour of understanding parents, teachers, headmasters, principals and guidance officers.

Qualifications of a Guidance Officer

A good Guidance Officer possesses many good qualities. He must have an understanding of young people and their problems, based on scientific knowledge but inspired with sympathy and the ability to look at life through the eyes of boys and girls. He should have special training in good counselling methods, mental hygiene and in the discriminating use of tests and school records. In the field of vocational guidance he should have an accurate knowledge of occupational opportunities and requirements. He must have ample time for conferences with pupils, parents and employers, and he must be fully familiar with the purpose and programme of the school and have the capacity to work in close co-operation with the teachers.

In all schools a good deal of guidance work will have to be done by the teachers in the class through informal contacts with their students. They can play a very important role in this respect. The Guidance Officer will gather much useful information from them helping him to understand students and their needs and problems. Likewise, he will furnish them with information which would enable them to fit class work more carefully to students' aptitudes and needs.

There are certain important points to be borne in mind in connection with education and vocational guidance. Personal differences which are of a permanent psychological feature at this stage must be recognised, understood and given due attention. Accurate, comprehensive and continuous information about occupations and about institutions of higher study should be made available to the pupils, as without his information they cannot intelligently determine their future line of action.

Vocational and educational guidance should be made available to the individual pupils at different stages because of the possible changes in his economic status, his aptitudes and interests as well as the changes that are likely to occur in the nature of the occupation. Care should be taken to see that students do not decide upon a vocation too early or too huriedly, but only after a careful study of the openings available and in the light of experience gained through trials.

There should, therefore, be provision for a reconsideration of their plans at the different stages of education.

In some States we found that investigations in Guidance have been started and experimental laboratories established, both for purposes of research and to train guidance officers. In States where a beginning has been made there are Career Masters attached to schools who have received a certain amount of training to enable them to discharge their duties as vocational counsellors. We are aware that in some universities the Students' Information Bureau are trying to collect necessary information for the use of their students. There are also in most States Employment Exchanges which may give information to those seeking employment. This is, however, a different thing from what is needed at the schools stage.

In most of the States there has been no serious attempt so far to make a scientific study of the available careers or to bring home to the pupils the possibilities open to them at the different stages of their education. It is not a question here of finding employment, but of seeking the knowledge necessary to equip students adequately for suitable types of work. It is at this stage that vocational guidance is required and Career Masters can be of help in placing these pupils in their proper position or in giving advice to pupils in the choice of vocation suited to their training and aptitudes.

The development of new types of visual aids provides unlimited possibilities for the pupils to obtain knowledge of the different occupations open to them at different stages of their educational ladder Thus to broaden the pupils' understanding of the scope, nature and significance of the occupations or industries, films should be available which not only depict the actual nature and conditions of work in a particular industry but also supplement this with information concerning the daily routine of the worker on the job.

Vocational guidance films are available in different countries to bring home to the young student the different types of employment that are available as well as what is expected of the employee who chooses a particular vocation. We believe that in this country there is urgent need to prepare such educational films showing the conditions of industrial, agricultural, technical and other vocations which will give the students information as well as guidance in the choice of their vocation.

It is not to be expected that every student will necessarily accept what the teacher or the headmaster or the counsellor may advise him to do. In some cases the parents' influence may out-weigh his opinion or the student may have a higher opinion of his own talents than the more sober and objective view taken by the guidance officer. We feel, however, that if the system is tried with tact and sympathy and the co-operation of all persons concerned, it will develop, in course of time, into a valuable method of avoiding the present waste of talent, and it will fit the trained aptitudes of students into types of work which they can do efficiently and through which they can achieve at least a certain measure of self-fulfilment

Role of Government Agencies

In all progressive countries, Government aims at a wide dissemination of facts concerning various occupations and constantly seeks to establish suitable agencies and techniques which will enable every individual to find employment suited to his inclination, ability, and skill. There should be in every region in India a centre for the training of Guidance

Officers and Career Masters and their services should be made available, in an increasing measure, to all educational institutions so that guidance may be given to students at different levels of education, particularly at the Secondary stage at which decisions about employment have to be taken by a large majority of students.

Career Conference

Among the agencies for imparting information about occupations is the "Career Conference" of teachers, parents, students, employers and successful persons from different vocations. Such a conference can stimulate interest, give fuller knowledge of vocational requirements and encourage students to avail themselves of the service provided by the vocational and educational guidance staff. At this conference successful men and women from various walks of life can be invited to discuss the requirements and opportunities in their special fields of work. The pupils too, should participate in it so that their interest may be stimulated and their curiosity fully satisfied. Often they do not know the further facilities available in Technical Higher education or the conditions of admission and the nature and duration of these courses, or the level of efficiency that they must attain if they are to pursue them success-fully. It would be the business of the Guidance Officers to provide necessary information and advise about all of these matters.

The Centre's Responsibility

We have referred briefly to the need for guidance, the place of Career Masters in schools, and the responsibility of the headmasters and teachers in regard to the future of their pupils. If this scheme is to be implemented satisfactorily, we are of the opinion that the Centre should take the responsibility of opening in different regions, institutions for the training of Guidance Officers and Career Masters to which each State should depute its nominees. It would be neither possible nor economical for each State to set up its own training centres. It may be possible to attach some of these centres to teacher training institutions so that, besides providing necessary training for Guidance Officers and Career Masters, they may also train the teachers in the general principles of educational and vocational guidance. This will help them to understand better the methods of observation to ascertain the aptitudes of the pupils under their care, and thus enable them to co-operate with the Career Masters more intelligently in the common problem of adapting instruction to the pupils and preparing the pupils more successfully for their future vocations.

In addition to the training institutions for Guidance Officers that we have envisaged we recommend that a Central Research Organization may be established for carrying out research in educational and vocational guidance and for the preparation of tests with particular reference to Indian conditions and the needs of the pupils concerned and the opportunities available to them from time to time.

In order to fulfil all the purposes we have in view we also recommend that in every State there should be a Bureau of Vocational and Educational Guidance whose duty would be to plan and coordinate the activities recommended above.

1. Educational guidance should receive much greater attention on the part of the educational authorities.
2. In order to broaden the pupil's understanding of the

scope, nature and significance of various occupations of industries, films should be prepared to show the nature of the work in various industries and this should be supplemented by actual visits.

3. The services of trained Guidance Officers and Career Masters should be made available gradually and in an increasing measure to all educational institutions.
4. The Centre should take up the responsibility of opening in different regions centres, of training for Guidance Officers and Career Masters to which each State may send a number of teachers or other suitable persons for training.

Gudiance and Counselling in Elementary Schools

Counselling and guidance programmes in elementary school is a recent development. The development of this speciality was slow for three reasons. First, many people believed that elementary school teachers should serve as counsellors for their students because they worked with them, all day and were in an ideal position to identify specific problems. Second, counselling at the time was primarily concerned with vocational development, which is not a major focus of elementary school children. Finally, many people did not recognise a need for counselling on the elementary school level.

Psychologists and social workers were employed by, many secondary schools to diagnose emotional and learning problems in older children and offer advice in difficult family situation, but full-time counselling on this level was not considered.

In 1964, Congress passed the National Defence Education Act (NDEA) Title V-A, and counselling services were extended to include elementary school children.

Two years later, the joint Committee on the Elementary School Counsellor (a cooperative effort between the Association for Counsellor Education and Supervision [ACES] and ASCA) issued a report defining the roles and functions of the elementary school counsellor, which emphasised counselling, consultation, and coordination.

Government grants to establish training institutes for elementary school counsellors were authorised in 1968; and by 1972, more than 10,000 elementary school counsellors were employed. During the 1970s the number of counsellors entering the elementary school counselling speciality levelled off and then fell temporarily due to declining school enrollments and economic properties.

In the late 1980s, however, accrediting agencies and state departments of public instruction began mandating that schools provide counselling services on the elementary level; and there was a surge in demand for elementary school counsellors. Elementary school counsellors are a vanguard in the mental health movement. No other profession has ever been organised to work with individuals from a purely preventive and developmental perspective. ASCAs role statement for the practice of school counselling lists five functions of elementary school counsellors:

1) Provide in-service training for teachers in hope of preventing serious problems among young children or minimising the impact of such problems
2) Provide consultation for teachers to help them build a healthy classroom environment
3) Work with parents to promote understanding of childhood growth and development
4) Cooperate in identifying and referring children with developmental deficiencies or handicaps

5) Direct older children's awareness to the relationship between school and work.

The elementary school counsellor is charged with facilitating optimal development of the whole child. The task involves many preventive and proactive services, such as classroom guidance, group counselling, consultation, and special intervention strategies for at-risk children.

A study in California of the perceived, actual, and ideal roles of elementary school counsellors found that the majority of counsellors who were surveyed spent a large portion of their time in counselling, consultation, and parental-help activities. Their actual and ideal roles were nearly identical. Schmidt and Osborne found similar results in a study of North Carolina elementary school counsellors, whose top activities were counselling with individuals and groups and consultation with teachers.

Morse and Russell also found preferences involving consultation, counselling, and group work when they analysed roles of Pacific Northwest elementary school counsellors in K-5 settings. Three of the five highest-ranked actual roles of these counsellors involved consultation activities while two of the five included individual counselling with students. These counsellors ranked four of their top five ideal activities as those that involved working with groups of students. Indeed, it appears that elementary school counsellors desire to spend more time working with children in groups.

The lowest-ranked and most inappropriate tasks that other school personnel try to assign elementary school counsellors include substitute teaching, monitoring lunch-rooms or playgrounds, and acting as school disciplinarian or student-records clerk. The emphases that elementary school counsellors place on such non-counselling services have important consequences for them and the children and schools they serve. If counsellors are used in such ways, they lose their effectiveness.

Elementary school counsellors engage in a number of preventive and remedial activities. Prevention is considered the preferred method because of its psychological pay-off in time invested and results.

Elementary school counselling programs strive to create a positive school environment for students. They emphasise the four Cs: counselling services, coordination of activities, consultation with others, and curriculum development. This last activity, which is both developmental and educational, focuses on formulating guidance classes on life skills and in preventing difficulties that might otherwise occur.

A first priority for elementary school counsellors is making themselves known as counsellors. School personnel are not usually viewed by young children as the first source of help.

Therefore, elementary school counsellors need to publicise who they are, what they do, and how and when they can help. This process is usually handled best through orientation programs for all children in the school, classroom visits, or both. The important point is to let children know that counselling and guidance services are a vital part of the total school environment. The sooner in the school year this is done, the better.

An increased concern and growth area among elementary school counsellors is preschool counselling dealing with 3 to 5 year-old children and their families. Many children in this age range face a multitude of detrimental conditions including poverty, family/

community violence, and neglect. In situations where very young children are part of the school environment, elementary school counsellors can offer special assistance by monitoring developmental aspects of children's lives and serve as advocates for them.

Counsellors can make sure that children's experiences enhance socialisation skills and positive self-concept rather than reflect diluted, cognitively focused, first-grade curriculums. This effort includes offering prosocial classroom guidance lessons in groups.

Furthermore, elementary school counsellors can consult with parents, teachers, and other mental health professionals to be sure that efforts at helping young children are maximised. It is especially important to work with parents and communities when children are at risk for developing either low self-concepts or antisocial attitudes.

Ways of combating potential destructiveness include helping parents become more aware of

(1) the developmental stages their children may go through and

(2) school resources, including the person of the counsellor, that are available to them.

There are also educational exercises and games that parents and community leaders can use in building up children's self-esteem and helping them develop healthy social attitudes. For instance, the National Organisation of Student Assistance Programs and Partners (NOSAPP) has produced a kit, Caring Connections, that is filled with activities for school professionals and youth leaders to help children from troubled homes.

After publicising their services, elementary school counsellors become active in classroom guidance. Myrick recommends a proactive, developmental, comprehensive approach to guidance programs: two to three large classroom meetings each week and twice as many small group sessions. These activities focus on structured learning activities, such as understanding oneself, decision making, problem solving, establishing healthy girt-boy relations, and learning how to get along with teachers and how to make friends.

Other preventive services include setting up peer counsellor programs and consultation/education activities. Peer counsellors are specially selected and trained students who serve the school and the counsellor in positive and unique ways. They may help students get to know one another, create an atmosphere of sharing and acceptance, or provide opportunities for other students to resolve personal difficulties by acting as counsellor assistants. In these ways, peer counsellors help elementary school guidance counsellors reach a number of individuals they might otherwise miss. They also enhance the overall cooperative atmosphere and problem-solving skills of the students.

By implementing consultation/education sessions for teachers, administrators and parents, counsellors address common concerns and teach new ways of handling old problems by getting many people committed to working in a cooperative manner. Promoting communication skills is crucial in this situation.

Parenting skills, on an individualised level, that emphasise effective communication procedures and behaviour management training are especially valuable. Skilled elementary school counsellors can even use their counselling role in preventive way by meeting regularly in individual sessions with at-risk children (those most likely to develop problems because of their backgrounds or present behaviours). Thus, counsellors can assess how well these children are functioning and what interventions, if any, might be helpful to them or significant for others. Preventive services are also necessary for gifted and talented students Although this subgroup of students may appear to function well, in reality individuals may have a number of concerns, such as underachieving, overextending, and handling stress.

In elementary school counselling, a number of activities come under the remediation heading. Among them are individual counselling, group counselling, and environmental changes and modifications. One way of determining what needs to be done is to use a needs assessment. Needs assessments are structured surveys that focus on the systematic appraisal of the types, depths, and scope of problems in a particular population. Needs assessments may be purchased commercially, borrowed and modified from others, or originated by an institutions's staff.

In school settings, counsellors can gain a great deal of useful information if they regularly take the time to survey students, teachers, parents, and support personnel. This knowledge helps them address specific problems in both a preventive and remedial way.

Typically, concerns uncovered through needs assessments fall into four main areas: school, family relations, relationships with others, and the self. Young children often respond best to counselling strategies built around techniques that require active participation. Play therapy and bibliotherapy are two strategic interventions that help counsellors establish rapport with young children and facilitate their self-understanding.

Play therapy is a specialised way of working with children that requires skill and training. It is covered more and more frequently in counsellor education programs.

Basically, children express emotions bymanipulating play media such as toys. When counsellors participate with children in the play process—that is,communication through acknowledgment of children'sthoughts and feelings—they establish rapport and a helping relationship. By expressing their feelings in a natural way, children are more able to recognise and constructively deal with volatile affect.

A number of approaches can be used in play therapy, but Jungian and person-centered are two of the most popular. When conducting play sessions with children, it is ideal to have a well-equipped playroom. But most schools do not have one, so counsellors usually need a tote bag in which to store their materials.

Play materials usually fall into one of three broad categories: real-life toys, acting out or aggressive toys, and toys for creative expression or release. Items frequently include puppets, masks, drawing materials, and clay. Sand play has been effective in working with children who have low esteem, poor academic progress, high anxiety, and mild depression. In some situations, counsellors may work with parents to continue play therapy sessions at home while in other cases counsellors may hold counselling sessions for students who are involved in play therapy.

A two-tiered developmental guidance approach has been recommended for working with children and the topic of divorce. In the first part of the model, the topic is handled through classroom guidance classes. The classes are general in focus but informationally humane in intent and are aimed at alleviating much of the negative stereotyping and myths that surround divorce.

The second half of the approach is more personalised and uses small groups to concentrate on specific children's needs. The counsellor focuses on dealing with the particular difficulties of children within the school. Groups for children experiencing divorce have been found effective in reducing dysfunctional behaviours, especially if both the custodial and noncustodial parents can be involved in this special service.

Children's self-esteem is related to self-concept (how individuals "perceive themselves in a variety of areas—academically, physically, socially, and so forth". Self-esteem results from the comparison of oneself to others in a peer group. To enhance self-esteem, counsellors need to focus on helping at-risk children improve in the following areas: critical school academic competencies, self-concept, communication skills, coping ability, and control. McWhirter *et al.* calls these the "Five Cs of Competency".

Counsellors can enhance self-esteem by having children look at themselves through the eyes of a special person. In this treatment modality, children pretend to be artists, drawing special people in their lives who love them. After the drawings are complete, the children pretend to be the special person whom they have drawn, thus seeing themselves through loving eyes. Through their drawings, children improve their self-concept, self-confidence, and social and academic possibilities.

When faced with children who have suffered abuse, elementary school counsellors work both preventively and remedially by using a bibliotherapeutic approach. Hollander suggests a number of books that can be used therapeutically with children who have been sexually abused, even at a preschool age.

Middle School Counselling and Guidance

Middle school counselling and guidance came into prominence in the 1970s as a hybrid way to offer services for students who did not fit the emphases given by either elementary school or high school counsellors. The idea of a special curriculum and environment for preadolescents and early adolescents was first implemented as a junior high concept: an attempt to group younger adolescents from older adolescents. Middle schools typically enroll children between the ages of 10 and 14 and encompass grades 6 through 9. Children at this age and grade level are often referred to as transescents or bubblegummers. In addition to experiencing the normal problems that exist in the family, school, and community, middle school boys and girls adjust to changes in the body, pressure from peers, demands by the school for excellence, conflicting attitudes of parents, and other problems with establishing self-identity.

There is little homogeneity about them and their most common characteristic is unlikeness. According to Dougherty, we know less about this age group than any other. Part of the reason is that very few middle school counsellors conduct research or publish their findings about this population. Yet the Gesell Institute of Child Development offers a description of cognitive, physical, and emotional factors that can be expected during this time. Too few counsellors avail themselves of this data. On a general level, however, most middle school counsellors are aware of the major physical, intellectual, and social developmental tasks that middle school children must accomplish. Thornburg outlines them:

1) Becoming aware of increased physical changes.
2) Organising knowledge and concepts into problem-solving strategies.

3) Making the transition from concrete to abstract symbols.
4) Learning new social and sex roles.
5) Identifying with stereotypical role models.
6) Developing friendships.
7) Gaining a sense of independence.
8) Developing a sense of responsibility.

Middle graders also must deal successfully with three basic stress situations. A Type A stress situation is one that is foreseeable and avoidable, such as not walking in a dangerous area at night. A Type B situation is neither foreseeable nor avoidable, such as an unexpected death. A type C situation is foreseeable but not avoidable, such as going to the dentist. Middle school children tend to experience more anxiety than either elementary or high school students. Therefore, they are at risk for not achieving or successfully resolving developmental tasks.

Thus, middle school counsellors can be most helpful in their approach to stressful situations because they can provide opportunities for children to experience themselves and their world in different and creative ways. They can foster a sense of identity with personal uniqueness and universality with common concerns.

Middle school counselling and guidance, like elementary school counselling and guidance, seeks to correct this imbalance by focusing on the child's total development. The emphasis is holistic: counsellors stress not only growth and development but also the process of transition involved in leaving childhood and entering adolescence. Their role responsibilities include the following:

— Smoothing the transitional process from the more

confining environment of the elementary school to the more open environment of the middle school.

— Identifying and working with teachers to incorporate developmental units into the curriculum.

— Organising and implementing a career guidance program.

These roles may be fulfilled more easily if counsellors develop capacities and programs in certain ways. The necessary capacities, according to Thornburg, include general information about developmental characteristics of middle schoolers and specific tasks students are expected to achieve.

In addition, counsellors must understand the specific child with whom they are interacting and his or her perspective on a problem. Finally, counsellors need to know how to help students make decisions so that students can help themselves in the future. The ideal role of middle school counsellors also includes providing individual counselling, group expe-riences, peer support systems, teacher consultation, student assessment, parent consultation, and evaluation of guidance services.

In a survey of Kansas principals and counsellors. Bonebrake and Borgers found that participants not only agreed on the ideal role of the middle school counsellor but also agreed on a counsellor's lowest priorities: serving as principal, supervising lunchroom discipline, and teaching nonguidance classes. This survey is encouraging because it shows the close agreement between principals and counsellors concerning ideal roles. After all, principals usually determine the role and function of counsellors within the school.

Yet outside the school, various groups have different perceptions and priorities about the purpose of middle school counsellors. To ease the tension that may arise from such evaluations, Bonebrake and Borgers recommend that counsellors document their functions and run "a visible, well-defined, and carefully evaluated program".

Middle school counsellors also need to be in constant communication with their various publics about what they do and when. Publicity as well as delivery of services is as crucial at this level as it is in elementary schools.

Working with middle school children requires both a preventive and a remedial approach. It is similar to dealing with elementary school children except that counsellors must penetrate more barriers if they are to be truly helpful in a holistic way. One of the most promising prevention programs for middle schoolers is the Succeeding in School approach. Composed of 50 minute classroom guidance units, this program is geared toward helping children become comfortable with themselves, their teachers, and their schools.

The approach is multimodal and asks children to participate actively in the learning process. Each lesson plan focuses in on a prosocial aspect of personal and institutional living, such as identifying with successful people, being comfortable in school, cooperating with peers and teachers, and recognising the bright side of life events. A complement to the Succeeding in School program is Morganett's group counselling activities for young adolescents.

These activities develop skills for living. Because her exercises for small groups can be used in various ways, middle school counsellors have flexibility in helping students deal with sensitive areas such as anger, grief, stress, divorce, assertiveness, and friendship.

Middle school counsellors can also use individual counselling, peer counselling, and consultation activities to foster problem prevention. All counsellors at the middle school level are constantly challenged to be creative in devising preventive materials for their students.

One of the best ways to work remedially with middle school students is to combine it with a preventive approach. According to Stamm and Nissman the activities of middle school counsellors are best viewed as services that revolve around "a Human Development Center (HDC) that deals with sensitive human beings". They recommend developing a rapport with these persons and coordinating middle school counselling and guidance services with others to provide the most productive program possible.

Stamm and Nissman outline eight service areas that they believe are vital to a comprehensive middle school counselling and guidance program. Each service cluster is linked with the others. But middle school counsellors cannot perform all the recommended functions alone, so they must delegate responsibility and solicit the help of other school personnel, parents, and community volunteers. A counsellor's job, then, entails coordinating service activities as well as delivering direct services when able.

The communication service cluster is primarily concerned with public relations. It is the counsellor's out reach arm and is critical for informing the general public about what the school counselling program is doing. Curriculum services, on the other hand, concentrate on facilitating course placements and academic adjustment.

Middle school counsellors need to help teachers

"psychologise" the curriculum so that students can deal with significant issues in their lives, such as peer relationships and values. If the curriculum is not relevant to children at this age, they often divert their energy to nonproductive activities. The assessment service cluster provides testing and evaluation services and is often linked to the career resource cluster, which focuses on the student's future goals and vocation.

The counselling services cluster and the crisis service cluster are also closely connected. Counselling services are provided on an individual, peer, and group level and are offered during off-school and in-school hours. Sometimes counselling activities are aimed at self-counselling, which is when people (including middle graders) think the ideas that they believe, then react to those ideas with logical emotional reactions and logical physical behaviours. Rational self-counselling is one research-based way to help students help themselves deal effectively with their emotions. At other times, peer facilitators help middle schoolers make friends and learn about their environments and schoolwork. There is also someone designated in the Stamm and Nissman model as a crisis person during the school day. This individual deals with emergencies and, with the help of the counsellor, finds an appropriate way to assist the child who is experiencing sudden distress.

The community contact cluster focuses on working with parents and other interested people to open the lines of communication between the school and other agencies. The professional growth cluster provides programs for school staff and paraprofessionals. This last task is critical to the counsellor's success. If the total school environment is to be positively affected, middle school counsellors must help teachers develop skills related to enhancing the students' self-concept and self-esteem.

4

Importance of Vocational Guidance

Vocational guidance is the assistance rendered by an individual to another in the latter's solving of problems related to his progress and vocational selection keeping in mind the individual's peculiarities or special abilities and their relations with his occupational opportunity.

Objectives

The following are the objectives of vocational guidance:

— To assist students to acquire knowledge of the characteristics, functions, duty requirements of occupations in which they are interested.

— To enable students to get relevant information about abilities and skills in terms of related qualifications and competencies required to take up the identified occupation.

— To enable students to understand their potentials and interest in relation to identified occupation or a group of occupations which they may take up.

— To assist students in developing abilities to analyse occupational information and make suitable choice by using appropriate career information effectively.

— To assist students in getting information about various post-educational and training facilities and apprenticeship schemes.

— To enable students to choose the right type of jobs.

— To develop entrepreneurship qualities in students for taking up self employment.

There has been a phenomenal growth of industries during recent times. Rapid industrialisation implies a higher man power requirement.

While industries both in the public, organised and unorganised sectors are concerned about recruiting the "right type of personnel" to carry out a variety of challenging and productive job, every student is bothered about getting the right job after successful completion of his education. The selection of the right person for the right job is a key factor in the technological progress of a country. Students desire to earn their livelihood after the successful completion of their education. They consciously work towards this.

For this purpose, they need to get adequate information about the job opportunities, job availability in the area of their study. Assistance provided in getting such information can be expected to go a long way in enabling students to enter the world of work. Students after completion of their study face many problems in the choice of an appropriate career due to inadequate information about career growth and development opportunities, suitability of the job to match their interest, aptitude, vocational preparation etc. With the limited information available through, newspapers and employment advertisements, some students may be fortunate enough to get a job while others may not. This results in frustration in those who do not get some suitable placement.

A person's performance for a vocation is influenced by the aspirations and choice of their parents. This may result in an unsatisfactory placement of the student. However it is important to note that the vocational choice should be decided more on the individual's ability, interest, aptitude, rather than on parental aspirations alone. Some individuals are often found to be dissatisfied in the work they are doing and are not properly adjusted to the work environment leading to frustration, state of stress, diminished productivity etc.

An unfavourable attitude of any individual is not conducive for the work culture in any organisation. Efforts must consciously be made by educational institutions to work towards developing a positive attitude towards work in their students. If this can be done in the institution, it can be expected that there would be a transfer of this in the work situation. The success or failure of a person in a vocation depends upon, many other factors, satisfaction one derives from the vocation. Satisfaction results from working in harmony with one's own potentialities, strengths, weaknesses etc.

Lack of an awareness of the self with regard to confidence, perception of reality, self-esteem, interest, personality etc., often leads to the setting up of unrealistic and unachievable goals to work. This in turn may lead to frustration in the work situation. An organised vocational guidance programme in the institution may be of great help to meet these problems. Through this programme students get necessary information about different careers. The world of work remains no more unfamiliar to them. Students get all sorts of information needed for a particular career or a group of careers in the vocational guidance programmes. Improper selection of courses of study , in the institution, inadequate information about job prospects, lack of knowledge of job training, unfavourable attitude towards work, mismatch of interests, aspirations to the job obtained are some of the factors which contribute to vocational problems.

Vocational guidance services offered on the basis of a proper understanding of the potentialities of the students in terms of their aspirations, acquired knowledge and skills in relation to the nature of the job can be expected to be of immense assistance to students in the choice of their careers.

Nature of Vocational guidance

It is known that students have individual differences in relation to their vocational choices. The nature of vocations are different from one another in terms of the nature of work, outputs, growth potentialities etc. Whenever any attempt is made to place a person in a job not suited for him, the result will be disastrous both to the individual and the job. In deliberately organising vocational guidance programmes, teachers must be careful enough to consider data about the students. The data may include the training obtained (knowledge and skills acquired) level of intelligence, special abilities, interests, aptitude, personal health details, personality details, economic status etc. Information regarding these and other relevant aspects must be collected objectively using suitable methods.

In the process of vocational guidance the individual is assisted to understand his abilities and limitations and accept them. Once he is aware of his potentialities, he is helped to make use of the available opportunities. For the effectiveness of vocational guidance, the students' goals, needs and interests are also taken into account. A well organised system of vocational information readily available to students and a set up which encourages students and trains them to find out the available information about careers form the basis for the choice of vocational guidance strategies.

Students may face many difficulties in the choice of vocation, vocational persuasion and vocational adjustment. This often leads to several ills such as students not getting proper jobs, encountering difficulties in getting on well with the job, etc. This implies that students should discover their capabilities. They must relate the information they acquire about their career to their own capabilities.

Vocational guidance strategies should be based on the following principles:

— Occupation is to be looked at as a source of income to people and a major source of satisfying needs and optimising aptitudes, competencies and interests.
— The individual needs to understand the total perspective of a vocation for which he has decided to prepare himself.
— The selection of a particular vocation is not confined to a single, fixed decision but a time extending process, involving a series of social and personal factors.
— Vocational guidance services should be based on the principle of individual differences.
— Different strategies need to be used to cater to the individual vocational needs of students.
— Vocational guidance service must fulfil the vocational needs of every student.

Vocational guidance can be given to an individual as well as to a group. When an individual faces any vocational problem like selection of a vocation, adjustment in vocation etc., individual guidance is given to him. On the other hand, if a similar vocational problem is faced by a group, a group guidance programme can be organised.

Group guidance in vocational area can not only be organised in problem cases but also, to prepare individuals for vocation. Various approaches are followed in organising vocational guidance. These include, career corner, career talk, career conference, industrial visit, simulated interview and vocational counselling.

Career corner

Career corner is a display place for imparting vocational information. A talk by a professional on various aspects of an occupation or a group of related occupations is career talk. A panel of speakers invited for discussion on a variety of careers in engineering, accountancy, agriculture etc., is a career conference.

The purpose of visit to industry organised in a vocational guidance programme is to enable students to get first hand experience on practical aspects of jobs.

In vocational counselling the assistance is given to the individual to understand and solve, his vocational problems. Simulated interview sessions are intended to train students to acquire the necessary skills for facing interview for jobs.Career corner is a display centre of different career books, pamphlets, posters and notices related to career information. The objectives of a career corner are:

— To enable students to get various information about occupations from a variety of career literature.

— To enable students to analyse their employment opportunities by consulting a career index.

— To enable students to get latest information about various job opportunities.

Phases of activities

— Selection of a suitable place for the career corner.

— Collection of career literature.

— Career Index preparation.

— Display of career literature.

— Periodical updating of literature.

A suitable place for setting up a career corner is very essential. The place should be such that it is easily approachable by students and that it is in a prominent place in the institution. An ideal situation would be to have an independent room. The room should have adequate furniture such as display tables, book racks, chairs, display boards.

If an independent room is not available, a portion of the library may be utilised for the purpose. Necessary career literature for display must be collected from various sources. These display materials may be in the form of career information booklets, pamphlets, advertisements in the form of paper cuttings, posters, charts, photographs of industries etc. Each of these type have specific purposes. The career literature may provide information to students about career opportunities, job requirements, career growth oppor-tunities, knowledge and skill requirements, job's pay package, work conditions, etc.

The large number of materials collected must be attractively displayed to catch the attention of the students. These are to be arranged in a systematic manner. All the career literature available in the career corner is to be arranged systematically. For this, a group of literature under a particular corporation, services, organisation may be placed together. For example, all the career literature available in railway services may be placed together.

Similarly all the career literature available in defence services may be placed together. Students usually demand easy and quick reference about job avenues and opportunities. This can be facilitated through Career Index Cards. Career Index Cards are cards which give information about the educational qualification, age, experience essential for a job.

It also contains information about the salary, promotional chances etc. Teachers must prepare these cards by collecting relevant information from the industries and store them in a card catalogue. These must be arranged in a suitable manner. The growth rate of industries is vary fast. The nature of the jobs available changes with the growth. With modernisation forming the backbone of industries knowledge and skill requirements by the industries from job aspirants will not remain the same. Hence, it is imperative that the career literature available must be constantly updated. Periodical updating of literature and discarding the obsolete one must be a continuous process.

Students can get information about vocation and career not only from different printed materials, but also directly from experienced persons in the field. Career talk is one of the methods of providing career information through lectures, seminars, and talks by professionals in the field. The value of books and pamphlets which are the principal sources of vocational information increases, if students get a chance to interact with professionals who are actually on the job. The following are the objectives of career talk.

— To enable students to get information about careers directly from an experienced person in the field.

— To enable students to get opportunity to clarify their doubts related to career through direct interaction with experts.

Phases of activities

— Decide the topic which has got importance.
— Prepare a brief note about what is expected from the visitor and send it to the speaker.
— Choice of suitable themes.
— Selection of the speaker.
— Decision of date and time.
— Preparation of career brief.
— Coordination of the career talk programme.

Success of career talk depends upon the care with which the theme for the programme is selected. The theme should be one of interaction and useful to a majority of students. The theme identified should cover all details about job opportunities. It is essential to note that the theme must cover a wide range of jobs instead of narrowing the same to any one job.

Some of the themes for career talk are "Career in Banking Services for Technical Diploma holders" "Career in Army Engineering Corps", "Start your own Small Scale Industry". The fact that appropriate speaker should be identified to give the career talk needs no overemphasis. The key to the realisation of objectives of career talk is the expert chosen for the talk. In choosing a person it is necessary to look for the following characteristics

— should have worked at different levels.

— have a thorough knowledge of all details of the job.

— be conversant with the latest developments in the industries.

— be a good speaker.

The next important step is to fix the schedule for the programme. One of the usual criteria for deciding the date and time would be the convenience of the identified speaker. Further the schedule must be such that most of the students will be able to attend the programme. It will be useful to arrange the same during the working hours of the Institute rather than after the institutions hours in order to ensure the attendance of a maximum number of students. The talk, should be considered as an integral part of the institutions activity to be deliberately organised. It may be useful to involve the student's union in organising this activity.

Careful preparation is essential for making the career talk useful to students. Both the institution and the identified speaker must make adequate preparation for this programme. In order that the speaker makes necessary planning he should be provided information such as the background of the institution, discipline of students attending the programme, number of students, their areas of interest, aspirations, total time set apart for the session, content expected to be covered etc.

The institution could prepare a brief note on the talk covering the details of time, date, speaker's name, objectives of the programme, content and points of discussion. Such a brief be made available to students in advance. The speaker may be requested to use audio visual aids for presentation.

Any photography, that he may want to exhibit may be collected well in advance and arrangements for their display. It will be useful and appropriate if teachers who are in charge of the progra-mme meet the speaker and discuss with him all details of the programme. Coordination of the programme is very vital if students should derive maximum benefit from it.

Some of the tasks of the programme may be, left to the members of the Student's Union. These may be arranging the lecture hall, receiving the speaker, arranging the display materials, distributing the programme brief etc. There should be a thorough follow up after the programme. The follow up may be in the form of visits to industries by a group of students, discussion sessions on identified themes.

As the very name suggests it is a conference of a few persons from various industries, teachers and students for the purposes of discussing the identified themes for vocational guidance. The main objectives of the career conference are given below:

- To enable students to get opportunity to collect information about different careers of their choice from a panel of experts
- To enable students to get the opportunity to have a direct interaction over a group of careers
- To enable students to get a broader perspective on various career opportunities.

Phase of activities

- Identifying the speakers

— Finalising the date, venue and time

— Monitoring the programme

— Evaluating the programme

— Constituting a organising committee

— Preparing a plan of activities

In order to facilitate smooth and effective organisation of the career conference programme, it is necessary to constitute an organising committee in the institution. This committee may consist of a teacher counsellor, one teacher from each of the disciplines, chairman of the student's union and two student representatives. This committee will be responsible for planning, conducting, monitoring and evaluating the programme. The various tasks of the committee include selection of the theme for the conference, (give examples of themes) identifying the participants for the conference from the industries to talk on different aspects of the theme, fixing the date, time, meeting identified speaker and getting their acceptance, extending invitation etc.

The schedule of the conference activities must be prepared well in advance. It is essential to organise a few career conferences and not just one. Each conference may focus on a discipline or a group of related disciplines. The schedule may be properly spaced out during the academic year. For each programme the plan of activities must be prepared.

Industrial visit

Industrial visit helps the student to get first hand information about the different aspect of the industry such as the tradition of work culture, organisational hierarchy facilities provided.

Objectives

- — Students get first hand information about their future working place.
- — Students get the opportunity to come in contact with their future employers.

Phase of activities

- — Select the industry to be visited.
- — Write to the personnel Manager of the industry/firm for fixing the date and time.
- — Prepare the students for the visit.
- — Conduct the visit.
- — Organise the feedback session after the visit is over.

Organisation

For industrial visit, the firm or industry may be selected from the nearby locality or from a distant place, depending on the purpose of the visit and the group which is going to visit. For example, if the visit is organised for electronics diploma students, there is no justification for visiting a fertiliser factory, which is situated very near to the industry. The visit to the same fertiliser factory by a group of chemical engineering diploma students will be very much useful. Therefore the selection of the industry or firm should be on the basis of the needs of the students.

Students who are going to visit the industry need some preparation. They are instructed to take necessary kits like note book, camera etc. The instruction, the uniform or dress is also given. Students are also asked to follow certain instructions like, they should not touch any machine without permission, they should not talk in the shop floor etc.

During the time of visit, the students are asked to note down the pertinent information. The personnel manager of the industry or firm is requested to give systematic briefing of jobs from employees' point of view. The details of machines and equipment can be heard from the foreman of the respective section. After the visit is over, the students are asked to submit a report on the industrial visit. A discussion session is organised for getting the necessary feedback.

Simulated interview

Simulation means artificial creation of the real situation. Sometimes it may not be possible to provide a real setting to the students for training to face interview. Interview is one of the methods followed by some organisations/ industries to recruit the most appropriate persons for various positions. The selection of the aspirants to jobs depends on how they perform in such interviews particularly if there are a large number of them with similar qualifications and experience. In such cases, candidates after short listing will be invited to appear in an interview by a staff selection committee.

In such cases, one who performs well the interview will be selected. It implies that students must know how to take an interview. Facing an interview and performing well by way of impressing the interviewing committee is an art. They should be necessarily trained in this so that they may learn all the behavioural requirements therein.

Objectives

— To enable students to get opportunity to acquire the necessary skills of facing an interview

— To enable students to get over complexes like frightening behaviour which come in the way of good at the interview performance.

Phases of activities

— Select the interviewer (s) and the interviewee

— Brief the interviewer (s) and interviewee about specific roles to be played.

— Organise the simulated interview session

— Obtain feedback from the candidates.

Organisation

Interview is a personal meeting between two individuals. The purpose of this may be evaluation, counselling, selection etc. In the meeting situation one is the interviewer and the other the interviewee.

It has been found that one interviewer is not sufficient in conducting interviews like selection interview and evaluation interview. Therefore a panel of interviewers is required to interview the candidate. This panel of interviewers form the interview board and conducts the interview.

In simulated interview, interview session is organised, in an artificial situation. Here, one or more persons play the role of the interviewer. While some other individual plays the role of an interviewee. Through simulated inter-view session, the interviewers try to explore the capacity of the interviewee in relation to a particular job. As soon as the interviewee presents himself before the interview board, the chairman of the board takes the initiative to start the session by asking him to take the chair.

To develop opening structure, the chairman may ask the candidate about his name, qualification etc. He then, invites other members of the board to ask questions. In the development phase of the interview, the interviewers skilfully ask probing questions.

This explores the capacity of the interviewee gradually. When the interviewers feel that the purpose of conducting the interview is achieved, the chairman once again takes the initiative to close the interview session. This he does by offering thanks to the interviewee for his participation.

Vocational counselling

In vocational counselling, problems such as selection of vocation, preparing for a vocation and progress in vocation are handled.

Every counselling session has specific objectives. Situational development influences every counselling session a lot. The major structure of any counselling session depends on the problem of the counsellee. However it may follow a general structure of activities. Phases are given below:

- Fix the time and date for the counselling session
- Begin the session as per schedule
- Create a congenial atmosphere through easy communication

— Assist the counsellee to explore his needs and potentialities
— Review the world of work with counsellee
— Assist counsellee to choose relevant occupation
— Get the feedback from the counsellee
— Terminate the session slowly.

In vocational counselling, the assistance is given by an individual to another to solve the latter's vocational problems. The individual who undergoes vocational counselling discovers his potentialities relevant to a particular vocation or a group of vocations. Several items of information like requirements and conditions of success in a vocation, advantages and disadvantages, compen-sation opportunities and prospects in several lines of work may also form part of the vocational counselling.

Through vocational counselling the self-awareness of the individual who comes for assistance is enhanced.The counsellor in vocational counselling, assists the individual to discover and evaluate his personal needs. Once the client realises his needs, it is necessary on the part of the counsellor to nurture his needs which make him more alert.

As a result of the counselling process, a sense of personal identity in relation to the world of work grows. The counsellor and counsellee, review occupations and works. In this review phase of the counselling process, only those occupations are considered which the counsellee feels relevant to him. The counsellee discovers himself in the light of his new experience.

Vocational Development

Vocational development is a mark of maturity. In a complex society such a development is in itself an achievement. Vocational planning precedes vocational experience, but competence in planning also requires abilities, which come with maturation. Vocational choice is a process of growth reflecting other phase of development.

Vocational choice

It is a very important decision a person must make for himself and this choice is a long process rather than a simple incident. Vocational interests and choices do not appear all of a sudden during adolescence, they appear as a result of developmental process. A number of theories have been advanced by psychologists and occupational analysts on occupational choice.

An individual never reaches the ultimate decision at a single moment in time, but through a series of decisions over a period of many years. The period during which the individual makes what can be described as a *fantasy choice;* the period during which he is making a *tentative choice;* and the period when he makes a realistic choice. The period of fantasy choice coincides in general with the latency period, between six and eleven, although residual elements of fantasy choice frequently carry over into pre-adolescent years. The period of tentative choice coincides, by and large, with early and late adolescence; with few exceptions, realistic choices are made in early childhood.

There are three basic elements regarding occupational choice:

(i) occupational choice is a developmental process; it is not a single decision made over a period of years--a process which takes place over a minimum of six or seven years, and more typically over ten years or more.

(ii) since each decision during adolescence is related to one's experience upto that point, and in turn has an influence on the future, the process of decision-making is basically irreversible.

(iii) since occupational choice involves the balancing of a series of subjective elements with opportunities and limitations of reality, the crystallisation of occupational choice inevitably has the quality of a compromise.

Vocational choices take place as a result of a developmental process. Very often this development can be traced to the influences exerted before birth. Child development studies have proved the powerful influence which the thwarted ambitions and frustrations of the parents have on the vocational choice of the individual. Vocation being the implementation of the self-concept, when the parents have failed to achieve it during their own career, they have sought it through the choice of career for their children.

Vocational development may be conceived of as beginning early in life and as proceeding along a curve late in life. Thus, a four year old child who plays the policeman or soldier is in a very early stage of vocational development and the old man of sixty who does not work for money but still keeps himself busy with writing books in the field of his specialisation is going through the late stage of vocational development.

Buehler has classified the vocational life stages as:

1) *growth* (birth to 14 years)

2) *explanatory* (15 to 24 years)—with the sub-stages of fantasy which may be tentative or realistic with appropriate attitudes towards work and occupation;
3) *establishment* (24 to 44 years)—beginning with trial and progressing into a stable position as the individual begins to make his place in the world of work;
4) *maintenance stage* (45 to 64 years)—characterised by stability in the field in which establishment has taken place earlier in life; and
5) *decline stage* (65 onwards)—characterised by deceleration during the early part and progressing into one of retirement.

The process of vocational development is continuous and ongoing and is essentially that of developing and implementing a self-concept; it is a compromise process in which the self-concept is a product of the interaction of inherited aptitudes, neural and endocrinal make-up, opportunity to play various roles, and evaluations of the extent to which the results of role playing meet with the approval of supervisors and fellows.

The process of compromise between individual and social factors, between self-concept and reality is one of role-playing whether the role is played in fantasy, in the counselling interviews, or in real life activities, such as school classes, clubs, part-time work and entry jobs.

The opportunities of exploring the occupational roles available in the world of work through actual participation are obviously limited-while part-time and trial jobs offer some real experience, only a very few occupational roles can be sampled in this way.

The material for these role playing activities can be came from a number of sources: the home, peers, friends and acquaintances who are in employment, the mass media, school/college/university, the career masters, counsellors, recruitment literature and so on. The inadequacies of these indirect sources and the unrealistic occupational perceptions which are gained from them often frustrate the most determined attempts to achieve a realistic compromise.

Work satisfaction and life satisfactions depend upon the extent to which the individual finds adequate outlets for his abilities, interests, personality traits and values; they depend upon his establishment in a type of work or work situations and a way of life in which he can play the kind of role which his growth and explanatory experiences have led him to consider congenial and appropriate.

Vocational preferences and competencies, the situations in which people live and work, and hence their self-concepts, change with time and experience, making choice and adjustment a continuous process. The vocational preferences of the developing child are subject to continual change.

For the young child, the chosen occupation is often one which is identified with adults. The process of occupational choice and adjustment does not end when a youngster enters his or her first job.

Occupational expectations will rarely be fully realised and some adjustment to the unexpected will be necessary. Even when such adjustment is achieved, the process is not complete. Regular work activities may facilitate the development of latent skills which the individual may subsequently want to utilise more fully.

A growing awareness of the world of work and the opportunities available may also motivate the individual to seek out what to perceive in better jobs. Even where a person remains in the same job for much of his life, a series of adjustments will be necessary to meet with the individual's changing concept of himself.

Factors Affecting Vocational Development

The nature of the career pattern is determined by the individual's parental socio-economic level, mental ability, and personality characteristic and by the opportunities to which he is exposed. Occupational choice and subsequent vocational development is greatly influenced by the experience a child undergoes. The individual is a product of his environment, his inherent aptitudes and neural endocrinal make-up.

Family

The most important social system which impinge upon the individual and influence his development, is the family in which he happens to be born and reared. The vocational development of the individual, which is a continuous process, beginning in early childhood and continuing into the late years of life, appears to be as much influenced by his family as are other aspects of his development.

The abilities, interests, physique and personality of the individual, which play such an important role in his vocational development, are partly determined by hereditary factors and the particular constellations of genes which the individual inherits depends upon his parents and ancestors.

Physical factors such as the geographical location of the home, the physical conditions prevailing in the home, and the health of various members of the family may, at times, have a significant effect on the vocational development of the individual. A boy coming from a home in a remote village will have much more difficulty in obtaining a college education than a boy residing in a town.

A person residing in a town which does not offer facilities for specialisation in a particular field will have to seek admission in another town, which obviously involves additional expenditure on board and lodging. If the family budget cannot accommodate this extra expenditure, the student has to change his educational-vocational aim and specialise in a different field or compromise by taking up a course of training at a lower level in the same field, if such training is available in his home town.

The location of the family residence also determines the type of vocational activities which the individual may take up. A person who has spent the formative years of his life in a project area—which is the centre of engineering activity—is likely to have more information about engineering, develop an interest in it, and see himself as playing a role in it, than a person who has lived far away from such type of activity.

Physical conditions in the family such as overcrowding, noise, lack of proper light and ventilation, and an inadequate diet may all have an injurious effect on the health of the individual as well as on his ability to concentrate on studies or work, and thus may adversely affect his vocational development.

Health of the members of the family may also have an indirect effect on vocational development. Crippling, ill-health or death of the breadwinner of the family may make it necessary for a youngster to discontinue his studies, no matter how bright he may be, and take up the first available job, whether it is suitable or not. Similarly, ill-health or death of the mother may make it necessary for a girl to spend so much of her time on household chores, that her studies or job are neglected, or, even to relinquish her studies or job altogether.

The social economic level of the family appears to exercise the most potent influence of all. The level and quality of education available and aspired to, as well as the level of work aspired to and accessible, are greatly affected by the family's finances and social contacts. Thus their children have higher aspirations either as a result of pressure from the parents or as a result of internalising parental pressures or both. If their intellectual endowment is good, their higher level of aspiration may be achieved. But if intellectual endowment is not commensurate with level of aspiration, conflict will arise; the individual will not be able to have an integrated self-concept, and vocational maladjustment is likely to follow.

At times, however, the reverse is true. Among very affluent families, the level of educational and vocational aspirations may be low, and a person with good abilities may not be sufficiently motivated to concentrate on studies and strike out a vocational path for himself, thus may fail to actualise his potentialities.

Person who belong to families from the higher economic strata also have better chances of finding employment at a higher level because their parents, and they themselves, have more contacts with people who are well-to-do and influential, people who are employers rather than employees.

In setting up a professional practice or business, too, individuals from the higher socio-economic strata are at an advantage because of the capital available to them as well as the well-to-do friends and acquaintances who are potential clients. The occupation information which a person picks up from his family will influence his vocational thinking and eventual choice of occupation. The types of occupations concerning which a family can provide information will vary with its socio-economic level—a person from a higher level family is in a better position to obtain more information about professional, business and admini-strative work, and one from a lower level family about skilled, semiskilled and unskilled work.

The types of cultural stimulation prevalent in the family, and the types of equipment available, which depend considerably on the socio-economic level of the family, will play a part in facilitating or hindering the development of the youngster's abilities and interests in certain directions, providing or failing to provide him with opportunities to test his self-concept through explanatory activities.

Identification of the individual with the socio-economic class to which his family belongs may also influence his self-concept. A person from a higher class family may find it difficult to work as a peon or clerk; while a person from a lower class family will tend to see himself in these or similar roles-if his vocational thinking is reality-oriented and not dominated by fantasy-and may find it difficult to see himself as a professional man or business man; an administrator or manager.

Family as a mediator of culture also influences vocational development. Caste and religion, mediated through the family, at times have a profound influence on vocational development. Caste often restricts the occupations open to its members.

This restrictive effect will play a greater part in the vocational development of a person who comes from an orthodox family in which conformity and obedience have been stressed than in the vocational development of a person whose family is un-conventional and regards its membership of a particular caste as a chance factor to which no importance need be attached. Family's religion too at times gives a bias to the choice of occupation. For example, the frequent choice of martial career by the Sikhs appears to be related to the militant nature of their religion.

Family is also instrumental in helping the individuals develop attitudes and values. It has been proved through researches that children are not born with attitudes but they acquire them gradually through various experiences and influences. Parents wittingly or unwittingly transmit attitudes and values to children.

Attitudes towards various types of occupations as well as towards work itself are learnt in the home, and play their part in developing in the individual preference for certain occupations and dislike for others. This is how people come to consider occupations as ranking high or low in prestige, as clean or dirty, as safe or risky, as purposeful or frivolous. For example, the individual who has grown up in a home where manual work is looked down upon as being uncultured and dirty, is likely to develop the attitude that manual work is beneath his dignity and to think that society will set less score by him if he takes up an occupation which involves manual work. This single factor is responsible for most of the People in our country seeking white collar jobs, and remaining unemployed while jobs requiring skilled and semi-skilled work go abegging.

Work values learned in the family can have a far reaching effect on vocational choice and adjustment. For ex ample, if concern for the welfare of people has permeated a home, the personality of an individual growing up in such a home cannot but be influenced by it, and he is likely to seek and find fulfilment in one of the social welfare occupations. If, on the other hand, monetary considerations have been predominant in his family, he will tend to go in for a type of work in which the monetary rewards are attractive.

A family in which aesthetic values play their part in daily living, children in that family will prefer artistic occupations. Children who come from a family in which intellectual activities and achievements are valued, are likely to be drawn towards intellectual pursuits in adulthood, whereas children who come from a home in which intellectual activities are not valued will tend not to be attracted towards such activities, or if there be an attraction on account of high intellectual abilities seeking an outlet, the attraction will not be without conflict.

Emotional currents in the family also have a subtle influence on vocational development. Inter-personal relations which prevail within the family, particularly during the individual's formative years, play a great role in shaping his entire personality and behaviour, including vocational behaviour. Conditions such as parental neglect or rejections, overprotection, parental disharmony or intense sibling rivalry can create insecure, unintegrated persons who find it difficult to make a good vocational adjustment; they find it difficult to make vocational decisions. Even when they make decisions, they are often unwise, and unstable; they have work inhibitions or an overbearing urge to achieve which defeats its own purpose.

Personality difficulties are the most frequent cause of vocational inefficiency and dissatisfaction and also of discharge from environment. Emotional needs fostered in the early interpersonal relations in the family tend to motivate the individual to seek their satisfaction through vocational activities. For instance, a child who has been over-protected by his family and grows up to have a strong need for security and dependence, will tend to avoid occupations involving outdoor life, leadership, taking risks, and so on.

Another person whose needs for self-expression and recognition have not been gratified within his family, may either seek a vocational situation in which needs can be gratified or he may become so cowed down and lacking in confidence that he may choose an occupation considerably below his ability level, or even drift into an occupation without planning. An exaggerated need of independence, developed in the course of his relationships with his parents, may make it difficult for a person to accept any salaried employment and impel him towards setting up his own business or go into some other independent venture.

Family provides the earliest adult role models with whom the individual may identity or whom he may reject. Normally the boy wants to be like his father and incorporates within himself the characteristics of the father, including his occupational role, work values and attitudes. As a child, he plays games in which he acts out the occupational role of the father, and later he wishes to take up the same occupation in earnest.

However, for the girl, the mother is a sex model rather than an occupational model, whereas for the boy the father is both a sex model and an occupational model. The bright girl who is aiming at a career thus often finds a suitable feminine occupational model lacking in her family; she may then identify with some female outside the family or with her father, or other male member of the family. In the latter event, the conflicting identifications may cause maladjustment in the vocational as well as in the personal-social sphere.

Frequently, such a girl compulsively seeks fulfilment through a career and is unable to seek fulfilment in the normal psycho-biological female roles of wife and mother. The boy, too, at times has conflicts arising out of identification with his mother as well as his father. The individual's self-concept emerges from and is greatly influenced by his family. Their judgement of his capacities and characteristics, the status and role he experiences in his relations with them, their acceptance or rejection of him as a person; it is from a myriad of such perceptions that the individual develops a concept of himself as a worker which he tries to implement in the course of his vocational development.

Ability

Ability is another important factor which matters in vocational development. Adolescents with higher intellectual ability tend to seek and prepare for jobs which require higher kind of intelligence, while the ones with lower mental ability go in for semiskilled jobs and continue in positions of almost no importance. The individuals who do not choose their careers according to their level of ability, land in failure because of poor competence.

Though no systematic and thorough study made on Indian samples is available, some foreign studies have produced results to illustrate the difference in vocational success of the intelligent and dull individuals. In one of the studies it was possible to follow-up eight individuals who had been diagnosed as feeble-minded or of borderline intelligence. Some eighteen years earlier, when their vocational achievement was studied, two of them were working as truck drivers; another was a taxi driver; a welder; a shipping clerk; a train repair man, and an assembler at an air plane factory. All of these persons were earning meagre money but each one of them was self-supporting and a productive citizen. Many of them were university teachers, physicians, lawyers, architects, authors, engineers and artists.

Personality

A social and an extrovert in all probability, would make a successful public relations officer but not a scholar or a librarian. Similarly, a quiet and an introvert would be unhappy if placed on the job of a salesman. Every job can be described in terms of the personality characteristics it requires for the person to be happy and satisfied in it. For example, good teachers are usually social, communicative, self confident, self-sufficient and aggressive.

Attempts have been made to measure people's personal suitability to a particular job through the study of their interest patterns, through their responses to questions in interest inventories and interest blanks. Prediction of the most suitable career for an individual is based on the numerous profiles of successful individuals in various jobs. The profile of the individual wanting guidance can be compared with those who have already been successful in that particular field.

The similarity and divergence between their personal qualities is a reliable guide for prediction of a career for the individual tested. Studies of reliability of these predictions have proved that young people changing a particular career have interest profiles markedly similar to those of the successful persons in that particular line. Study done by Norton has also shown that persons most stable in their jobs showed interest patterns most suitable to work of their choice.

A significant difference has been found in the earnings of persons in jobs most suited to their personality characteristics and the ones who have been placed in jobs not suited to their interest patterns. In addition to the job satisfaction, suitable personality and interest patterns provide the individual with an opportunity for the development of vocational drive. Mere work skills and abilities are not the sole determinants of success of the individual on the job; good personal adjustment and skills of inter-personal communication are also a must.

Economics plays an important role in the vocational choice and development of an individual. While planning the career, the individual, naturally, avoids the vocations with low wages and low prestige even though these may be the ones in which he is interested the most. Business cycle is another economic factor affecting the vocational development of young persons as well as the vocational pattern and adjustment of older adults. It is an established fact that business completes a cycle of success and failure. The business expands and brings the society to the condition of complete prosperity followed by another period of prosperity.

This cycle has definite effects on the vocational development and employment of the individual. A young adult who completes his education during depression is faced with the strain of scarcity of employment which is unfamiliar to another young man who may have passed college during more prosperous times. The two are forced to make very different vocational adjustment.

During depressions, there is a general downgrading which results in dissatisfaction among the workers. During prosperous times, on the other hand, there is scarcity of suitable individuals, so there is a trend of upgrading. Persons with ordinary qualifications, are able to secure good and above-expectation jobs.

Industrialisation

Another factor which influences vocational development of an individual is industrialisation. Many new jobs come up due to industrialisation. The people are not usually familiar with these jobs. They had never aspired for them neither have they had the opportunity to explore their interests and aptitudes for these jobs. Industrialisation also effects the workers already settled in jobs. For many it may mean getting uprooted and looking for the main jobs; for the others it may mean acquiring new skills to fit into the positions requiring skilled labour.

Public policy

Public policy has its effect on the vocational development of the individual. Reservations both in admission and jobs proves an important factor for scheduled castes to go in for particular vocations—in spite of the fact that they are not well-qualified. Similarly, those from other castes may not be able to go in for medicine or engineering in spite of fairly good merit as compared to the Scheduled Castes. Hence change in vocations in spite of interest, aptitude and ability for these lines.

State patronage for a particular industry in a backward area acts as a boost while similar industry in an advanced area may suffer an obvious setback. Changes in fashion and style also affect the vocational development. New styles of dresses, hair cuts, make-up, furniture and household equipment, create new vocations and may affect the vocational development. Natural calamities as floods, earthquakes, droughts also affect the vocational development.

Vocational adjustment

The aim of all vocational guidance programmes and activities is vocational adjustment. As far as adjustment to a vocation is concerned it is necessary that the individual should have a pleasant feeling and tone while doing his occupational work and that he should acquire a reasonable amount of facility in that work. Vocational adjustment in case of some individuals also means that the individual should be able to express his personality adequately through his work.

The occupation should provide him with enough remuneration to meet his economic needs. The work should also enable him to enjoy some social status and allow him to play a certain type of role in society in conformity with his values and personality needs. Vocational adjustment cannot be judged merely by satisfaction and facility in work. Such criteria of adjustment tend to be narrow and neglect the "global" aspects of adjustment. Vocational adjustment means adjustment not only to work involved in the occupation but to all social, economic and physical situations connected with the occupation.

An occupation brings with it many social relationships with colleagues, superiors, subordinates and the public. An occupation also creates for the individual a social atmosphere in which he lives and works. Hence vocational adjustment means adjust-ment not only to work but to these social relationships and the social atmosphere prevailing in the place of work. A good deal of satisfaction is derived from social relationships. A worker may be very good in his work but if he is not adjusted to the social atmosphere, he should be considered as vocationally maladjusted.

Conversely, a worker may not be quite competent by virtue of his aptitudes in the work but if he is able to derive satisfaction from the social relationships he may be well-adjusted to the work situation as a whole. Social status is considered a factor more important in occupational adjustment than economic gain. Professional and technical competence is not enough for vocational success or adjustment. There are many occupations—professional and technical in nature—which call for the qualities and competencies other than those required in the technical execution of work.

People lose positions or fail to attain positions even when they are competent to perform the technical duties involved in their jobs. Conversely, technically incompetent persons may be retained or achieve advancement because other qualities offset the lack of technical competence.

Vocational adjustment also involves the implementation of a part of the individual's self-concept in the world of work. By self-concept is meant the complex of ideas and attitudes which an individual has about himself and to the world around him. Thus, self-concept defines the locus of the individual in the field of his relations to the social and physical world. In simpler words, it is the picture of the individual as it appears to him or the way he looks at himself.

Super in his memorable article "Vocational Adjustment—Imple-menting a Self-Concept" explains how the self-concept is involved in vocational adjustment. He redefines vocational guidance in terms of self-concept when he says, "vocational guidance is the process of helping a person to develop and accept an integrated and adequate picture of himself and of his role in the world of work, to test this concept against reality, and to convert it into a reality, with satisfaction to himself and benefit to society".

Individuals vary in the degree of need for implementation of their self-concept in the occupational world, with the result that at the lower extreme, there would be individuals who could obtain satisfaction from several types of work within the range of their capacity. Some thinking has also been directed to the problem of fulfilment of emotional needs of the individual in his occupational world and the role of emotional needs in vocational choice.

Gratification of these needs is regarded to be the psycho-dynamic factor in vocational choice and adjustment. This need may be felt by the individual consciously or may operate from the unconscious as an impelling force. Some of the needs, as stated by Murray, are abasement, achievement, acquisition, affiliation, aggre-ssion, autonomy, cognizance, escape, nurturance, recreation, succourance, and so on. It may be assumed that the persons' interests are focused on activities which seem likely to permit the satisfaction of their strongest need.

If so, it may further be presumed that adjustment in a particular occupation involves the satisfaction of a particular need or a particular combination of needs. However, it seems that different individuals tend to satisfy the same need in different occupations. For example, the need for achievement may be satisfied by one individual in medicine whereas the same need may be satisfied by another individual in a technical occupation. Conversely, it may be stated that different individuals or different types of individuals gratify different needs in the same occupation. The need for creativity plays an important part in vocational choice and adjustment. By creativity we mean the need to create new objects, maintaining and fostering them. Different individuals seek different ways of gratifying this need.

An expert advisor for vocational guidance

We developed a multimedia program which combines a vocational encyclopedia and a testing facility to foster adequate career decisions. The testing facility is designed to suggest the same careers which a given number of experts would have suggested, if presented with the same user's input. Our vocational database includes imprecise data like expert ratings enabling the calculation of suggestions of career options. The most important group of users of software for vocational guidance are young adults, who are about to leave schools.

The test facility has been implemented on several CD-ROMs, a short quiz to identify occupational fields, and a wide range of surveys which are responded by letters. 43 students participated in an experiment to investigate the understanding and acceptance of the information provided by the system. The results show that students are able to judge, whether careers match their individual interests or not. Furthermore, we explore whether the system is able to reconstruct 38 experts´ ratings. The system shows a good performance in reconstructing the experts´ data - except of one academical career which was not described very clearly. In a recent study, we tested the influence of the testing facility on recall of information and individual acceptance (n=75). Acceptance and recall of information about career options is clearly enhanced when studying individualized materials compared to more general information.

Many people feel a lack of competence in career decision making. A lot of programs provide help but most of them cover selected topics and are judged to be of poor quality. We developed a multimedia program which combines a vocational encyclopedia and a testing facility to foster adequate career decisions. The testing facility is designed to maximize the probability to suggest careers which a given number of experts - based upon the same user input - would have suggested. The testing facility and the vocational encyclopedia have been implemented on microcomputers using Windows 3.1, Windows 95, and on UNIX machines.

Although knowledge based systems and intelligent tutoring system (ITS) are well established tools, there are hardly any implementations of systems for vocational diagnosing and counseling. Psychological testing procedures including computer-supported diagnosis are used to conduct aptitude tests in personnel selection, adaptive testing optimizing economy and performance of personality, aptitude, and ability tests, and decision analysis applied to management diagnostics.

Although there are numerous tests which check for individual interests, and aptitude, there are hardly any computer-based, psychological testing procedures addressing vocational guidance. This does not mean, however, that there are no software products available: Counseling software guides list 200 programs, approximately, that are designed to support self assessment, job finding, and job keeping. About 70 titles incorporate surveys or self-testing facilities in order to provide the user with information about his or her career alternatives and career satisfaction. Most of these program address restricted topics like nursing professions or writing successful job applications. Additionally, many programs are judged to be of a poor quality in terms of completeness, accuracy and counseling efficacy. Despite several shortcomings career counseling software is considered to be useful:

— The software can offer both instruction and practice (e.g. interviewing for jobs).

— Some programs have quizzes or exercises allowing an evaluation of career maturity or job hunting skills.

— The program can access information from large databases of occupational fields or careers.

— A large group of software allows users to answer questions about likes and dislikes and match them to careers.

— Some of this programs take the repetitive work and tedious jobs away from the counselor, hence, enabling him or her to focus on interactive career counseling.

The most common complaints regarding these programs are:

— Poor usability in terms of screen layout and functional design,

— long response and searching times,

— a lack of adaptability to the audience,

— too few or inadequate assessment questions,

— and a lack of complete and up-to-date information.

Models for vocational guidance

Recent tendencies of the job market force young adults to acquire a high qualification in order to get adequate jobs. Additionally, the transition from school to work life gets more difficult and protracted. Therefore, improvements in educational and psychological counseling are required. A core concept of career counseling is the assessment of vocational interests and abilities. Interests play an important role in career decision processes. They are considered to be that part of the self concept that matches personal traits and job structures. Therefore, vocational interests are effects of cognitive decision processes when judging about objects and actions which are relevant for jobs. Bergmann found reliable correlation between the dominating personal traits and the profession. These findings are theoretically explained by person-environment models which suppose that people tend to reduce dissonance between personal and environmental conditions.

Vocational interests of young adults

The most important group of users of software for vocational guidance are young adults, who are about to leave schools. An important factor of career decision making is the knowledge young adults can access to in order to come up with valid decisions. 426 pupils participated in two studies designed to identify structures within job related interests and aptitudes. The results of a cluster analysis of 156 items show that the interests of pupils from secondary schools are poor structured and do not fit the situation on the job market: Production, technical equipment, and the notion of "dirty work" form one cluster, "clean" and social professions form another cluster. Working in offices, e.g. commercial professions, are supposed to be between "dirty" and "clean" work.

Students of high schools have even simpler images in mind when judging about jobs in crafts and industries: They simply divide in "dirty" and "clean" jobs, and they are much more fond of getting a clean job than students of secondary schools are. Academical jobs, however, were described in complex and highly interrelated patterns. Figure 1 displays the results of the cluster analyses conducted with the data from highschool students judging non-academical jobs. This structure is compared to the structure derived from the experts´ ratings.

Knowledge and system engineering for vocational guidance

Students are novices with respect to career decisions, because they have no experiences which help them to evaluate their own vocational orientation. Experts tend to be over-specific and cannot take a "naive" point of view. Thus, an ideal system supporting vocational guidance should reduce and transform inputs from experts and students into profiles which can be compared automatically. Based upon this considerations a system to support career decision making can be constituted by an interactive test or quiz to match interests and preferences with job characteristics, and an encyclopedia or database to inform the user about relevant job characteristics like tasks, educational programs, work load, income, and so on.

Our decision support system is not designed to mimic the full range of an interpersonal counseling process. Rather, it shall provide the user with a variety of career options which match his or her personal interests and preferences. The knowledge engineering process covered five project phases:

1. The relevant factors of the experts´ reasoning about careers were identified using interviews and surveys. More than 800 German careers and educational programs, about 50 items like "Is this job physically demanding?", and 118 interviews with experts were included in this first step.

2. The data revealed from this investigations were reduced to dimensions that discriminate between careers by means of statistical measurements. We calculated Principal Component Analyses (PCA) which are standard procedures of multivariate statistics in order to identify main sources of variances in multi-dimensional data sets. We identified seven factors for academical career and nine factors for non-academical careers. Thus, 16 factors are sufficient to calculate discriminating profiles for each career in our expert system.

3. We wrote short statements like "I would like to explain new products to customers" which were dedicated to describe one of our 16 factors. 12 Items per factor were written and reviewed by a team of eight vocational experts resulting in an item pool of 192 statements.

4. 426 students filled in surveys about their state of information, their vocational interests and responded to our item pool. By means of a multiple regression procedure we identified those items which described a single factor most clearly. This step resulted in a reduced item pool of 80 statements, 5 items per factor.

5. In the last step, we implemented a database containing relevant information about 800 German careers and educational programs: Task descriptions, special demands, agenda of educational program, income wages, prognostic data, and the job profile relying on the reduced expert data.

The database serves a the basis of our expert advisory system. In particular, we aimed to meet the following conditions:

1. The probability should be maximized that our system

generates the same list of careers which our 118 experts would have suggested, if presented with identical input data.

2. The implemented module should be small and fast - that is, the program should be small enough to be stored on a single floppy disc including basic data about 600 German professions and educational programs; additionally, system response times should not exceed 2 seconds.

3. The model should be able to incorporate information from our vocational databases like average income, prognostication of the job market etc.

4. The data of the model should be updated and maintained easily. This is a crucial point for all systems supporting career decisions, because vocational databases have to be updated and modified quite frequently.

Calculating the goodness of fit

The core component of all career guidance systems is to inform the user about the goodness of fit of his or her vocational interests and a variety of career options. Katz tries to give a feedback about goodness of fit by performing a multiplication of self-ratings and expert ratings.

Self-ratings (RSelf) refer to the variations of the importance attached to each dimension by the user, e.g. how much she or he likes team-oriented working. Expert ratings (RExpert) are judgments of experts about how important each dimension is in every-day work life, e.g. the proportion of time spent by team-oriented work. More sophisticated models rely on a measurement of the distance between self rating and expert rating. These model mostly use the City-Block distance or other forms of Minkowski metrics.

Parameter c has to be greater than or equal to 1; with c=1 the term calculates the City-Block distance and with c=2 the Euclidean distance is calculated. Simple distance models, such aas describes in and , have several shortcomings: (a) The functions are not monotone and the distances measurements are far from being equi-distant. (b) There are no information about positive or negative matches but only about how much self and expert ratings fit. (c) It is hard to introduce preference models, e.g. to take into account whether a certain item or dimension is judged to be more or less important compared to another item or dimension. (d) The scores expressing distances between self ratings and expert ratings cannot be compared directly - that is, scores derived from multiplication like in and Minkowki metrics like in are probably not contained in comparable scales.

An of the paradox consequences of these simple distance models is that the more conflicting interests the user has got the more careers are fitting the user's profile. Consider a user who states that she or he likes to work in an office and at the same time she or he likes to work open-air. According to Minkowski metrics all careers are appropriate that can be carried out either in an office or open-air. A more adequate response would be to suggest careers that fulfill both conditions: partly to work in an office and partly to work open-air, e.g. security staff in big companies.

Al models to match careers to individual interests

As mentioned before, there were no systems at hand based on classical AI methods to guide or implementation process. We reviewed rule-based expert systems, neural networks, genetic algorithms, fuzzy logic, and advanced statistical systems in order to check their appropriatnes for our purposes.

1. Neural networks are superior to many statistical methods because they provide an easy way for non-linear forecast. They are effective in recognizing patterns in noisy or incomplete data. Therefore, neural networks are suited for career counseling where clear rules cannot be formulated. Unfortunately, it is impossible to explain the reasoning of neural networks to users. Explanation of the underlying reasoning, however, is a crucial point in career counseling.

2. Genetic algorithms are successful in searching huge databases and large optimization problems including timetabling, job-shop scheduling, and data-mining. Moreover, genetic algorithms can provide explanations of the decisions they produce. The performance of genetic algorithms, however, is strongly affected by the representations schemes employed. Additionally, setting the parameters such as mutation rate and crossover need extensive experimentation. This contradicts our goal to develop a algorithm which is simple to use and simple to maintain.

3. One of the obvious advantages of fuzzy systems is their capability to deal with imprecise data using a rule-based knowledge base which is easy to understand and explain. This advantage, however, tuns out to be a problem if clear rules can not be elicited.

4. While interviewing 118 experts for career counseling, we learned from the interviews that the experts use rules to guide the counseling process, but they do not rely on any detectable rules when matching career options and personal traits. Thus, we had difficulties to translate their expertise into simple If-then-rules.

Our statistical analysis of the expert data revealed that only very few statistically significant factors are discriminating hundreds of career options. We aimed to take advantage of this fact and reviewed statistical methods to match multi-dimensional data sets. We looked for an algorithm which allows easy explanation of reasoning, easy updating and maintainance, and incorporation of precise and imprecise data. Above all, no paradox results should be obtained by the system.

Implementation of the expert advisor

We developed a system which embedded the following components:

1. An easy quiz or test about vocational interests and experiences.
2. Rating data and dimensions derived from a PCA (Principal Components Analysis; Stevens, 1992) of the expert ratings.
3. An algorithm based on a GLM (General Linear Model) to compare user and expert ratings.
4. A component to enter additional preferences and to modify the results of the GLM.
5. Finally, a report module generates an assorted list of suggested professions or careers.

Although there are more comprehensive databases about educational programs in Germany than ours, our database is the only one which includes imprecise data like expert ratings enabling the calculation of commendable career options. There are two ways to incorporate additional information into the calculation: (a) Precise data like student fees and income wages are considered by looking up the appropriate data tables. (b) Imprecise inputs like individual preferences are used to modify the distances measurements.

We decided to rely on distance measurement models from multivariate statistics providing information about strength and direction of matches, enabling easy modifications and transformations into appropriate scales. The most simple form to express a directed goodness of fit is to calculate a linear regression.

This score expresses the distances of the ratings by means of the squared distances of individual ratings and the arithmetic mean and can be transformed into statistically comparable values. The covariance can be adapted to the standard deviations of the ratings (s Self and s Expert) – resulting in the linear correlation coefficient r – and can be fitted to the normal distribution by a Z-transformation – resulting in the value Z .

Z expresses an directed and normalized measurement of the linear fit of self ratings and expert ratings within a range from -1 (negative fit) to +1 (positive fit). As the Z-value is fitted to a normal curve, it can be used even in sophisticated statistical procedures. Profiles of single careers can be included in or excluded from the database without affecting the comparison algorithm. The system does not produce paradox results because conflicting interest ratings lead to a general decrease of the correlation coefficients. Furthermore, the coefficients can be easily adapted to individual importance ratings attached to different dimensions: In one implementation of our expert advisor the users could move sliders from 0 (low preference) to 100 (high preference) to express the importance of their ratings. Our system represents variations of the importance attached to each dimensions by an modified covariance formula [5] with l being the importance rating (e.g. raging from 0 to 100):

After having been modified the covariance can be used in statistical procedures like normal covariance coefficients. Finally, Z-values allow for an exact definition of the cut-off point separating career options that match individual interests from those that do not: We defined the peak of the Z-value distribution (the "bell curve") to be the cut-off criterion. The peak can easily be calculated by comparing the differences between the Z-values of two neighboring careers: The peak of the distribution is reached when the preceding difference is smaller than it's successor.

System implementation and product development

UNIX-computers using the programming language C because of its portability. This C-program was modified, extended, and incorporated in several products: A series of CD-ROMs for Windows-PC, a short quiz to identify occupational fields, and a wide range of surveys which are responded by carefully.

Medialog produces a series of eight CD-ROM for microcomputers equipped with Windows 3.1 or Windows 95. Each CD-ROM applies to a certain occupational field like "Economics and Law", "Natural Sciences", and so on, and contains a vocational encyclopedia combined with the testing facility. In the beginning of a session the user enters his or her personal qualifications and conditions in order to allow the program to come up with reasonable suggestions and information. The user decides whether he or she wants to examine occupational fields, to explore the index of the encyclopedia, or to take a job quiz. The quiz provides the user with up to 80 simple yes/no assessments. After having responded to 20 items the system signals to the user that it is ready to suggest jobs and educational programs. If the user accesses the list of suggested items he or she may jump into the encyclopedia by a simple mouse click and retrieve information about qualifications, tasks, work load, income, prognoses, and so on. All occupational fields and many jobs are illustrated by videos and photos in order to elaborate the text and give an realistic impression of work life.

A multimedia program containing our testing facility has been produced and published in charge of an international bank. The program contains a wide range of information: In the final version the program informs the user in short about 300 jobs and educational programs, psychological testing procedures, preparing job applications, studying in Europe and North America, how to improve decision making, and about 1500 relevant addresses. Furthermore, the program is equipped with a testing facility combining preferences concerning interests, income, and job security: The user can take a quiz about his or her interests responding up to 60 questions.

Two sliders enable the user to compare his or her interests (1) to the preference to get a high income and (2) the preference to get a high job security. The slider can be put into any position between "0" (less important than interests) to "100" (more important than interests). The user can choose between lists of suggested job fields, single jobs, or university studies. A short description can be accessed for each suggestion.

A third version of our system has been implemented in charge of a international chemical trust. The company wants to present its educational programs and career opportunities in schools motivating students to start their career in the chemical industry. The program is used as a point-of-information with a sophisticated graphical user interface including maps, charts, photographs, and sounds.

Evaluation of the expert advisor

There are several psychological inventories dedicated to measure career development and vocational maturity. One goal was to make valid prognostications of the career development and the vocational success. Most of the studies, however, show essential validity for short-term predictions, only. Therefore, most investigations focus on enhancing construct validity. High construct validity, however, gives little support to career decision making and vocational guidance. Therefore, we evaluated our testing facility for its practical validity – that is, how are the system´s responses accepted by students and counseling experts. 43 students participated in an experiment to investigate the understanding and acceptance of the information provided by the system. Furthermore, we explore whether the system is able to reconstruct 38 experts´ ratings.

We asked the students to rank four different job lists according to their judgment, whether the lists match their vocational interests or not. The students were told that the four lists were generated by four different computer programs. In fact, only one list was calculated by our computer system, three list contained random selections: A short random list with 6 suggestions, a long random list with 20 suggestions, and a list with a random selection of 12 popular jobs. The results show that students are able to judge, whether careers match their individual interests or not: They preferred individually calculated job lists compared to random lists. But they were not able to tell them apart from the list which consists of popular jobs which do not match their interests. Therefore, the students´ judgments rely on weak criteria (sometimes) leading them to wrong conclusions.

More information makes students more critical and keen to get more information. This is the result of a study in which 156 high school students participated. The students filled in a survey about their actual state of information and their need for information.

In a recent study, we tested the influence of the testing facility on recall of information and individual acceptance. The testing facility enabled the participants to enter their vocational interests and to receive a list of suggested jobs and educational programs from a multimedia encyclopedia. Additionally, all participants received the same list of jobs. The study has two parts: During the learning phase the participants read information about jobs and educational programs; during the testing phase, all participants completed two surveys: (a) They rated the overall acceptance of the program, its functions, and its information. (b) They completed a cued-recall task which consists of five questions about the job's description, income, distribution of age groups, usability indices, and unemployment rates.

The results confirm that individualized information effects acceptances ratings positively: The students considered all information about recommended jobs to be more interesting and valuable. Additionally, recall is clearly enhanced when studying individualized materials compared to general information. Students tend to recall more information about careers that match their individual interests.

Multimedia have potentials to enhance and facilitate career decision making. Most of the recent multimedia systems, however, show small positive effects or none at all. The effective use of multimedia is influenced by many internal and external factors, like motivation, knowledge, mode and contents of media, learning strategies, features of the task, etc. Making multimedia applications effective means to start from the user's perspective: Mostly, this implies to conduct a study about needs and abilities of the intended users.

Expert advises provided by the system clearly increases acceptance and performance of the system: Users pick up more information about career options that match their interests and they consider this information to be more valuable. The more information they have gathered and elaborated the more the loose their notion of knowing and develop a critical approach to expert advisory. Multimedia applications should not be designed to provide "something for everyone", but they should provide exactly that piece of information which is needed in a particular state of the decision making process. Multivariate statistical methods can complement (or partly replace) AI methods where they are not fully applicable.

Our system does not address the students´ inability to make reasonable judgments as a whole but tries to motivate careful consideration of as many career options as possible. In order to achieve this goal system responses have to be valid in terms of the students´ understanding and the experts´ valuation.

Three steps of the development of our testing facility ascertain its validity: (1) a comprehensive database containing precise and imprecise data, (2) examination of the items and testing procedures with the intended users, and (3) applying an adequate algorithm which refers to expert knowledge. Recently, a German bank charged us to develop a new testing facility addressing career decision making amongst non-students, namely professionals who want to make a shift within their company. In the future, we will test whether our approach can be extended and applied to different target groups and career options.

Placement services and vocational guidance

Placement services and vocational guidance, implemented in the LOs, includes various tasks and activities, which can be devided into a number of groups:

- receiving, registering and providing information to the unemployed;
- formulating employment plans;
- monitoring, counselling and placing clients into active employment policy programmes;
- placing clients in jobs and cooperating with employers;
- issuing work permits for foreign workers.

As in previous years, professional work on placement services and vocational guidance remains one of the priorities of ESS. After the new Employment and Unemployment Insurance Act was adopted, ESS began pushing for a transition from passive forms of dealing with unemployment issues towards encouraging and supporting the active involvment of unemployed people themselves, which brings new tasks and obligations to ESS staff.

New tasks appear mainly in the following areas: a more comprehensive and more exacting employment programme for all the registered unemployed should becompleted. The unemployed person should be actively seen and advised at least once a month. All the expenses, connected with searching for employment, should be approved. In order to improve job placement and because of employers' request to cooperate with ESS, the cooperation between these parties should be improved.

Vocational guidance and scholarships and CVIG

ESS vocational orientation has recently experienced some radical changes. The year 1998 was a turning point for the area of vocational guidance for the unemployed. The number of individual sessions has increased sixfold in the last two years. In 1998, for the first time, the number of sessions held with adults was higher than the number held with young people. It can be seen that vocational guidance is a lifetime process.

The year 1999 is a turning point for the area of vocational orientation for schoolchildren. In autumn 1998 Employment and Unemployment Insurance Act was changed. Article 71, which defined some activities and relations with schools, was omitted.

In 1999 the Vocational Guidance and Scholarships programme for schoolchildren does not actually provide for some activities: eighth-grade pupils enquiry by means of a questionnaire, collecting and processing of eighth-grade students' intentions, attending of the secondary school students' incorporation and success (the testing of seventh-grade students' intellectual abilities will, in accordance with the agreement between ESS, the Ministry of Labour, the Family and Social Affairs and the Ministry of Education and Sport, be implemented through a modified procedure). It has to be emphasized that only in this case, some tasks are eliminated since schoolchildren still are one of the Vocational Guidance and Scholarships Office's target groups.

Centre for Vocational Guidance and Information (CVIG)

The first CVIG in Slovenia was founded in 1998 in Ljubljana,

Smoletova ulica 12. It offers information necessary for planning educational and career paths to all who are interested. It is also intended for unemployed and surplus workers, who need in-depth vocational guidance, to young people who are making decisions about their study paths and professions and who need a great deal of information from vocational counsellors, and to any others who wish to obtain similar information.

At the moment there are more than 160 descriptions of professions available. In the CVIG library there is also information about courses and training at all levels, as well as information on financial assistance for the education available in the EU and other countries, as well as other tools and instructions on how to seek employment.

In addition to written, audio and visual resources, other forms of assistance are available every working day from ESS professional counsellor: individual counselling on designing a career or study path; descriptions of professions for the unemployed and young people.

Active employment policy programmes

After the new Employment and Unemployment Insurance Act active employment policy programmes were given a new dimension, which is shown in the increased importance of active employment policy measures to co-ordinate discrepancies in the labour market. On the basis of the new law, active employment policy measures can now be implemented by employers, authorised organizations and labour funds, in addition to ESS and the Ministry of Labour, Family and Social Affairs.

The following active employment policy measures are being carried out by ESS:

- training and education;
- public works;
- training and employment for disabled people and medical services;
- support for the self-employment;
- refunds and repayment of contributions;
- shared funding of regional projects;

Mostly the unemployed benefitted from these programmes and were therefore made more competitive in the labour market. ESS also applied various measures to prevent transitions into official unemployment from occuring:

- shared funding of sheltered companies;
- sharing the costs of the training and the additional training of surplus workers;
- participation in the government staff restructuring project and the prevention of transitions into official unemployment;
- labour funds;
- professional tasks to invitation for applicants to share the costs of new jobs and company restructuring.

Unemployment insurance activity

Within the unemployment insurance activity ESS resolves the entitlements arising from unemployment insurance, it apportions them and pays out money to those entitled. The entitlements arising from unemployment insurance are as follows:

- unemployment benefit;
- unemployment assistance;
- reimbursement of travel expenses;
- entitlements to health,
- pension and disability insurance.

The majority of administrative affairs are connected to decision-making procedures and paying out unemployment benefit and unemployment assistance (recognition and apportionment, stagnation, ceasing and reducting of the entitlement, etc.)

Insured people may exercise their entitlements for the period during which they are jobless through no fault of their own or against their wish. This entitlement to get unemployment benefit can be exercised provided they have unemployment insurance, that they were employed for a period of at least 12 months in the 18 months prior to the termination of employment, and that no suitable employment is available. An insured person becomes entitled to unemployment assistance after the end of their unemployment benefit, or after the trainee period, if shorter than 12 months. The conditions to assert the entitlement is in accordance with the income (80.0% of the guaranteed wage per family member) and with social/property census.

ESS ceases to pay unemployment benefit or unemployment assistance, among other things, if the person issuedit rejects suitable employment, rejects participation in the active employment policy programme, does not actively search for a job, is not available, etc.

People entitled to unemployment benefit have a right to basic health insurance as well as pension and disability insurance. Contributions for basic health insurance, pension and disability insurance and income tax deposit are deducted from the unemployment benefit. People entitled to unemployment assistance have a right to medical services.

An unemployed person is entitled to repayment of travel expenses (while searching for employment) and for registered post. Applications for expense repayments are presented at the LOs where decisions about the entitlements are made. Payment of the acknowledged expenses is guaranteed by the Insurance Implementation Office.

Legal affairs

ESS legal affairs department conducts all legal affairs, its own internal affairs, property and status-related issues and it partly implements the unemployment insurance. The tasks include the following in particular:

- legal support for ESS as a legal entity through the regulation of relationships and the formulation of internal general acts;
- legal support for activities and employment programmes through the preparation of uniform instructions and interpretation and examination of contracts;
- harmonisation of the legal practice of the ROs in the implementation of the unemployment insurance system, and other legal issues relating to employment programmes (registers of job-seekers and the unemployed);
- advice on scholarships, appeals procedure and entitlements of the unemployed and employers;
- legal exaction of debts.

Basic analytical work is related to the provision of correct, punctual and up-to-date information on the phenomena and events taking place in the labour market. With this aim in mind, special attention was devoted to a single methodology and approach for the processing of data on the registered unemployed, on demands for workers and trainees, on job placements for workers and trainees, and on the activities of ESS which fall within the scope of active employment policy measures. A great deal of attention was devoted to improving the methods of monitoring the work of ESS in achieving their objectives. The methodological aspect of monitoring the achievement of objectives was standardised, as was the method of presenting and publishing the selected indicators.

In 1998 a standardised classification of occupations was introduced on a trial basis. The coding key used as a classification tool in recording the titles of qualification was changed to coincide with the introduction of new professional titles and qualifications.

In keeping with its legal obligation, ESS conducted a survey (Employment Plan) in all companies and private businesses employing ten or more staff. Based on the survey results, an analysis of employers' employment plans was performed and an assesment made of the expected influx of redundant workers into unemployment.

At the end of each year an analysis of employment and unemployment trends and of the structural aspect of unemployment, with an emphasis on the critical groups of the registered unemployed, is carried out and a forecast of the conditions in the labour market in the forthcoming year made.

Monthly information is regularly published and the preparation of material for press conferences continues. In addition to involvement in the preparation of the Annual Report, we prepare material for use by the state and other bodies at the national, regional and local levels throughout the year, and also participate in the international exchange of data and experiences on collection methods. We publish relevant data on ESS internet and on the Web site. Part of the Analytical Department's work is associated with running the internal library and documentation facilities. The library uses the standard method for keeping records of books and other publications, periodicals (foreign and Slovene), videotapes, CD-ROMs, and ESS documentation.

Computerised information system

The purpose of the information technology centre is to provide computer support for ESS staff in the implementation of programmes and measures, and to provide support for the efficient functioning of ESS as a service and for its function as information provider. The major part of the work of the staff of the Information Technology Centre and departments revolves around the provision of support for the implementation of programmes and measures.

The Informational Technology Centre works on upgrading computer support for ESS information system. A start has been made on establishing standards for the computer environment within which the overhauled computer support system will operate, and the minimum hardware and software required for test operations; training was provided for staff at the Information Technology Centre, who will be the ones working hardest on overhauling the computer support system. A joint database model was prepared, and several concrete solutions for merging data from existing computer programs into a joint database were put forward.

Finance and accounting

The Accountancy and Finance Department deals with all ESS activities in operative financial accountancy. Its basic tasks are:

- realization of all necessary procedures for the expenditure of budgetary resources;
- providing information related to the financial situation (resources, obligations to sources), monetary and financial streams, reporting on the influx and expenditure of funds, according to purposes;
- providing mid-year analysis and operative reports for internal and external users and ESS annual balance sheet;
- monitoring of the financial-accountancy area, tax policy, employment and other ESS areas, as well as preparing various instructions and regulations as well as the interpretation of procedures;
- operational and even partly supervisory function in the implementation of providing resources for subsidizing students' nutrition through the Students' Organization of the University of Ljubljana and the Students' Organization of University of Maribor.

Personnel

Personnel department operates uniformly for ESS and co-ordinates some local offices' activities. Beside standard tasks, procedures dealing with job relations, one of the tasks is also the introduction of Regulations on Promotion changes, the Regulation on Education, and Regulations on Internal Organization and Job Systematization.

Through the new Employment and Unemployment Insurance Act the Personnel Department was given a task connected to contents preparation, the organization and implementation of expert examinations. According to the law, each employee who attains the sixth or the seventh level of education, working on employment, unemployment insurance, active employment policy and scholarships, has to pass the expert examination.

According to the new Employment and Unemployment Insurance Act special concern is focused on ESS staff education and training.

General affairs

General Affairs Department operates in the following areas:

- investments and keeping of ESS business premises and equipment;
- supply, records and stocktaking;
- central supply and records of supply and usage of office material;
- publishing;
- housing problems of ESS staff;
- social standards;
- keeping of business premises of ESS Head Office;
- office management, records and preserving documentary material;
- implementation, control and records of public orders.

Public relations, information and publishing

The Public Relations Co-ordinator mostly deals with systematically providing the public with information on ESS activities and its competence. Some of our forms and methods of providing the general public with information are:

- organizing regular monthly press conferences at the Head Office and ROs;
- providing informative material, such as leaflets, brochures, books, posters etc.;
- informing ESS staff through monthly bulletins and ESS Intranet system;
- active participation in different television broadcasts;
- systematically providing the public with information through the media;
- integral promotion of new ESS activities;
- taking part in the organization of consultations with other institutions;
- organizing various consultations and round tables;
- upgrading the free information helpline service with permanent topic-days;
- taking part in different fairs of local or state character;
- production of CD-ROMs containing information on the tasks and areas of ESS responsibility etc.

Due to numerous changes brought by the new law the following forms of informing were upgraded and intensified: ESS free information helpline service, ESS Intranet and Webpages, taking part in fairs, systematically (weekly or monthly) providing information via the mass media with ESS's own columns and creating the special television broadcast Slu•beni vhod (Business Entry).

Publishing is given an emphasis by ESS. At the moment 31 different leaflets are being used throughout Slovenia in ROs, LOs and other institutions (libraries, information offices, job clubs, schools etc. Leaflets are published two or three times a year, according to changing needs.

Organization, development and modernization of the institution

An Organization and Development Department supporting the activity service for organizational solutions provides organizational rules, instructions, authorizations etc., assistance with applications for users, editing, updating and publishing, participating in project teams and the monitoring of their work, and assistance to organizational units.

Essential contents, development and organization-related questions are solved within projects through which the Organization and Development Department offers professional and technical assistance with connection and co-ordination.

International cooperation

The ESS international activities are numerous and diverse. The ESS actively co-operates with public employment services and similar institutions abroad. Work on Phare projects has become more and more intensive, as well as on other European Union programmes, particularly within Leonardo da Vinci.

The central activities of international co-operation include:

- activities within the World Association of Public Employment Services (WAPES);

- participating at professional meetings and workshops within established co-operation between public Employment Services in Central Europe - Austria, the Czech Republic, Hungary, Germany, Slovakia, Poland, Croatia and Slovenia;
- activities for accession to the European Union - EURES Network, European Structural Funds, especially European Social Fund, adoption of acquis communautaire;
- participating in Phare projects and programmes, containing intensive forms of cross-border co-operation with regional offices of public Employment Services in Austria, Italy and Hungary; co-operation with Croatia has started as well.

Supervisory body

According to the new Employment and Unemployment Insurance Act the legal basis for a foundation of a new department within ESS was given. Professional tasks of the Supervisory Body are:

- implementation of supervision;
- acquisition of necessary data from other institutions;
- co-ordinating work with other institutions;
- proposing measures subsequent upon supervision;
- proposing changes and supplementary action dealing with relations between ESS and the unemployed;
- proposals of supplements and changes to laws and regulations.

The Supervisory Body is supposed to inspect approximately 2% of the unemployed registered at ESS. Those people who fail to accomplish their obligations are crossed out of ESS records and the right to participate in active employment policy programmes is denied them.

Internal revision

Internal revision is an independent evaluating activity which analyses tests and evaluates the internal control system.

ESS internal revision is directly subordinated to ESS Managing Director. In accordance with its establishment the internal revision informs ESS management and advises how to abolish the irregularities.

5

Career Counselling

Herr and Cramer stress that a career-counselling viewpoint must be integrative. Five major career-counselling models are often used in working with individuals trait-and-factor, client- centered, psychodynamic, developmental, and behavioural. Several career counselling specialists, among them Crites, Super and associates, and Krumboltz, have attempted to develop their own more comprehensive approaches. Career development theories try to explain why individuals choose careers. They also deal with the career adjustments people make over time. Modern theories, which are broad and comprehensive in regard to individual and occupational development, began appearing in the literature in the 1950s. The following four theories are among the most prominent:

Career Development Theories

Trait-and-factor theory

The origin of trait-and-factor theory can be traced back to Frank Parsons. It stresses matching an individual with a job that fits that person's talents. Its most widespread influence occurred during the Great Depression when E. G. Williamson championed its use. It was out of favour during the 1950s and 60s but has resurfaced in a more modern form, as reflected in the work of researchers such as John Holland.

The trait-and-factor approach has always stressed the uniqueness of persons. Original advocates of the theory assumed that a person's abilities and traits could be measured objectively and quantified. Personal motivation was considered relatively stable. Thus, satisfaction in a particular occupation depended on a proper fit between one's abilities and the job requirements. In its modern form, trait-and-factor theory stresses the interpersonal nature of careers and associated life-styles as well as the performance requirements of a work position.

Holland identifies six categories in which personality types and job environments can be classified: realistic, investigative, artistic, social, enterprising, and conventional. Personal satisfaction in a work setting depends on the degree of congruence between the personality type and the work environment.

For example, an artistic person will probably not fit well into a conventional job environment, such as that of office manager. There are exceptions, of course; and as Salomone and Sheehan point out, it is likely that some non-psychological factors, such as economic, social, or cultural influences, account for why many professional and nonprofessional workers accept and keep their jobs.

Psychodynamic theory

Psychodynamic theory is best exemplified by the writings of Anne Roe although Robert Hoppock outlines some similar ideas by stressing the importance of unconscious motivation and meeting emotional needs. Roe theorised that vocational interests develop as a result of the interaction between parents and their children. Career choices reflect the desire to satisfy needs not met by parents in childhood. From the psychodynamic point of view, the first few years, of childhood are primarily responsible for shaping the pattern of life. Roe believes there is an unconscious motivation from this period that influences people to choose a career in which these needs can be expressed and satisfied. Three different parent-child relationship climates The first is characterised by an emotional concentration on the child. The pattern takes one of two forms.

One is overprotection, in which the parents do too much for the child and encourage dependency. The other is over-demanding, in which the parents emphasise achievement. Children who grow up in these types of environments usually develop a need for constant feedback and rewards. They frequently choose careers that provide recognition from others, such as the performing arts.

There are two extremes within child-rearing pattern. One is neglectful parenting, in which there is little effort made to satisfy the needs of the child. The other is rejecting parenting, ill which no effort is made to satisfy the child's needs. Roe speculates that children reared in such environments will concentrate on careers that involve scientific and mechanical interests as a way of finding gratification in life. They are more prone to deal with things and ideas. The final pattern of child-parent relationships is acceptance of the child. Acceptance may be casual or more actively loving; in either case, independence is encouraged. Children from these families usually seek careers that balance the personal and nonpersonal aspects of life, such as teaching or counselling.

Developmental theories

Developmental theories are generally more inclusive, more concerned with longitudinal expression of career behaviour, and more inclined to highlight the importance of self-concept. Super believes that career development is the process of implementing a self-concept. People's views of who they are reflected in what they do. He suggests vocational development unfolds in five stages, each of which contains a developmental task to be completed.

The first stage is growth (from birth to 14). During this stage, with its substages of fantasy (ages 4-10), interest (ages 11-12), and capacity (ages 13-14), a child forms a mental picture of the self in relation to others. During the process of growth, the child becomes oriented to the world of work. The second stage is exploration (ages 15-24). It has three substages: tentative (ages 15-17), transition (ages 18-21), and trial (ages 22-24). The major task of this stage is a general exploration of the world of work and the specification of a career preference. The third stage is known as establishment (ages 25-44). Its two substages, trial (ages 25-30) and advancement (ages 31-44), constitute the major task of becoming established in a preferred and appropriate field of work. Once established, persons can concentrate on advancement until they tire or reach the top of the profession. The fourth stage, maintenance (ages 45-64), has the major task of preserving what one has already achieved.

The final stage, decline (age 65 to death), is a time for disengagement from work and alignment with other sources of satisfaction. It has two substages: deceleration (ages 65-70) and retirement (age 71 to death).

Cognitive and social-learning theories

In the 1960s cognitive and social-learning theories of career development were formulated Two of the must prominent cognitive models have a developmental base. Tiedeman and O'Hara outline a seven-stage model of career decision: exploration (ages 14-18), crystallisation (ages 18-21), choice (ages 18-25), clarification (ages 18-25), induction (ages 21-30), reformation (ages 21-30), and integration (ages 30-40). There is some overlap among these stages, but each requires the individual to make a decision.

This emphasis on the cognitive restructuring of the person from "within to without" is Tiedeman's unique contribution to career development theory. Knefelkamp and Slepitza also focus on a hierarchical structure of cognitive development 'in describing the development of career decision making in college students. Their model of career planning takes into account nine variables, such as locus of control, analysis, synthesis, and openness to alternative perspectives. A major weakness of the theory is its lack of measurement of the processes on which it focuses.

Career counselling has not enjoyed the same degree of prestige that other forms of counselling or psychotherapy have. This is unfortunate for both the counselling profession and the many people who need these services. Surveys of high school juniors and seniors and college undergraduates show that the counselling service they most prefer is career counselling. Brown also points that career counselling may be a viable intervention for some clients who have emotional problems related to nonsupportive, stress-producing environments. The contribution of career counselling to personal growth and development is well documented. Crites lists important aspects of career counselling, which include the following:

1) The need for career counselling is greater than the need for psychotherapy.
2) Career counselling can be therapeutic.
3) Career counselling is more difficult than psychotherapy.

Types of Career counselling

Client-centered career counselling

Client-centered career counselling was inspired by the writings of Carl Rogers and developed by C. H. Patterson. Client-centered career counselling deals in a complex but systematic fashion with both the emotional and cognitive aspects of making a career choice. Its major shortfalls are a failure to consider thoroughly the influence of outside phenomena on the career decisions of clients and an inconsistency in conveying career information to clients in a nondidactic Rogerian fashion.

Psychodynamic career counselling

The model underlying psychodynamic career counselling was constructed primarily by Bordin. His view, which is based on psychodynamic theories such as Anne Roe's, holds that career choices involve a client's needs and are developmental in nature. A major limitation of the approach is its strong emphasis on internal factors, such as motivation, and its lack of attention to external variables. The process of career counselling from this perspective is considered overly complex.

One offshoot of psychodynamic career counselling, which is more concrete but still complex, is based on the work of Murray Bowen and has been amplified by McGoldrick and Gerson. According to this approach, the uniqueness of people is interconnected with their family of origin. One way of mapping family-of-origin patterns is to draw a genogram. Okiishi used genograms and a psychodynamically based theory to provide career counselling for undergraduate students. Okiishi's results were successful, illustrating that complex psychodynamic career counselling can still be pragmatic.

Developmental career counselling

The major contributions of developmental career counselling are its emphases on the importance of the life span in career decision making and on career decisions that are influenced by other processes and events in a person's life. This "life pattern paradigm for career counselling encourages Counsellors to consider a client's aptitudes and interests in a matrix of life experiences, not just in comparison to some normative group".

The developmental approach can be conceptualised as career-pattern counselling. While this method has been criticised for its historical and descriptive emphases, these features, along with the conceptual depth of the theory, have also been considered strengths. Overall, developmental career counselling is strong. With the further elaborations of Super and his associates, an even more comprehensive rainbow theory has emerged.

Comprehensive career counselling

Crites developed a model based on the five major approaches just discussed; the more general systems of counselling and psychotherapy, such as those described by Corsini and Wedding; and his own wide experience as a career counsellor. Counsellors make three diagnoses of a client's career problems: *differential* (what the problems are), dynamic (why problems have occurred), and *decisional* (how the problems are being dealt with). Such diagnoses result from a close working relationship between client and counsellor and are facilitated by open communication. Once made, diagnoses form the basis for problem-resolution strategies that can be expected to produce more further functioning individuals-intellectually, personally, socially, and vocationally.

Crites employs eclectic methods in his career counselling. He uses client-centered and developmental counselling at the beginning to identify problems. The middle stage of his process is dominated by psychodynamic techniques, such as interpretation, to clarify how problems have occurred. The final stage of the process uses trait-and-factor and behavioural approaches to help the client resolve problem areas. Comprehensive career counselling also advocates the use of tests in working with clients. The focus in test use, however, is on interpreting the tests without the tests: that is, letting the client and counsellor share responsibility for interpreting what the test results mean independently of standardised norms.

Finally, this model of career counselling stresses the use of career information and recommends that counsellors orient clients to such information and reinforce them when they make use of it.

Career Counselling with Diverse Population

Career counselling and education are conducted with a wide variety of individuals in diverse settings. Brown observes that career counselling typically is offered in college counselling centers, rehabilitation facilities, employment offices, and public schools. He thinks it could be applied with great advantage in many other places as well, including mental health centers and private-practice offices.

Jesser agrees and asserts there is a need to provide career information and counselling to potential users, such as the unemployed, the learning disabled, prisoners, and those released from mental hospitals who seek to reenter the job market. Reimbursement is a drawback to offering career counselling outside its traditional populations and settings. Career concerns are not covered in the DSM-IV, and most health-care coverage excludes this service from reimbursement.

The concept of careers encompasses the life span, Counsellors who specialise in this area find themselves working with a full age range of clients, from young children to octgenarians. Consequently, many different approaches and techniques have been developed for working effectively with select groups. The process of career development begins in the preschool years and becomes more direct in elementary schools. Herr and Cramer cite numerous studies to show that during the first six years of school, many children develop a relatively stable self perception and make a tentative commitment to a vocation. These processes are observed whether career counselling and guidance activities are offered or not.

Nevertheless, it is beneficial for children, especially those who live in areas with limited employment opportunities, to have a broad, systematic program of career counselling and guidance in the schools. Such a program should focus on awareness rather than firm decision making and should teach children that they have career choices.

Levels of career awareness in elementary school children may be raised through activities such as field trips to local industries, bakeries, manufacturing plants, or banks. When such trips are followed up with appropriate classroom learning exercises, children become aware of a wider spectrum of related occupations.

Other ways of expanding children's awareness of careers are through parent career days or class visitors. "This is an opportune time to introduce the concept of school as work and students as workers". Splete outlines a comprehensive program for working with children that includes parent education and classroom discussions jointly planned by teacher and counsellor.

There are three key career development areas at the elementary school level: self-awareness (that is, one's uniqueness), career awareness and exploration, and decision making. Well-designed career guidance and counselling programs that are implemented at an early age and coordinated with programs across all levels of the educational system can go a long way toward dispelling irrational and decision-hindering career development myths, such as "a career decision is an event that should occur at a specific point in time".

To meet the career needs of adolescents, the American School Counsellor Association developed a role statement on the expectations and responsibilities of school Counsellors engaged in career guidance. The five-point statement emphasises that school Counsellors should involve others, both inside and outside the school, in the delivery of career education to students.

Cole stresses that in the middle and junior high school, career guidance activities should include the exploration of work opportunities and student's evaluation of their own strengths and weaknesses in regard to possible future careers. Assets that students should become aware of and begin, to evaluate include talents and—skills, general intelligence, motivation level, friends, family, life experience, appearance, and health.

Applied arts curriculum such as industrial arts (applied technology), home economics (family life education) and computer literary classes... offer ideal opportunities for integrated career education. Libraries and/or career centers may have special middle level computerised career information delivery systems (CIDS) for student use". At the senior high school, career guidance and counselling activities are related to the maturity of students.

The greatest challenge and need for career development programs occur on this level. Herr and Cramer state that, in general, there are three emphases of career counselling at the high school level: "stimulating career development, providing treatment, and aiding placement". More specifically, Counsellors provide students with reassurance, information, emotional support, reality testing, planning strategies, attitude clarification, and work experiences, depending on a student's needs and level of functioning.

Several techniques have proven quite effective in helping adolescents crystallise ideas about careers. Some involve the use of fantasies, such as imagining a typical day in the future, an awards ceremony, a midcareer change, or retirement. More concrete exercises might include completing an occupational family tree to find out how present interests compare with the careers of family members.

Another career focus within high schools is youth apprenticeships, a popular approach that provides work-based learning for adolescents. They help students who are not college-bound make a smooth transition from high school to the primary work environment. While apprenticeships hold much promise, they pose several tasks for career Counsellors:

(a) helping clients learn adaptive skills that will enable them to change with change, (b) helping clients find ways to acquire the kinds of work [identified in government reports], and (c) helping clients to develop a personally meaningful set of work values that will enable them to humanise the workplace for themselves-and thus receive the personal satisfaction that comes from true work.

In addition to helping youth in school, career counsellors must make special efforts to help the estimated 15-29 percent of high school students who leave school before graduation. These young people are at risk of unemployment or underemployment for the rest of their lives. Educational programs, such as Mann's *four Cs* (cash, care, computers, and coalitions), can help students at risk become involved in career exploration and development.

According to Bloch, successful educational counselling programs for students at risk of dropping out should follow six guidelines:

1) They make a connection between a student's present and future status (that is, cash-students are paid for attending).
2) They individualise programs and communicate caring.
3) They form successful coalitions with community institutions and businesses.
4) They integrate sequencing of career-development activities.
5) They offer age and stage-appropriate career-development activities.
6) They use a wide variety of media and career-development resources, including computers.

Career counselling with college students

Undergraduates are likely to visit college counselling centers for career counselling. Career-counselling services are valued by college students at all levels of study For example, a study conducted at the University of Georgia revealed that career-development needs far outweighed student's purely personal and academic concerns. Even students who have already decided on their college majors and careers seek such services.

Counselling center activities range from creating alumni career consultation programs to writing weekly informational columns for student newspapers. Herr and Cramer list a number of services that a comprehensive career guidance and counselling program in an institution of higher education attempts to provide. Among them are help with the selection of a major field of study; offering self-assessment and self-analysis through psychological testing; helping students understand the world of work; facilitating access to employment opportunities through career fairs, internships, and campus interviews; teaching decision-making skills; and meeting the needs of special populations.

Another important service is exploring with students the role of leisure in proposed career and life-style plans. Anticipating problems related to work and intimate relationships, such as preparing to live in a dual-career family, have also been proposed as career-counselling services for college students.

Career counselling with adults

Career interest patterns tend to be more stable after college than during college. Nevertheless, many adults continue to need career counselling. Indeed, adults experience cyclical periods of stability and transition throughout their lives, and career change is a developmental as well as situational expectation at this stage of life.

Adults may have particularly difficult times with their careers and career decisions when they find themselves unhappy in their work yet feel appropriately ambivalent about switching directions. In such situations they may create illogical or troublesome career beliefs that become self-fulfilling and self-defeating.

There are two dominant ways of working with adults in career counselling, the differential approach and the developmental approach. The differential approach stresses that "the typology of persons and environments is more useful than any life stage strategies for coping with career problems".

It avoids age-related stereotypes, gender and minority-group issues, and the scientific and practical difficulties of dealing with life-span problems. At any age, the level and quality of a person's vocational coping is a function of the interaction of personality type and type of environment plus the consistency and differentiation of each. A career counsellor who is aware of typological formulations such as Holland's can predict the characteristic ways a given personal cope with career problems.

For example, a person with a well-defined social/artistic personality (typical of many individuals employed as counsellors) would be expected to have high educational and vocational aspirations, to have good decision-making ability, to have a strong and lifelong interest in learning, to have, moderate personal competency, and to have a marked interest in creative and high level performance rather than in leadership.

A person with such a profile would also have a tendency to remold or leave an environment in the face of adversity. A major advantage of working from this approach is the ease with which it explains career shifts at any age. People who shift careers, at any point in life, seek to find more consistency between personality and environment.

The developmental approach examines a greater number of individual and environmental variables. The experiences people have with events, situations and other people play a large part in determining their identities (i.e., what they believe and value, how they respond to others, and what their own self images are) Developmental life-span career theory proposes that adults are always in the process of evaluating themselves in regard to how they are affected by outside influences (such as spouse, family, and friends) and how they impact these variables. The theories of Donald Super and John Crites are prime examples of Viewpoints that address developmental career concerns.

Likewise, Okun and Gladstein and Apfel believe the interplay of other people and events strongly influences career decisions in adulthood. Gladstein and Apfel's approach to adult Career counselling focuses on a combination of six elements: developmental, comprehensive self-in-group, longitudinal, mutual committment, and multimethodological. These elements work together in the process of change at this stage of life. This model, which has been implemented on a practical level at the University of Rochester Adult Counselling Center since 1977, considers the total identity of the person over time. In a related model, Chusmir stresses the interaction of multiple factors in the process that men undergo when choosing nontraditional careers. Whether or not careers are nontraditional, the fact is that many forces enter into career decisions.

Career counselling with women

Women and cultural minorities have historically received less adequate career counselling than white males have. The reason has often involved stereotypical beliefs and practices connected with these two groups. For example, society has generally assumed that women will have discontinuous career patterns to accommodate the needs of their families. This trend is changing, although gender-based differences in American society will continue to exert an influence for years to come. These differences should not be overlooked in the evolution of career and work environments.

Gender-based career patterns have changed for several reasons. In 1987 the Hudson Institute issued a report, *Workforce 2000,* which calculated that, from the late 1980s to the year 2000, nonwhites, women, and immigrants will make up more than five-sixths of net additions to the U.S. work force. These statistics, along with growing social activism among women and cultural minority groups, are helping to challenge constraining negative forces.

Since 1970, there has been a dramatic rise in research on and interest in the career development of women. The trend parallels the increase in women's participation in the work force, from roughly 50 percent of all women in the early 1970s to approximately 75 percent in the 1990s. Unfortunately, most theories of career development cannot be appropriately applied to women because they were formulated for men or are incomplete. In working with women, counsellors need to watch out for occupational sex-role stereotyping, even at the elementary school level.

Many people often assume that as a group females prefer social, artistic, and conventional occupations.

Therefore, girls and women are sometimes not challenged to explore their abilities and possibilities. As a result, many women fail to develop their abilities to the fullest.

Consequently, they never work; develop a low or moderate commitment to work; or focus on "safe," traditional, female-dominated occupations such as teaching, nursing, or social work. Only a relatively small portion of women are pioneers who become highly committed to working in nontraditional occupations. To understand why many women choose career paths as they do, Scott and Hatalla surveyed an extensive number of women from a large, urban, mid-Atlantic university 30 years after their graduations in 1959 and 1960. They found that three factors were common to the sample group, regardless of work history: "the contingency factors of Perception of Interests and Awareness of Skills, and the chance factor of Unexpected Personal Events".

These researchers believe the last factor, Unexpected Personal Events, needs further investigation and exploration. Another area that needs counsellor's attention is demographics and trends. Analysis of labour market trends through the year 2000 indicates a major shift from goods-producing to service-producing industries". Service jobs are those such as sales clerk and computer operator. If young women take these jobs rather than pursue higher-paying, nontraditional careers in skilled trades, they will be subjected to economic forces such as poverty, social welfare, and dependence on men that are not in their best interest or society's.

Therefore, there is "an urgent need for career counselling interventions" offered through live or video modelling "that will persuade young women to consider the economic benefits of nontraditional career choices".

In addition to girls and young women, two other groups of women workers displaced homemakers and late entrants have received and should continue to receive considerable attention. Displaced homemakers, who enter the job market out of necessity, and late-entry or delayed-entry women, who decide to enter the job market after considerable time at home, pose considerable challenges for career counsellors.

The displaced homemaker often finds herself in a financial strain, uninformed about current job market trends, without a support system, and with a shaky self-concept. Career counsellors must first help women sort out or resolve some of these problems before dealing with major career decisions. In the process, they may assist the women in finding temporary employment, but long-term solutions to career satisfaction take time. Late-entry women, because of their own motivation and status, do not face the same problems to the same degree. Nevertheless, they usually need more information on careers and, like displaced homemakers have to identify skills and deal with self-concept and family responsibilities.

Counselling of Cultural minorities

Cultural minorities are so diverse that it is impossible to focus on all the factors that career counsellors must deal with in working with them individually or collectively. Many minorities (and women) have difficulty obtaining meaningful employment because of employer's discrimination practices, lack of marketable skills, and limited access to informal networks that lead to good jobs.

The interest patterns of cultural minorities (as a group) tend to fall within Holland's social, conventional, and enterprising categories, which can limit their choices for meaningful work. While about 27 percent of adults in the United States expresses a need for assistance in finding information about work, the rate is much higher among specific minority populations.

Counsellors must remember that cultural minorities have special needs in regard to establishing themselves in careers. Counsellors must be sensitive to such issues and at the same time help individuals overcome artificial and real barriers that prohibit them from maximising their potential. For instance, some African-American youths who have lived in poverty all their lives are characterised as vocationally handicapped because "they have few positive work-related experiences, limited educational opportunities, and frequently lack positive work role models". Structured programs for these individuals use positive role models and experiences to affirm cultural or ethnic heritage and abilities, thus working to address and overcome traditional restrictions.

A special minority group not often considered in career counselling are those individuals with gay, lesbian, or bisexual life-styles. These individuals face unique concerns as well as many that are common to other groups. Of special concern to many gays, lesbians, and bisexuals is whether to be overt or covert in disclosing their sexual orientation at work. Persons with minority sexual orientations face personal and professional developmental concerns, including discrimination, if they openly acknowledge their beliefs and practices.

Importance of Career Guidance

Psychology has provided counselling a theoretical base for understanding and changing human behaviour. These factors do little to separate counselling from educational psychology as elaborated earlier in this book. However, a strong case could be made for the striking lack of commonality between counselling and educational psychology.

Educational psychology has become less interested in application whereas counselling is by definition oriented toward change and the application of principles of change. Educational psychology has always been closely tied to undergraduate teacher education, its very existence arising from the early application of psychology to teacher training. The scope of its knowledge base is reflected in, if not identical with, the content that undergraduate teacher trainees are expected to master . No such direct tie between teacher training and counselling exists. Counselling is almost exclusively a graduate program with, in some cases, no tie to colleges of education.

In looking at the history of guidance and counselling psychology, a plausible case could be made for including a number of contributive events in a story of complex developments. It is difficult to look back and select those people, circumstances, and events that provide a history for guidance and counselling. In like manner, it is difficult to look forward from a place in history and trace the impact of particular people, events, and cultural circumstances. A particular key event may have direct and indirect consequences for not only guidance and counselling, but may also be part of the history of other areas as well.

In order to limit the historical scope, one must first determine the phenomena one is attempting to explain. Counselling professionals are trained at undergraduate, masters, and doctoral levels, with the majority of direct service providers being trained at the masters level. Each of the levels is based on different assumptions and resultant models of what is needed for effective intervention. This description will restrict itself to those professional areas variously described as:

a) counselling psychology,

b) counsellor education, and

c) guidance and counselling.

The counselling psychology area includes only those doctoral programs meeting APA-accreditation standards. The counsellor education area includes all other doctoral programs in counselling. Guidance and counselling will be used as an inclusive category for all subdoctoral programs, including such programs as school counselling, agency counselling, college counselling, marital and family counselling, and rehabilitation counselling. We will look first at the status of counselling psychology as a professional field.

The American Psychologist lists doctoral programs as being either fully accredited or provisionally accredited. Of these programs nine were accredited in the 1950s, three in the 1960s, 11 in the 1970s, and 18 have received accredited status in the 1980s. Obviously, the impetus to become an accredited doctoral program has greatly increased and generally reflects an increased identity with psychology in those programs. The identity with psychology has been greatly influenced by the credentialing process. Licensure laws for psychology exist in 48 states, with graduation from an accredited program allowing for access to the examination process in most states.

Access to third-party payments for the provision of mental health services is also greatly enhanced by graduation from an accredited program. Further, the majority of 275 accredited predoctoral internship training programs in psychology either require or highly prefer applicants who have graduated from accredited programs. It appears that the professional stature and access provided by the doctoral degree in counselling psychology clearly make it the preferred degree for counselling professionals.

Both career and training opportunities are enhanced by credentials made more available through APA accredited programs. Further, it appears that those programs with adequate strength and resources have moved in this direction. In fact, some of the more recently accredited programs were not too long ago identified as leading counsellor education programs. The identity w psychology has also required curriculum that ensures adequate psychology content. Hollis and Wan summarize the APA criteria:

Professional psychology programs generally are located in universities or schools of professional psychology that offer doctoral training and are approved by one of the six regional accreditation bodies recognized by the Council on Post-Secondary Accreditation (COPA). Program must be clearly identified and labeled as a psychology program and must be a recognizable, coherent organisation entity. Faculty must be well qualified and must have clear authority and primary responsibility for all aspects of the program. The plan of study must be integrated and organized with assurance of breadth of exposure to the field of psychology including a curriculum with equivalency of at least three academic years of full-time resident graduate study. The course-work must include scientific and professional ethics and standards, research design and methodology, statistics and psychological measurement, biological bases of behaviour, cognitive-affective bases of behaviour, social bases of behaviour, individual bases of behaviour, and courses in specialty areas.

Supervised practicum, internship, and field or laboratory training must be included. The minimum practicum experience is 300 hours, of which at least 150 hours are in direct service experience and 75 hours of formally scheduled supervision. Internship must be full-time for one year or the equivalent with an experience of at least 1500 hours.

Counselling psychology as a recognized specialty in psychology is also represented by a research literature through the Journal of Counselling Psychology and The Counselling Psychologist. The Journal of Counselling Psychology is primarily concerned with "reporting the results of empirical studies about counselling processes and interventions, theoretical articles about counselling, and studies dealing with the evaluation of applications of counselling and counselling programs". The Counselling Psychologist is a theme-oriented journal that requests and approves proposed issues dealing with timely topics related to counselling. Division 17 of APA represents the Counselling Psychology field within APA and also to the public. Membership in Division 17 of APA lists 224 Fellows, 2,182 Members, and 148 Associates.

The American Board of Professional Psychology offers diplomate status in Counselling Psychology with 262 individuals so recognized. Another parallel professional group is the Council of Counselling Psychology Training Programs. This group is concerned with training issues and with representing counselling psychology student and program interests with the Association of Psychology Internship Centers (APIC), state licensing boards, the Veterans Administration (VA) and with other specialty areas in psychology.

Counsellor education

In USA Hollis and Wantz surveyed 506 institutions and 584 administrative units offering counsellor preparation programs. Units surveyed offered a wide range of counselling specialities. From the reported data, Hollis and Wantz extrapolated that 222 doctoral degree programs are offered. From the large number of programs it is not difficult to conclude that nearly every university, college, or professional school that offers a doctoral degree offers one in a counselling related area.

From this frequency it could also be assumed that counselling doctoral programs are cost efficient from the institution's perspective,. From the graduates surveyed, 19% of them were identified with counselling psychology. The other 81% were identified as counselling, counsellor education, counselling and guidance, or some other related designation.

Counsellor education doctoral programs are more diverse than those in counselling psychology so it is more difficult to assess the status of these doctoral programs. Counsellor education programs are best represented by the Association of Counsellor Education and Supervision, a Division of the American Association of Counselling and Development.

AACD is the major professional organisation representing counsellors at the masters level and counsellor education at the doctoral level. Although AACD membership is predominantly made up of master's level professionals, membership in ACES is primarily doctoral. ACES first approved training standards for Advanced Preparation in Counsellor Education in 1977. Hollis and Wantz summarize the standards as follows:

> The doctoral program consists of a minimum of four academic years of graduate preparation, including the entry program and a year of internship. A minimum of one academic year of full-time graduate study beyond the entry program (masters and specialists) is required. Supervised experiences include the completion of at least one academic year (36 weeks) of full-time internship.
>
> Competencies in statistics, research design, and other research methodology are to be obtained by all students. In addition to the core areas of preparation, students are to gain a depth of knowledge and skills in one or more areas such as learning theory, career guidance, research, testing, or evaluation.
>
> Beyond coursework and seminars students are to be provided opportunities to participate in conferences, workshops, special training programs, and other professional activities that will assist in bridging the gap between the campus and the professional world. Sixteen programs have received accreditation for doctoral studies from the Council for Accreditation of Counselling and Related Educational Programs.

Thus, only a minority of doctoral level counsellor educators have graduated from a program that has met national training standards and been the subject of external peer evaluation. The utility of CACREP accreditation is still uncertain. Certainly such standards assist a doctoral training program in self-evaluation studies, but whether it serves a credentialing function for graduates is unclear.

Many graduates of non-APA approved doctoral programs seek licensure as psychologists, often unsuccessfully and frequently with a great deal of questioning from state licensing boards. Several states have passed counsellor licensing bills, but these have not clearly facilitated the collection of third-party payments or allowed the licensed counsellor any special privileges. They have served to restrict the title and thus protect the public by ensuring that those with such credentials have met minimal standards. Counsellor Education as a professional field is represented by the Journal of Counselling and Development and other AACD publications.

The Journal of Counselling and Development has been primarily a practitioner-oriented journal with little theoretical, empirical research reported. However, with the recent change of editorship a more scholarly emphasis is evident. The editor, associate editor, and column editors are also professionals with heavy involvement in counselling psychology. Current leadership in AACD and its divisions is decidedly void of individuals who also are leaders in counselling psychology. This has not always been the case as early leaders in APA Division 17 and AACD were often drawn from the same leadership pool.

Based on the 418 units analysed by Hollis and Wantz, 407 programs offered one or more masters and specialists degrees. They estimated that more than 24,000 master's students with some type of counselling major are graduated each year. Of these, approximately half seem to be prepared for jobs in school settings, although not all these graduates are finding employment in schools. The remainder are preparing for positions outside the school setting in such areas as rehabilitation counselling, student personnel development, and community and agency counselling. Again, it would not be presumptuous to conclude that nearly every post secondary institution offering graduate degrees offers a master's degree in guidance and counselling or a similarly named field.

Many of the programs began in response to a tremendous demand for counsellors in the schools and once developed, have continued to graduate large numbers of counsellors despite an imbalance between demand for graduates and the number of graduates. One response has been a great expansion of the number of specialties offered by the programs. Many employers have also gradually raised requirements from the paraprofessional level to the master's degree as the preferred entry level preparation.

Vocational rehabilitation counselling increased its standards during the 1970s and the same change is currently evident in the substance abuse area. Alcohol treatment centers are increasingly seeking people with greater credentials and training, with a similar trend becoming evident in correctional settings. The master's degree in counselling and guidance is also viewed as a robust degree.

Teachers, needing additional coursework for advancement, see a counselling degree as a way to increase salary and expand options, With the degree, the person is eligible for a position as a school counsellor and also has a credential that may allow for work outside the elementary/secondary school environment. Addit-ionally, many people find master's degree programs interesting and applicable to their own lives and their environments. They are perceived as providing a set of skills that can be used in a range of noncounselling settings from real estate sales to business management.

Unfortunately, because of the demand/graduate imbalance, students with more focused vocational goals may find that the degree fails to result in the career credential sought.

The Association for Counsellor Education and Supervision accepted standards for the entry preparation of counsellors and other personnel services specialists in 1973. Hollis and Wantz summarize the training standards as follows:

— The Program must have objectives that were developed by the faculty in the institution of higher education where offered. The institution must provide a graduate program in counsellor education with opportunity for full-time study throughout the academic year.

— The program of study includes a core of courses with content applicable to the following areas: human growth and development, social and cultural foundations, helping relationship, groups, lifestyle and career development, appraisal of the individual, research and evaluation, and professional orientation.

— The program must provide specialized studies necessary for practice in different work settings so that each student may gain skills needed to work effectively in the professional setting where the student plans to practice.

Supervised experiences include laboratory, practicum, and internship. The minimum practicum requirement is sixty clock hours extended over a minimum nine-month period. Internship is a postpracticum experience where the intern spends in the field placement a minimum of 300 clock hours on the job under supervision by a qualified supervisor. Research facilities must be available within the counsellor preparation institution to faculty and students. A small percentage of master's level programs are accredited by ACES. However, several others have met AAMFT, CORE, or other standards and a large number of them meet minimal standards set by their state departments of education in order to recommend graduates for credentials as guidance counsellors.

These programs differ widely in the extent of psychological content in their curriculum. Some by virtue of administrative location include significant coursework in psychology or educational psychology whereas others, often housed independently from a psychology or educational psychology department, may be openly antagonistic toward psychology and are regarded with disdain by psychologists on campus.

The controversy over the relevance and adequacy of psychology as the primary discipline base for counsellor training has been a controversial one and the "gulf between counselling psychology and counsellor education appears to be growing" over this issue. Master's degree training of counsellors often exists within the context of teacher training. The genesis of many of the programs was the training of school counsellors; thus, these programs developed almost exclusively in colleges of education.

Several recent national studies of education have suggested that teacher training would be improved if many of the less equipped institutions would get out of the business. This same recommendation would certainly apply to graduate training in counselling. There are far too many programs with less than minimal faculty and other resources, with ill-defined curricula, and without adequately supervised practicum experiences producing poorly prepared graduates. The training of master's degree counsellors is, however, an important function.

In nearly all situations, a great percentage of direct services are provided by subdoctoral personnel. A master's degree program can provide entry level preparation for these roles. As identified earlier, many areas are undergoing increased corrections and the master's level professional represents a level of formal training well beyond the current, typical service provider. Just as the position of school counsellor evolved from the teacher who showed a knack for counselling, to the 90-day wonder with limited training, to the master's degree as the minimal entry requirement, the master's degree represents a significant increase in professionalisation in many settings.

There is, however, no longer a need for programs that cannot provide rigorous, well-developed academic and practical experiences. What is labeled as counselling is diverse and wide-ranging. An analogy from the geography of the United States seems descriptive of the current status of counselling and its history.

Vocational guidance movement

The mountain beginning of counselling was clearly the vocational guidance movement. This interesting and robust heritage, itself the product of diverse sources, grew from a period of social problems, but yet one that was characterized by optimism. Rockwell and Rothney stated that the "guidance movement was born in the swelter and confusion of protest, reform, utopian idealism, and defences of the status quo which were rampant in the late nineteenth and early twentieth century". The industrial revolution resulted in a concentration of the workforce, a demand for a skilled workforce, and uncertainty in the labour market. Subsequently, there was a growth in secondary school enrolment and a challenge to the relevance of a classical education for preparing a skilled workforce. Brewer identified four social cues that led to the development of vocational guidance including:

a) the division of labour,

b) the growth of technology,

c) the extension of vocational education, and

d) the spread of democracy.

People such as Frank Parsons at the Civic Service House in Boston and Jesse B. Davis in the schools of Detroit and Grand Rapids began to develop approaches to vocational guidance that allowed a person to study self and aptitudes and occupations and to make wise decisions based on this study.

Vocational guidance was not only viewed as assisting the development of individuals, but was also seen as a means for achieving social goals. The contribution of psychology to the vocational guidance movement was described by Brewer "the psychologists and their researches did not lead to the organisation of a systematic plan for guidance; the plan came from the work of the publicist, the social worker, the teacher, the promoter of adult education" and "while the practice of vocational guidance has been greatly aided through the researches of the psychologists, in no sense can it be said that experimental or the psychology contributed to its actual origin" The importance of Frank Parsons' thin reflected in his 1908 book Choosing a Profession must be emphasized.

6

College Counselling

College counselling and student services involve understanding how college students of all ages learn, grow, and develop. Many entry-level and not a few seasoned professionals know little of student development theory or practice. This fact is unfortunate because working with students effectively requires specialised knowledge. Even among professionals with the best of intentions, ethically or legally questionable behaviour may cause harm if one is not closely attuned to this specific population. There are a number of theoretical models that attempt to guide professionals in college counselling and student services. From an ideological viewpoint, there are three dominant traditions: in loco parentis, student services, and student development. In loco parentis gives faculty and staff the parental role of teaching moral values.

Student services emphasises the student as consumer and mandates services that facilitate development. This approach stresses a cafeteria-style manner of program offerings that students select according to what they think they need. Student development focuses on creating research-based environments that "help college students learn and develop". Student development is proactive because it makes opportunities available for special groups of students. Within student development, there are at least four kinds of developmental theories that guide professionals' activities: psycho-social, cognitive-structural, person-environment interaction, and typological. *Psychosocial theories* are embodied most thoroughly in the writings of Arthur Chickering. He contends that there are seven specific developmental tasks of college students: competence, autonomy, managing emotions, identity, purpose, integrity, and relationships. These tasks are in line with Erik Erikson's ideas about the developmental processes of youth.

A major strength of Chickering is that he elaborates and specifies Erikson's concepts in such a way that college counsellors and student-services personnel can plan and evaluate their practices and programs around three key issues: career development, intimacy, and formulation of an adult philosophy of life.

For example, freshman and seniors differ in their specific levels of development, with freshmen being more preoccupied than seniors with establishing competence, managing emotions, and developing autonomy. Seniors, on the other hand, concentrate more on issues such as establishing identity, freeing interpersonal relationships, developing purpose, and establishing integrity.

Cognitive-structural theories focus on how individuals develop a sense of meaning in the world. They deal with perception and evaluation and are best described in the moral and intellectual models of Perry and Kohlberg. These models are process-oriented, hierarchical, and sequential.

For example, Perry's model assumes growth from "simple dualism (positions 1 and 2) through multiplicity (positions 3 and 4) and relativism (positions 5 and 6) to commitment within a relativistic framework (positions 7 through 9)." Kohlberg's model "outlines three levels of moral development: the preconventional, the conventional, and the postconventional". According to these theories, each new stage contains the previous one and is a building block for the next one. Cognitive, discomfort is the impetus for change.

The person-environment interaction model "refers to various conceptualisations of the college student and the college environment and the degree of congruence occurs when they interact". Congruence is believed to lead to "satisfaction, stability, and perhaps, development". The theories, in this model stress that development is a holistic process that involves all parts of the person with the environment in an interacting way. It is similar to the psycho-social approach in assuming that development in one area of life can facilitate growth is another.

For example, when students participate and take leadership positions in student organisations, their life-management skills develop more positively than those students who are more passive. Likewise, students, who volunteer in community-service initiatives become more informed about environmental needs, less egocentric, and more empathetic.

Unlike psychosocial theories, person-environment theories "are not developmental per se" In many ways they are rooted in Kurt Lewin's (1936) formula: B = f(P

E), where behaviour (B) is a function (f) of person (P) and environment (E).

Typological theories focus on individual differences, such as temperament, personality type, and patterns of socialisation. These differences are assumed to persist over time, and most often individuals are combinations of types. Patterns of personality influence individuals to vary in their developmental growth patterns and are related to their motivation, effort, and achievement.

Professional Preparation

Because there is such diversity in the functions of student-service professionals, no single professional preparation program can meet the needs of all graduate students. Because those who enter this speciality "do not need the same kind of graduate work," CACREP provides different speciality standards for the field. CACREP accreditation under Student Affairs Practice in Higher Education (SAPHE) includes programs with the following three emphases: counselling (SAC), developmental (SAD), and administrative (SAA).

The specific course work and experiences needed for graduation have been outlined by the Council for the Advancement of Standards for Student Services/ Development Programs. Individuals who plan careers in student affairs have a choice regarding the courses they take. It is vital that specialisation decisions be made as soon as possible in one's graduate career because the outcomes of each course of study vary considerably Traditional student-services preparatory programs tend to focus on counselling and human-relations skills regardless of the ultimate speciality.

Roles of Student-services Providers

Student services concentrated on helping new students adjust to campus life. This focus still exists but now includes a focus on older returning students and an increased concern for all aspects of the college/university community, such as working with ethnic minority students and those whose culture differs from the institution. There is a humanistic quality among individuals who choose college student services as a profession: they try to maximise, personalise, and individualise the higher education of students, helping them fully use the environment to promote their development. An important by-product of this process is that students are greatly assisted in making successful transitions from their communities to institutional life and back again.

Thus, student-services personnel are institutional integrators who facilitate the accomplishment of student and college/university goals. There are times during the college year (orientation, midterm examinations, and the end of the term) when the work of student-services professionals increases dramatically. Although certain problems are universal regardless of one's developmental age or stage (including health, anxiety, and depression), other concerns are related directly to specific college-student populations. For example, college freshmen may especially need help during their initial months in college.

Graduation from high school involves a loss of identity and a need for re-evaluation and goal commitment that is often unavailable to entering students before they matriculate. "Some of the most commonly reported crises in the fresh man year involve difficulties in social adjustment manifested as feelings of homesickness and loneliness". Another unique problem is Greek rush. The rush system of fraternities and sororities, while exciting and fulfilling for many students, may also produce feelings of depression among students who are not offered bids. In helping students during these times, student-services personnel need to be sensitive to individual needs offer support, and try to help rejected students find a fulfilling peer group.

In line with transitional problems, Grites found that 12 of the 43 items on the Social Readjustment Rating Scale almost exclusively apply to college freshmen in their adjustment to a new environment. When translated into life-change units, these factors yield a combined score of 250, which the authors of this instrument consider to be in the "moderate life crisis" category. As a group, individuals in this category have a 51-per cent greater risk of a deteriorating health change than those who score 150 or below.

New students who face other changes outside the college/university environment (for example, the death of a family member or friend) are likely to move into the "major life crisis" category, becoming an even greater risk for a detrimental health change. Whether there is change in one's physical health or not, there is often the experience of psychological pain because of the disruption in established friendship networks.

Therefore many colleges and universities now employ special student-services staff to work with each incoming class to enhance the freshmen experience and promote positive individual development as well as a sense of community. Regardless of such attempts at prevention, approximately 10 percent of all students encounter an emotional difficulty during their years in college (perhaps the death of a friend or marriage) that is serious enough to impair academic performance. Stress on college students to pass examinations or get into a professional school increase the incidents of major depression in this population. If appropriate intervention is not offered (for example, training in appropriate anger expression or stress management), student, experience emotional, social, or academic problems to such a degree that they drop out of school. Between 40 and 60 percent of students who begin four-year institution, do not graduate.

Some of the strongest predictors of staying in school, such as academic achievement and commitment to the goal of graduation, are amenable to student support services. To help students have a successful and productive college experience, student-professionals offer campuswide programs and individual assistance. The goal of comprehensive programs is to make a positive impact upon students and help them identify problems or concerns at strategic points where intervention strategies may be most beneficial.

The emphases and roles of student-services personnel are aimed at helping sensitise students to the multiple issues that face them and constructively deal with these unfolding issue, and themselves. For example, college students face the challenge of maintaining some form of separation from their parents and families while establishing their own identity through individuation.

There is a correlation between student adjustment to college and attachment to parents. "Research suggests that college students benefit from (a) secure attachment to parents in which there is mutual trust, communication, and little conflict or alienation, and (b) relationships with parents in which their separateness and individuality are mirrored, acknowledged, and supported". By informing students of the need to separate positively and connect with their families and offering strategies and support for doing so, student-services personnel assist students in their overall adjustment and achievement at college and beyond.

The activities of student-services professionals are related to the speciality area in which they work: administration, development, or counselling. "The administrative model is based on the premise that the student services profession is an administrative, service-oriented unit in higher education that provides many facilitating and development activities and programs for students". Examples of these services include admissions, records, food, health, and financial aid. The developmental model is one that stresses education, such as helping students learn decision-making skills by offering leadership seminars or facilitating increased autonomy in residence- life activities.

Finally, the counselling model is one that emphasises social and emotional growth in interpersonal and vocational decisions and includes conducting highly personalised seminars around a topic of interest, such as dating, careers, or stress. Not all student-services activities are conducted by professionals.

These paraprofessionals are "under-graduate students who have been selected and trained to offer services or programs to their peers. These services are intentionally designed to assist in the adjustment, satisfaction, and/or persistence of students". Student paraprofessionals are frequently employed in residence halls and orientation programs; they also work with crisis lines, student judiciaries, academic advising, financial aid, international student programs, and student activities. Student-services professionals directly and indirectly offer them leadership opportunities, improve the quality of life on campus, and accomplish critical tasks. By 1987, more than 600 U.S. colleges and universities were offering students some type of formal leadership training.

But Roberts and Ullom note that certain core beliefs, underlying principles, and necessary curriculum topics must be dealt with before any such activity can be effective. Student-affairs professionals have become increasingly interested in improving their leadership abilities at the same time that they have devoted additional time and effort to helping students in this area.

The roles of college counsellors vary and are influenced by the models under which they operate. There are four main models of counselling services that college/university counselling centers follow:

Counselling as psychotherapy: This model emphasises long-term counselling with a small percentage of students. The counsellor deals with personality change and refers other vocational and educational concerns to student academic advisers.

Counselling as vocational guidance: This model emphasises helping 'students productively relate academic and career matters. The counsellor deals with academic or vocationally undecided students and refers those with personal or emotional problems to other agencies.

Counselling as traditionally defined: This model emphasises a broad range of counselling services, including short- or long-term relationships and those that deal with personal, academic, and career concerns. The counsellor's role is diverse.

Counselling as consultation: This model emphasises working with the various organisations and personnel who have a direct impact on student mental health. The counsellor offers indirect services to students through strategic interventions. Few college counselling centers concentrate on implementing just one service model. Instead, most offer a variety of services, including outreach programs, in order to help their diverse client populations. The ASCA role statement for postsecondary counsellors concurs with this divergence, emphasising counsellors' three main tasks:

1) Participate in a comprehensive program of student-support services 1 to help students meet needs (for example, financial aid)
2) Offer students the opportunity to participate in deliberate psychological educational experiences that promote inter and intrapersonal growth and development
3) Assist students at various levels of ability and maturity to identify and use school and community-based resources for vocational growth

The activities of college counsellors are similar to those of student-services professionals in comprehensiveness and variety. Some even overlap. Lewing and Cowger identify nine counselling functions that generally dictate the agendas of college counsellors:

— Academic and educational counselling

— Vocational counselling

— Personal counselling

— Testing

— Supervision and training

— Research

— Teaching

— Professional development

— Administration

Three of these activities—personal, vocational, and educational counselling-account for more than 50 percent of counsellors' time. Most of the counselling theories covered in this book are implemented in college counselling centers. For instance, Thurman finds that rational-emotive therapy, including the use of rational-emotive imagery, can be effective in reducing Type A behaviour among college students and help them become healthier achievers. Watkins on the other hand, finds a person-centered approach to be most effective in helping students evaluate present and future plans and decide whether to stay in college.

Even systems theory most often used in marriage and family counselling, has proven effective in helping students understand family dynamics and patterns of interaction and how family patterns continue to influence important decisions about education. Brief therapy, a form of systems theory, has been employed in college counselling centers to help expand the "therapeutic framework to include nonfamilial members [who] can affect therapeutic progress" for better or worse. In this treatment, conflictual nonfamily members within a campus community are brought together to form meaningful relationships and make changes in problematic situations. The idea behind the treatment is that students within a campus can help eachother to solve their problem and make their environments healthier through the resolution of problem behaviours. In the process, blaming and scape-goating cease.

One challenge that college counsellors face is a constantly changing student culture. Behaviours among college students change with each generation. The culture of "Generation X" (the current student population) is not the same as its predecessor. Therefore, both educational and preventive programs must regularly be modified to help students handle their current issues. There is great benefit involved in such modifications: as a group, students who receive counselling services tend to graduate at a higher rate than those who do not. They are less likely to drop out of college for academic reasons if they choose to withdraw.

When services are varied and numerous at the professional level, everyone benefits. The College Adjustment Scales is a means of screening college students for common developmental and psychological problems. These nine scales measure psychological distress in the following areas: anxiety, depression, suicidal ideation, substance abuse, self-esteem problems, interpersonal problems, family problems, academic problems, and career problems, Peer counsellors are another effective way of reaching students. As a rule, students turn first to friends for help, then to close relatives, before finally turning to faculty and counselling services.

Ragle and Krone found that freshmen who had previously undergone a summer orientation program at the University of Texas at Austin were, as a result, overwhelmingly at ease in talking with peer advisors over the telephone about various concerns. Furthermore, they felt that contact with peer counsellors was helpful and indicated that it made the university seem less impersonal. Sometimes peer counsellors take the role of resident assistants (RAs). In this arrangement, RAs are assigned to live in selected residence halls. Their services, which include dealing with remedial, preventive, and developmental issues, are given high exposure.

RAs provide crisis intervention, short-term counselling, conflict mediation, and referral services. They help students keep favourable attitudes toward counselling and counselling-related services and, at the same time, become more aware of opportunities offered by college counselling centers.

In addition, RAs sponsor programs for residents on mental and physical health topics, bringing in faculty and staff from across the campus to give presentations. RAs usually receive ongoing professional training and supervision from the campus counselling center. This arrangement benefits the RAs, students in the residence halls, and the campus as a whole because of its integrative and preventive focus.

College counsellors can offer services and programs in conjunction with other student-services personnel. Two of the most needed services relate to alcohol and sexual abuse and violence. Alcohol-related problems include the abuse of alcohol and its concomitant disorders. Binge drinking is a prevalent problem, and one in three college students drinks primarily to get drunk.

Included in the wide array of addictive behaviours and problems associated with alcohol abuse is growing up in a dysfunctional alcoholic family. Alcohol abuse is likely to bring students in contact with counsellors and other student-services personnel. Systematic steps are usually implemented to help students get through denial and realise their need for help in correcting out-of-control behaviour. Intervention is sometimes done individually, but often it involves a group.

When students experience problems related to growing up in an alcoholic family, counsellors often use other strategies. Specific interventions include helping students define more clearly the roles they played in their family-life dramas and then helping them break nonproductive patterns of interaction. Sexual assault and violence, including incest and rape, are matters that many, students, primarily women, must deal with during their college experience. The dynamics surrounding sexual crimes have similarities and differences. A common denominator in many cases is alcohol abuse: 90 per cent of campus rapes occur when alcohol has been consumed by the assailant, the victim, or both. There are at least two stages in the recovery process:

(1) the acute, which is characterised by disorganisation, and

(2) long-term reorganisation, which includes dealing with the pain of trauma and rebuilding one's life through support.

In addressing these issues, college counsellors in cooperation with student-services professionals can take preventive action on tertiary, secondary, and primary levels. "*Tertiary prevention* is akin to remediation and includes direct services to victims". It includes encouraging the reporting of aggression and helping the victim use available resources. Secondary prevention is geared toward problems, such as date rape, already in existence on campus and is aimed at raising consciousness and setting policies to stop known abuses.

Primary prevention is aimed at stopping problems from ever developing. It involves modifying the physical environment as well as addressing causes and providing training to create awareness and change values. For example, to reduce alcohol abuse and the resulting sexual violence, student-services personnel might persuade students that excessive or binge drinking is not "cool" or a "rite of passage".

In addition to working with college counsellors address the needs of nontraditional students. These may be older students, first-generation college students, or even student athletes. In all likelihood, those who are today called nontraditional students will become the norm in the early part of the 21st century.

Many nontraditional students are adults who are older than the traditional college age. One-third to one-half of undergraduate students and more than 50 percent of all graduate students are over age 30.

As a group, they are highly motivated, prefer interactive learning, have family and financial concerns, view education as an investment, and have multiple commitments and responsibilities that are not related to school. Within this large group there are two basic subgroups: students ages 25-50 and those ages 50-80. The first subgroup is usually motivated to return to college because of changing job or career requirements or opportunities that include family life transitions. Building up self-esteem and providing academic and social support are particularly important for these younger nontraditional students. The latter subgroup, often called senior students, come to campus for many purposes, which include obtaining degrees and finding personal enrichment.

When working with senior students, student-services personnel must take several factors into consideration. They include modifications to the counselling environment (perhaps brighter lighting or warmer room temperatures), the developmental stage of the client (for example, dealing with issues of generativity or integration), the pace of the counselling sessions (slower may be better), potentially difficult areas in counselling (such as transference), and the use of counselling techniques (such as bibliotherapy or journal writing). With an increase in the number of older people, the numbers of senior students will most likely continue to grow.

Regardless of how fast the number of senior students grows, the overall number of nontraditional students will increase because of business down-sizing, the rapid advance of technology, and increased opportunities for professional development. As is the case with traditional student, more females than males will enroll, there will be an increase in the number of part time students, and more cultural and racial minorities will seek a college education. All these events will test the limits of counselling and other student services. A second group of nontraditional students is first-generation college students. The individuals in this category come from a wide variety of backgrounds including second-generation immigrants and upwardly mobile poor. Their needs include help in understanding student services and study skills. Furthermore, they need support in bridging the gap between their communities and the college environment.A third group of nontraditional students is student athletes. Many of these students have "problems in relating to the university system and the larger society". They are often seen by others as problem students who have trouble relating either socially or academically.

In addition many are from minority cultural groups and are the first within their families to attend college. A sports-oriented environment may foster dependence on a coach or a team. Therefore, these students may become isolated and alienated from the mainstream of college life. Teaching time management and social skills are areas where counsellors can help. When student athletes lose their athletic identity through loss of eligibility or because of injury, they need assistance in making an integrative transition back to college life.

Educational measurements

The nature of educational measurements is the same as that of all scientific measurements. Educational measurements usually lack zero points and have ill-defined units of measurement. Carefully made measurements could be of great practical use to educators.

According to Edward L. Thorndike, measurements of many sorts would be indispensable in scientific research on educational problems. He was among the first to develop scientifically based procedures of measurement for such research. With his *Introduction to The Theory of Mental and Social Measurements* he was the first to offer a treatment, comprehensive for its time, of statistical methods in educational research. Space does not permit presenting a complete history of the beginnings and development of measurement in educational psychology. There are numerous sources for facts and interpretations of this history. Joncich's biography of Thorndike gives an illuminating account of his role in the development of educational measurement. Monroe contrasted the status of educational measurement in 1945 with that in 1920.

In the early years of its existence, the National Society for the Study of Education published several year-books devoted to educational measurement issues; for example, Whipple edited one on the measurement of "educational products" in which Thorndike contributed the previously quoted homily on educational measurement and its uses. The periodic reviews of educational and psychological testing research in the Review of Educational Research, starting with that in Volume 3 and ending with that in Volume 39 can be consulted for details and bibliographies.

The development of contemporary methods of testing has had a long and tortuous history. From time immemorial-even in ancient China, Greece, and Rome—the traditional way of assessing students' progress learning has been some form of oral or written examination, and this mode of testing is still widely used, though perhaps with more observance standards and safeguards than in earlier times.

Examinations have been many kinds, ranging from simple spelling and arithmetic tests to the writing of long essays response to questions or problems posed. But even the written examination was not widely used until means of writing became readily available in schools in the 19th century. It was not until the 20th century that the use of "new-type" or "objective" examinations became at all prevalent. The objective or new-type test, consisting of series of completion, true-false, or multiple-choice items, grew mainly out of early efforts to measure mental abilities. Ebbinghaus, was the originator of the completion or fill-in test-the forerunner of the cloze technique later developed by Taylor to measure the readability of prose. Using the completion technique, Trabue developed scales for measuring the level of language knowledge and understanding.

Other types of objective test items were derived, in part from the work of Binet, by Yerkes, Bridges, and Hardwick. Just before the entry of the United States into World War I, Otis had developed a group intelligence test for elementary school children that was completely objective in the sense that it could be scored by checking responses against an answer key.

His tests, and related materials, were models for the Alpha and Beta examinations rather hastily constructed for testing mental abilities of Army recruits. Otis published an account of his group intelligence test, interesting for the statistical methods of scaling and item analysis that he used. The success of objective-type items in the measurement of abilities encouraged educators to import this type of test into the measurement of school learning and achievement. McCall described "a new kind of school examination" that was actually nothing more or less than the true-false test.

The multiple-choice type of achievement-test item started to become prevalent in the mid 1920s. It was also in this period that test standardisation procedures were developed and became widely used, although even as early as 1917 a textbook on educational measurements by Monroe, DeVoss, and Kelly listed "standardized" tests in a variety of school subjects—tests that did not, however, generally use objective-type items. Methods and guidelines for the actual writing of objective tests were slow to appear. Little or no information on this matter is to be found, for example, in the text by Monroe et al. just cited, but McCall treated the topic fairly extensively. Starting in 1927, Ruch and Rice conducted a nationwide contest in the construction of objective examinations; they published an extensive sample of examinations that were awarded prizes.

In evaluating the entries, no explicit consideration was given to whether the examinations covered specified educational objectives; apparently appropriateness to educational objectives was taken for granted. Much more consideration of educational objectives, and methods of writing items to test them, was given in a collection of articles edited by Hawkes, Lindquist, and Mann under the auspices of a committee of the American Council on Education.

In these articles, authors suggested ways of testing understanding and other "higher mental processes," but in general, the many achievement tests constructed during the 1930s were limited to the testing of elementary skills and factual knowledge. The tests used in the well-known Pennsylvania Study of high school and college students' subject-matter attainments were of this type. A departure from this tradition came with the tests constructed for the so-called Eight-Year Study, to measure higher mental processes, social sensitivity, appreciation, and personal and social adjustment. During the early years of educational measurement, there was considerable ambiguity and confusion as to what kind of measurement could be called objective.

At first, objectivity was defined simply in terms of "freedom from personal opinion in scoring." McCall stated that "a test is perfectly objective when identical results are secured from two applications of the same test to the same pupils by different examiners. " Later, objectivity came to be defined in terms of whether tests could be scored by clerks, or even by machine. Restricting attention to the process of test writing, there are at least two important trends in the period since about 1935:

1) Gradual acceptance and implementation of the idea that tests must be closely geared to the measurement of specified educational objectives. Bloom's Taxonomy of Educational Objectives played an important role here, as did later work on the specification of behavioural objectives, inspired by programmed instruction and similar developments. Tests were planned in terms of grids or outlines specifying contents and item types in relation to objectives. Standardized achievement tests paid more attention to common elements in curricula nationwide, and this led to criticisms of these tests as forcing undue uniformity of curricula and as not adequately reflecting local curriculum variations.

2) There was more knowledge about, and greater appreciation of, characteristics of good as opposed to poor test items in terms of wording, format, dependence on the objective to be tested, and the influence of specific determiners. In the 1930s and 1940s, there was much research on characteristics of various types of objective items, and on their validity

> as compared to that of free-response and essay tests. Manuals of item-writing techniques also became available, a trend culminating in such more recent works as those of Bormuth and Roid and Haladyna offering a technology for test-item writing.

Although test item writing may have become more of an established discipline for professional test constructors, it is anybody's guess how well this discipline has penetrated into the actual practices of teachers in the schools. To be sure, departments and colleges of education have long offered courses in educational measurement and statistics for teachers, and occasionally schools conduct workshops on the subject for their staffs, but there has been continued failure on the part of many teachers to address themselves to the preparation of well-designed classroom tests and the use of simple statistical procedures, such as item analysis, to make effective diagnostic and evaluative instruments.

Measurement theory

In his *Introduction to the Theory of Mental and Social Measurements* which may be characterised as an early textbook on statistics rather than one on educational measurement—Thorndike pointed out the "special difficulties" of mental measurements, "due chiefly to

- the absence or imperfection of units in which to measure,
- the lack of constancy in the facts measured, and
- the extreme complexity of the measurements to be made".

His chapter "Units and Scales" pointed out "common

defects in scales for measuring mental and social facts, " such as the arbitrariness of a scale from 0 to 100 or from 0 to 10. He distinguished objective from subjective scales, absolute from relative scales, discrete from continuous series, and absolute from arbitrary zero points. He hinted at notions of reliability and, validity of measurements, although he did not use those terms. In Thorndike's early work, the ideal scale for an educational measurement was perceived as one that presented specimen educational products of different degrees of quality from very poor to excellent, with numbers assigned to these different products in such a way that they formed approximately what would now be called an interval scale with equal units of measurement.

Thorndike presented a handwriting scale following this scheme. In use, samples of handwriting were to be matched as accurately as possible to specimens on the scale. The equality of units was established by analysing judges' ratings according to Fullerton and Cattell's theorem that differences that are equally often noticed are equal.

Inspired by this work, scales for other kinds of educational products, such as drawings and English compositions, were constructed by Thorndike or his students, and apparently put into fairly wide use. It seems, however, that in the subsequent history of educational measurement relatively little use has been made of this technique, at least not in the careful way that Thorndike and his students employed it. For example, the technique can be used in the measurement of public speaking performances, foreign language speaking and writing proficiency, and the excellence of mathematical proofs.

The problem of measurement scales arose in a more critical way when points were assigned to answers to a series of discrete items, resulting in test scores. Here there was no satisfactory way, as Thorndike realized, to assume equality of units. Based on statistical work done in the 19th century on distributions of personal attributes like height and weight, it was widely assumed that underlying distributions of ability and school achievement would approximate normality; witness a statement by Monroe, DeVoss, and Kelly: "It is a well-known fact that when a group of pupils is measured with respect to a mental or physical characteristic they are found to be distributed as shown in."

There was concern, therefore, with how test scores could be evaluated with reference to a normal distribution. Thorndike presented methods for translating scores into percentiles and then to normal curve equivalents. Monroe et al. presented a method of translating test scores into school mark scales. There was also the question of assessing and scaling difficulty of particular questions, exercises, or items. Monroe et al. refer to methods used by Buckingham Trabue , and Woody in translating percent of correct responses into P. E. equivalents.

Apparently these authors were the first to convert proportions correctly into normal curve equivalents, at least to create something like a reasonable interval scale. Strangely, however, they were also concerned with establishing an absolute zero point on this basis. Monroe et al. state that to express the absolute value of an exercise a zero point must be established. This is done by constructing an exercise which calls for zero ability. The other exercises are then compared with this one.

According to current theory, of course, such a procedure makes little sense, or would be considered invalid. These early procedures formed the basis for expressing scores in terms of norms, whether in percentiles, P. E. scores, T scores or scaled scores. By the 1960s, many tests were being criticized as "norm-referenced" because their results could be interpreted only with reference to norms. Yet, it should be pointed out that early educational measurers had a strong desire to express tested educational outcomes in terms of what would now be called criterion referencing, that is, in terms of what actual kinds of performance a score would refer to.

In the early years of the century, there were many attempts to make test scores criterion-referenced in the contemporary sense of the term. The logical problems of establishing measuring scales began to be formalized with the work of Stevens in distinguishing four basic scale types: nominal, ordinal, interval, and ratio. This work has had more importance in the use of measurement scales in statistical research than in the actual construction of classroom tests.

The importance has been in connection with the assumptions underlying various statistical procedures, such as correlation or analysis of variance. It has been argued that data that are no more than ordinal are inappropriately analysed with parametric statistics, or at least, that much caution must be used in using such statistics with them.

The question of the necessity of observing rules about scale types has been debated for many years. The latest exchange has been between Gaito and Townsend and Ashby, the former arguing, with Lord, that "the numbers do not know where they come from" and therefore that they can be treated as pure numbers without regard to type of measurement scale, and the latter pointing out that ignoring scale type can, at least in some circumstances, lead to serious errors in interpreting statistical results.

On the other hand, even though many test scores are technically no more than ordinally scaled, most educational researchers believe that it usually does little violence to use parametric statistics with them, providing their distributions are approximately normal. Even more formal considerations of measurement problems have been made by philosophers and logicians who have attempted to construct an axiomatic system for defining scales.

However, any of this work has as yet influenced educational measurement or educational research. One basis for establishing a scale of ability, proficiency, or achievement is to select a series of tasks, all of which are considered or demonstrated to measure the same trait, but which vary in apparent difficulty or complexity, and then to determine the proportion of individuals in some representative sample who are able to perform, solve, or master each task.

The ability scale is then formed by arranging the tasks in order of proportion correct. On the assumption that the underlying ability is normally distributed in the sample of individuals tested, the tasks are assigned difficulty values in terms of normal deviate units corresponding to the proportions. Kelley presented a curve relating "proportion missed" to the difficulty of spelling words.

In their work on the construction of a scale of intelligence, Thorndike, Bregman, Cobb, and Woodyard were impressed with the fact that for a group of persons at any given ability level, there was a regular curve of relation between task difficulty and percent correct for that particular group. In fact, by shifting origins for different groups, curves for different groups coincided and appeared to have the same form. It was on this basis that Thorndike et al. established a scale for specifying the "altitude" of an individual's intellect. A problem with this approach was that the procedures did not guarantee that the scale was unidimensional. Almost any series of tasks, as long as they have some correlation among themselves, could generate an "altitude" scale like Thornlike's. The tasks assigned to different levels, however, might measure somewhat different traits. The first breakthrough in solving this problem was made by Walker in a series of papers appearing in the *British Journal of Psychology*.

Walker noticed that at least for certain tests, the students' answers followed a systematic pattern when they were studied in relation to item difficulty. Students who were able to perform the most difficult tasks could also perform all or nearly all tasks of less difficulty. Likewise, students who failed easy tasks also failed all or nearly all tasks of greater difficulty. Tests that had this characteristic, according to Walker, were called "unig"; tests that did not were said to have an element of "hig".

Thus, Walker anticipated the work of Guttman who regarded a series of tasks or items showing the previously described answer pattern as being unidimensional. In fact, the scalograrn technique developed by Guttman is simply a way of seeing the extent to which Walker's "unig" pattern is displayed by a set of data. Perhaps the so-called Guttman scale should be renamed the Walker scale. Eventually there were further developments along these lines; for the most part, the various contributors were unaware of each other's work.

A Walker scale was assumed by Ferguson and Carroll in their work on the variance and correlational properties of such scales. Ferguson was concerned with the effects of using tasks on such scales in item factor-analysis: Carroll considered the additional complications introduced when items, or sets of them, could be passed by chance guessing.

Mosier related such mental test scales to psychophysical scales, by pointing out that they constituted a relation between the nature of the stimulus and the individual's characteristic level of ability. Loevinger's index of homogeneity was a measure of the extent to which a test conforms to the properties of a perfect Walker-Guttman scale; Carroll pointed out, however, that Loevinger's index could be seriously depressed by unreliability and chance guessing effects.

Test theory

Test theory concerns the particular problems of statistical analysis associated with the construction of tests and other kinds of variables dealt with in psychological and educational research, such as ratings, questionnaire responses, and the like. The problems dealt with in the preceding section, on units of measurement, have close relations with problems of test theory; it is difficult to draw the line, in fact. Nevertheless, in test theory it is possible to distinguish between problems having to do with variables as such, and problems having to do with composites of variables, which is, in reality, what many tests are.

Much of test theory concerns how tests should be constructed as composites of items, each item usually consisting of a stimulus and a response that is scored dichotomously, that is, as either 1 or 0 depending on whether the response is considered correct or incorrect. The total test score is a sum of the item scores, or sometimes a sum of the weighted item scores. First we consider that part of test theory that concerns scores, ratings, or other measures as variables rather than as composites.

Later theories of test scores as composites of items somewhat more recently than the former Actually, all of this theory is considered as p classical test theory, as opposed to what has to be called item response theory. Most of classical test theory can be derived certain elementary theorems about the correlation of sums, the sums being regarded as containing both true scores and error scores. It thus harks to a period when applications of correlation t were being developed. It is perhaps difficult present-day student to realize that the theory correlation is less than 100 years old.

As discussed by Walker the idea of correlation the mind of Francis Galton, but the actual mathematical formulation of the theory was done by Karl Pearson, an a ate of Galton, around 1895. The ordinary, fa correlation statistic is called the Pearsonian product moment correlation because it was form by Pearson as the mean of the products of standard deviation scores of two variables. Pearson a students also developed variants of the correlation coefficient such as the biserial and the tetrachoric coefficients, and worked out the theory of multiple partial correlation. Thus, the groundwork was already laid for developing a theory of test reliability when, shortly after 1900, Charles Spearman his studies of tests of mental abilities.

The basic theory of reliability was set fort paper by Spearman. The term reliability was not used in that paper, however; it di appear in print until 1910, when Spearman defined it as "the coefficient between one-half an other half of several measurements of the thing." The modern student of test theory, working through the derivations presented by Spearman and others see this development as rather tortured; the derivations given by Spearman seem much more complicated than they need to be. Nevertheless, the idea of a test score as a composite of a true and an error score is certainly implicit in man's discussion in 1904; in fact the other that Spearman published that year, concept of intelligence, provided an example of the use of what would now be called the correction for attenuation.

The correction for attenuation and the so-called Spearman-Brown prophecy formula, however, were not formalized until 1910 in papers independently published by Spearman and Brown coincidentally in the same issue of the *British Journal of Psychology*.

Use of the term reliability as referring to the correlation between equivalent measures, and thus as an indication of the accuracy of a measurement, was slow to penetrate educational measurement procedures in the United States. Even in the revised edition of his textbook on mental measurements, Thorndike used the term only to refer to standard efforts of statistics. Similar use of the term was made by Rugg in his text on statistics.

Monroe, DeVoss, and Kelly's text used the term in its general sense, but not with reference to actual coefficients of reliability. Otis concluded that the most "reliable" measures of an ability are obtained by using items for which there is an average of 50% correct answers. He also remarked that he believed it was better to express the unreliability of scores in terms of a median deviation or "probable error" of the scores than in terms of a coefficient of correlation, since the latter is affected by the degree of heterogeneity of the group. Working without knowledge of Spearman and Brown's efforts, Truman Kelley developed a formula for the "index of reliability", and in a footnote offered a formula similar to the Spearman-Brown prophecy formula. It was not until about 1921, however, that usage of the term reliability as the name of a particular kind of correlation coefficient began to be standardized and widely recognized among test constructors.

Only by the time of Kelley's Interpretation of Educational Measurements can one find a more or less complete discussion of reliability coefficients and their use, including formulas for the standard error of measurement and the effect of the range of talent on the reliability coefficient. Kelley even went so far as to specify certain values for "minimal satisfactory reliabilities as measured by a reliability coefficient determined from the pupils in a single school grade" for tests serving different purposes. One of the clearest, simplest presentations of classical test theory, with derivations, was given by Thurstone; later and more advanced presentations are those of R. L. Thorndike and Gulliksen.

In the first several decades of the test movement there was much controversy and empirical research concerning the accuracy and utility of the Spearman-Brown prophecy formula in predicting the reliability of lengthened tests. Some of this research was briefly treated by Osburn and subsequent reviewers in the Review of Educational Research. Evidently the problem was not really resolved until Gulliksen pointed out that the accuracy of the formula depends on the degree to which its assumptions are valid for a particular use of the formula. Prior to the work of Kuder and Richardson, estimates of test reliability were generally made by split-half, test-retest, or alternate form techniques.

Using theorems associated with variances and correlations of sums, Kuder and Richardson showed how test reliability could also be determined from internal item statistics. Their formulas 20 and 21 are now regularly used in this connection, although the assumptions underlying their use are not always recognized. For about the next 10 years, the journal Psychometrika contained numerous articles concerned with issues of test reliability.

Articles by Wherry and Gaylord are of note, concerned with the effect of factorial composition on reliability. An article by Tucker led to concern with the "attenuation paradox" to the effect that under certain conditions test validity can seem to decrease as reliability increases, contrary to classical test theory predictions. This problem was not resolved until the advent of Lord and Novick's item response theory; it was seen that the paradox arose because of the incorrect assumption of linearity in test validity coefficients. Early educational researchers occasionally encountered the problem of assessing the reliability of multiple measures, such as a series of ratings. Commonly this was done by finding the average correlation among such measures and using the Spearman-Brown prophecy formula to estimate the reliability of the composite of the ratings; Edgerton and Toops presented a short-cut for these computations.

It was not until 1951 that Ebel perceived the applicability of ANOVA techniques to this problem. Already in 1941 Jackson and Ferguson had applied such techniques to test scores. Later presentations by Stanley and Winer have shown how variances due to trait, item difficulty, rater bias, and error can be computed and used in the assessment of the reliability with which a variable is measured. In the meantime-in fact as early as 1908 with Stone's arithmetic tests-test constructors were concerned with the properties of particular test items as contributing to measurements of variables. One problem was the distribution of item difficulties.

Otis's observation that the most reliable test would be composed of items of 50% difficulty. This seemed, to some, to be contrary to common sense and logic, and the usual practice among early test constructors was to compose tests from items graded in difficulty from fairly easy to fairly difficult. Others, however, felt that all items should be fairly easy, in order to detect pupils who were not able to pass items "crucial" for a given grade.

For most of the history of test construction, the tendency has been to use item difficulty distributions peaked at about the mean difficulty level expected for the sample or population to be tested, although it can be shown that this policy is unwise under certain conditions. In assessing the validity of an item-that is, the effectiveness of an item in measuring a trait or an educational achievement, techniques in an almost startling variety were devised. J. A. Long and Sandiford's survey and analysis of these methods will be found instructive. One easy method was to split the total score distribution at the median and compare percents correct in the two halves. A somewhat more sophisticated technique was developed by Flanagan on the basis of a proof by Kelley that in general, and under certain assumptions, maximum accuracy would result from comparing percents correct from the upper and lower 27% portions of the distribution.

Brigham used the Pearson- and Kelley-developed biserial correlation in his work on developing the Scholastic Aptitude Test.

The central idea of item response theory (IRT), as introduced in Lord and Novick's classic that subjects' likelihoods of correct response item can be described by a functional equation that may have one or more parameters-usually The most important parameter is one representing the item's overall level of difficulty on the scale of the latent trait measured by the item. Two other parameters are one describing the slope of the function as ability varies a representing the probability of correct response a subject whose ability is infinitely low, but who may nevertheless perform the item ci through guessing or other chance phenomena.

IRT has many applications, as in developing more reliable, better tests, in equating tests, in using "tailored in studying item bias, and so forth. IRT i highly technical computations, and generally requires large samples to fit and test models. Its main virtue is that it resolves, or claims to resolve, many of the difficulties presented in classical test. Test theorists have divided into several of thought and interest. One school, led by and Stone, puts emphasis on a one parameter item response model derived from the Rasch. Another school of I led by Popham, Berk, and has devoted its attention to the develop criterion-referenced tests based on domains of items.

A criterion-referenced test is on outcomes help to indicate and describes performances with reference to educational objectives more directly and substantively than scores of norm-referenced tests, which only indicate students' performances relative to nor claimed that special procedures for determining liability and validity are required for such criterion-referenced tests. Cronbach, Gleser, Nanda Rajaratnam elevated reliability the what they call generalizability theory, concerned with the replicability of measurements samples of items and examinee populations.

In the midst of the excitement, many were startled to see Lumsden's evaluation of test theory as having "few major "dominated by an inappropriate and model." What Lumsden seems to have been calling for would be a test theory more concerned with construct validity and trait measurement t matters of reliability, scaling, and other nice mathematical properties. In some ways, Lumsden's critique brings test theory full circle back to the concerns voiced by Edward L. Thorndike in the early years of the century. But even Thorndike was perhaps unduly distracted by his attempts to develop "scientific" measurements with defined, equal units.

Factor analysis

The term factor analysis refers to a collection of techniques for determining the latent dimensionality of a set of measures applied to a sample of persons or objects and for assessing the extent to which each variable measures each of the latent dimensions. In simple terms, factor analysis can help one decide how many different kinds of ability traits or dimensions of learning there are, and how different tests measure those traits or dimensions. Although the variables studied in factor-analytic investigations have most often been measures of mental abilities and attributes of personality, they have also included measures of students' educational achievement, attributes of schools or school systems, and characteristics of educational materials and products.

Factor analysis originated in a famous paper by Spearman, which presented an analysis of a small matrix of correlations among certain tests of sensory discrimination, reaction time, and school marks. Spearman claimed that his matrix could be accounted for by a single latent dimension of general intelligence, especially if the correlations were corrected for errors of measurement. Over the years 1904 to 1927 Spearman developed his two factor theory of intelligence, which proposed that any test of intelligence measured a factor of general intelligence, designated g, and a factor specific to that test, designated. This theory was presented in detail in his book The Abilities of Man, but the term factor analysis does not appear in that book. Nevertheless, various British statisticians addressed the mathematical problems Of testing the two-factor theory and determining factor loading coefficients, sometimes criticizing Spearman's theory.

Gradually, factor analysis became a recognized field of statistical psychology. It seems that Thurstone was the first to use the term factor analysis. During the period of Spearman's domination of the field, the principal debate concerned whether intelligence could be satisfactorily accounted for by the two-factor theory. Even Spearman was finally led to admit that some group factors of intelligence existed alongside g. In the United States, Holzinger developed a methods of factor method of finding factors and factor loadings.

Kelley was another American educational psychologist who developed methods of factor analysis that could yield multiple factors. Holzinger and Kelley's methods, however, did not gain wide acceptance, partly because they seemed to present computational difficulties and partly because they did not have the clarity and force of the multiple factor analysis model presented by Thurstone. Over the period 1935 to about 1970 the dominant model and method of factor analysis was Thurstone's; as characterised by Tucker it would now be called a model and method for exploratory factor analysis, as opposed to confirmatory factor analysis.

Exploratory factor analysis proposes to take any given correlation matrix and determine the number of meaningful common factors in it, as well as the coefficients of equations specifying the factorial composition of the variables. Thurstone recommended use of his centroid method for determining an orthogonal factor matrix that would approximately reproduce the given correlation matrix; the coordinates on which this factor matrix was based were then to be rotated to what Thurstone called simple structure.

Thurstone and his students conducted a number of classic factor-analytic investigations using this method. He saw that it was often desirable to allow factors to be correlated. In this way, one could arrive at second- and higher-order factors to account more satisfactorily for the correlations of a set of variables. Schmid and Leiman developed this idea further to arrive at hierarchical factor solutions in which the independent contributions of higher-order factors could be expressed in the factorial equations for variables.

After Thurstone's death in 1955, research workers continued to perform many exploratory factor analysis studies using his model and methods. Thurstone had been aware of the contribution of Hotelling in developing the principal component method, that relied on finding the eigen-values and eigen-vectors of the correlation matrix.

For large matrices, this method could not readily be used with hand computation methods, however. When high-speed computers became available, the principal component method, or several variants of it were applied to numerous data sets. The question of whether principal component or principal factoring procedures are preferable is still unresolved.

Thurstone's concept of simple structure has given rise to much controversy and investigation. Although the principle of simple structure has generally gone unquestioned, some workers have questioned whether factors should be allowed to be correlated. A number of investigators, being dissatisfied with the largely subjective, graphical methods developed by Thurstone, have attempted to develop more objective, "analytic" methods of factor rotation.

Kaiser's Varimax solution became the most generally accepted procedure for orthogonal rotation of axes, but it has not been possible for research workers to decide which of numerous available procedures is preferable for oblique rotation to correlated factors. Exploratory factor analysis has been plagued with the number-of-factors problem, that is, the decision as to the number of significant common factors to be analysed in a correlation matrix. With his scree test, Cattell has offered one solution to this problem, as have Montanelli and Humphreys, but experience with applying these criteria to real data sets does not indicate that any final and general solution is yet in sight.

It has been claimed that most of the problems of exploratory factor analysis vanish when confirmatory techniques are employed. Confirmatory techniques derive initially from the work of Lawley and Maxwell , and others, in providing maximum likelihood methods of factor extraction, accompanied by statistical tests of hypotheses as to number of factors and factor structure.

Even statistical tests, however, merely indicate probabilities, which are a matter of degree. Confirmatory techniques have receive their greatest development at the hands of Joreskog and his associates. With his techniques, and with use of the so-called LISREL program, it is possible to set up and test hypotheses concerning the factorial structure of set of variables, and to gain information as to how those hypotheses might be modified to obtain more satisfactory fit of model to data. Because of the recency of these developments, they have not as yet been applied to sufficiently varied samples of data to permit definitive evaluations of their utility, but it can be said that they are highly promising.

Despite the methodological problems inherent in factor analysis, of either the exploratory or the confirmatory kind, factorial results cannot be dismissed as having little or no significance. If methods are used carefully and intelligently, the findings have the same general patterns with different methods, and can make a distinct contribution to the understanding of educational measurement data.

Test validity

The idea that a test, or other educational measurement procedure, should yield information on what is claimed to be measured is a very old one, certainly implicit in discussions going back to the days of E. L. Thorndike or earlier. Nevertheless, it was not until the 1920s that the term validity acquired anything like the technical meaning it possesses now, nor can one find extended discussion of the concept of validity before that time. Validity was viewed as being supported by either or both of two kinds of evidence:

a) chiefly in the case of achievement tests, judged faithfulness of the test content to the curricular objectives covered, and

b) chiefly in the case of mental ability and aptitude tests, correlations of measurements with external criteria, such as other measurements intended to measure the same thing, school achievement, or judgments of job performance.

The former came to be called content validity, and the latter, predictive validity. As an example of predictive validity, we may cite the concern of the developers of the Army Alpha test to demonstrate its high correlations with individual scales of intelligence such as the Binet.

One of the first extended discussions of the concept of validity was given by Kelley. He felt that tests—even particular items in tests—should be shown to be valid in terms of both content and correlations with external criteria. Among other matters, he discussed the relative emphasis that ability and achievement tests should give to "speed" and "power," pointing out that speed elements might often interfere with valid measurement of the abilities and achievements one might wish to tap.

Further discussions of test validity can be found in works by Hawkes et al. and Smith. The validity of particular tests, and the evidence or lack of evidence for it, was a favourite topic for test reviewers in the Mental Measurement Yearbook series initiated by O. K. Buros in 1935.

More modern concepts of validity developed out of much experience in attempting to evaluate the validity of various types of tests-mental ability, scholastic aptitude, school achievement, and personality tests, among others-in a wide variety of situations. It was recognized, for example by R. L. Thorndike and Cureton, that the concept of validity presented many logical and even philosophical problems, in addition to statistical ones such as that of cross-validation.

The first edition of Technical Recommendations for Psychological Tests and Diagnostic Techniques distinguished four types of validity-content, predictive, concurrent, and construct, and noted that "the vagueness of construct is an inevitable consequence of the incompleteness of current psychological theory, and cannot be rectified faster than theory grows and is confirmed.

The next version, compilation of which had been conducted with the collaboration of educational measurement groups, collapsed predictive validity and concurrent validity into a single category, criterion- related validity. The evolution of the concept of validity was influenced by considerations from the logic and philosophy of science as reviewed by Cronbach and Meehl; an advanced treatment of the topic is to be found in a chapter by Cronbach.

Research design

Most research designs in educational psychology prior to about 1950 would be regarded as relatively primitive by contemporary standards. Often they involved small groups matched on some variable thought to be in need of experimental control. If it was necessary to evaluate a difference in means, most often a "critical ratio" of the difference to its probable error was determined and evaluated.

Monroe stated that "a difference is commonly called statistically significant when it is equal to or greater than four times its probable error. " Because a critical ratio of 4 is approximately equivalent to a t value of 2.7, $p < .005$ for 40 degrees of freedom, early statistical tests of significance may be characterised as suitably conservative in avoiding Type I errors. Occasionally more involved designs were used; for example Campbell and Stanley cited a study by Thorndike, McCall, and Chapman that used a "rotation experiment" design that was essentially equivalent to what would now be called a Latin square.

Campbell and Stanley praised McCall's book How to Experiment in Education as "an undervalued classic," pointing out that it recommended random selection as the best procedure for obtaining equated groups. In the meantime, more sophisticated procedures of experimental design were being developed in Great Britain by R. A. Fisher, chiefly in agricultural research.

The introduction of Fisherian designs, small-sample statistics, and analysis of variance and covariance (ANOVA) procedures into educational and psychological research was slow. Rucci and Tweney, in a comprehensive historical analysis of the period from 1925 to 1950, suggest three stages:

a) an initial, expository phase lasting until the onset of World War II,

b) a wartime interregnum during which use of ANOVA declined, and

c) a postwar resurgence, characterised by the institutionalisation of ANOVA training.

Leaders in introducing these techniques included Jackson, working in an educational research setting in Toronto, and Lindquist, with influential textbooks on statistics and experimental design. Deemer and Rulon conducted one of the earliest large-scale educational experiments using the Johnson and Neyman technique to find regions of an aptitude space where differences in performance were significant as a function of type of training in short-hand, but use of the Johnson-Neyman technique is still fairly infrequent, even in aptitude-treatment interaction (ATI) studies. It was recognized that small-sample statistics and ANOVA techniques had the possible draw back of requiring strong assumptions about the scaling and distributional characteristics of variables.

As one way of circumventing this drawback, educational researchers were introduced to nonparametric statistics by Siegel. It is probably not worthwhile to recount the more recent history of experimental design and statistical methods in educational and psychological research. A classic statement on experimental and quasi-experimental designs in research on teaching was published by Campbell and Stanley; it has continued to have a strong influence on research practices. Increasingly complex designs have come into use, and many researchers have become thoroughly familiar with various forms of multivariate analysis as detailed in texts like those of Cooley and Lohnes and Tatsuoka.

It is almost banal to remark that most of the present-day advances in educational measurement technology could not have come about had it not been for advances in devices for performing computations and various data collection and clerical functions, mechanically or electronically.

Nevertheless, present-day students need to realize that around the beginning of the century, desk-top hand calculators had only recently become available. These machines were used by Pearson and his students in performing statistical calculations and preparing statistical tables. Presumably, they were also available to Thorndike and other early researchers; yet, Thorndike deemed it advisable to supply his readers with multiplication and square root tables to aid in hand calculations.

Until well into the 1950s, most psychological and educational research computations were performed either by hand, by slide rule, or with the aid of desk-top mechanical calculators. Motor-driven calculators facilitated such work from about 1930 on. Correlations were often computed with the use of various worksheets whereby one would make a scatterplot of the data and follow certain rather involved algorithms to find the value. All such computations were highly error prone and it is indubitable that substantial numbers of published results were inaccurate. Early in the century, the U. S. Census Bureau began using machines for tabulating data recorded on punched cards. Warren and Mendenhall developed a method for using tabulating machines for computing the sums and sums of squares and cross-products required for correlation tables, but the final computations still had to be done with hand calculators. These and related procedures were extensively employed in the personnel research programs of World War II. It was not until the advent of high-speed electronic calculating machines, in the middle 1950s, that educational and psychological researchers were readily able to process large quantities of data and make elaborate statistical computations.

For example, Lord reported using the Whirl-wind computer, sponsored by the Office of Naval Research, to perform a factor analysis of 39 variables by Lawley's maximum likelihood method. Since that time, various computer packages for performing all sorts of statistical computations for educational and psychological research have become available, and the speed of mainframe computers has increased by several orders of magnitude.

The latest advance, of course, has been the introduction of microcomputers and associated software. Unfortunately, the available hardware and software is not always used as competently and intelligently as it might be, and some software programs continue to have errors and bugs of various sorts that unsuspecting users may not recognize. Similar technological advances have been made in the scoring of tests and the handling of test data. The test scoring template, for use with objective tests, was introduced in 1918 for the Army Alpha examination and shortly after World War I most published standardized tests began to include scoring stencils in sets of materials for users.

In 1935, the IBM Corporation marketed a test scoring machine based on measuring the conductivity of graphite marks made by examinees on special answer sheets. These IBM scoring machines were in wide use until about 1970, when optical scanning machines for test scoring had become perfected.

Since 1970 or even earlier, there have been attempts to use computers for scoring and otherwise evaluating outcomes of tests and examinations other than those of the purely objective type, for example, essays and English compositions. Thus far, there has not been unqualified success in this effort. However, mention should be made of uses of computers in the administration and scoring of "tailored" tests in which items are presented and sequenced dependent on examinee's responses. As of this writing, both the underlying measurement theory and the hardware technology are available, but tailored testing with computers is only beginning to be put into wide use.

Measurement has taken somewhat different directions in departments of psychology and in departments or schools of education, although actually the connections have generally been close. In psychology, the study of measurement and statistics has usually been part of the regular training of all psychologists, though only a small proportion of psychologists have specialized in it. Departments of psychology where there was a strong emphasis on psychological measurement in the first decades of the century included those at Clark, Columbia, Johns Hopkins, and Stanford Universities. Later, psychometrics flourished notably at Stanford University, the University of Chicago, and the University of Southern California.

In education, the main line of development derives from E. L. Thorndike's work and teaching at Teachers College, Columbia University; many Ph.D. dissertations appeared under his auspices in the Teachers College Contributions to Education. Many of the early standardized tests in education were developed by Thorndike's students. Since the early decades of the century, there has been a gradual evolution of educational measurement as a specialty. Lindquist remarked that in

1945 very few institutions offered advanced graduate level courses in educational measurement. At present, however, many university departments and schools of education maintain programs of graduate study in measurement.

The earliest organisation devoted to educational research as such, and thus incidentally to problems of measurement, was the Society of Educational Research, founded in New York City in 1903, but it was short-lived. A more successful organisation was the National Association of Directors of Educational Research, founded in 1915 and devoted largely to problems of conducting school surveys-a prevalent concern in those days. This association became a department of the National Education Association (NEA) in 1930, and at that time changed its name to the American Educational Research Association (AERA). Shortly thereafter, in 1931, the AERA founded the journal Review of Educational Research, which, as has been mentioned, published periodic reviews of educational research and measurement topics for many years.

As the AERA became more interested in scholarly, psychological, and technical issues, in 1968 it severed its ties with the NEA and formed divisions of membership, one of which was devoted to measurement and research methodology. In its publication program, the AERA exhibited its strong interest in educational research and measurement, continuing the Review of Educational Research and founding such journals as the American Educational Research Journal and the Journal of Educational Statistics. Still another organisation devoted to measurement was the National Council on Measurements Used in Education, responsible for publishing the Journal of Educational Measurement.

The American Psychological Association, which had been founded in 1892, had in 1945 formed itself into divisions, Division 5 being that devoted to psychological and educational measurement. Psychological and educational measurement concerns were centered in the APA's publication of the Journal of Educational Psychology (which it took over from a private publisher in 1957) and a statistical section of the Psychological Bulletin.

Independent of the APA, scholars concerned with psychological measurement, especially factor analysis and test theory, founded the Psychometric Society in 1935, which has published the increasingly technical journal Psychometrika since 1936. There is also a Society for Multivariate Experimental Psychology, founded by R. B. Cattell in 1960, which has concerned itself extensively with psychological and educational measurement problems, publishing the journal Multivariate Behavioural Research from 1966. Thus, persons interested in psychological and educational measurement have increasingly had a wide choice of organisations, conventions, and journals, to the point that it is now quite difficult to keep abreast of the great diversity of activities and journal articles.

Test publishing

The first successful commercial test publication in the United States was that of the Courtis Standard Research Tests in Arithmetic, by the World Book Company, in 1918. Starting as early as the 1920s, a number of publishers have had extensive test development departments devoted to the construction, analysis, and standardisation of tests. The Psychological Corporation, founded in 1921 by J. McK.

Cattell, E. L. Thorndike, and R. S. Woodworth, has provided an outlet for many psychological tests; it has now been acquired by Harcourt Brace Jovanovich. Science Research Associates was another large commercial test publishing organisation, now a division of the IBM Corporation. Important non-profit testing organisations have included the Cooperative Test Service, the Graduate Record Examination, and Educational Records Bureau; in 1947 these three organisations were absorbed into the newly founded Educational Testing Service, which has continued important practical and theoretical work in measurement.

The role of profit and non-profit testing organisations in education was examined by Holmen and Docter. They concluded that despite some shortcomings and problems, the influence of these organisations on education has been generally salutary and wholesome. They remarked, however, that "the good practices at the test-research and development level are not sufficient at this time to offset testing system inadequacies at the test user level".

There has been a persistent problem in monitoring the testing industry, and all makers of tests, even individual scholars, for the quality and excellence of the products. Probably the most important and effective method of meeting this problem is represented in the series of Mental Measurement Yearbooks edited by O. K. Buros over the period 1934 to 1978. Expert reviews have served to out to the profession, and to test users, strengths and weaknesses of published tests other measurement procedures. In the long run has improved the quality of these materials. Parallel to this, professional organisations have published, starting 1954, guidelines and standards for psychological and educational tests ; it hardly be questioned that these standards have an important influence on test makers publishers. Even with such arrangements to maintain integrity and scientific excellence of the testings profession, many tests in print fail to meet h standards, and there is a certain tendency for tradition and inertia to cause undesirable or outdated materials and techniques to persist after their time.

In parallel with psychologists' interest in education, educators have consistently afforded developmental psychology a place in educational theory. This is not the place to consider the general nature of educational theory, except to comment that at least some aspects of it must be value-laden, since the essential process of education is intended to be directed towards the attainment of valued ends. The definition of these ends and the specification of the means by which they might be attained are informed by a wide range of considerations including conceptions of the nature of man and society, conceptions of the forces which shaped educational organisations, and theories of how institutions and individuals work. Whilst in this light the place of developmental psychology seems assured in the student teacher's curriculum, there are many problems in translating from the essentially descriptive findings of psychology to the prescriptive business of education.

These issues have long been recognised but have rarely been given the exhaustive treatment they merit before being used in teacher education. The first thing that must be established is the quality of the informing psychological theory. Whilst recognising some consonance between his educational principles and those of Rousseau, Piaget none the less emphasised that Rousseau's view was'... no more than a sociological belief or a polemical weapon...' and that I what Rousseau lacked in order to constitute a science of education was a psychology of mental development'. It is the claim to scientific validity which underpins the developmentalist's right to a hearing on educational matters. Unfortunately, there is no body of developmental theory which is not open to fundamental reservation. For example, extensive criticisms of Piaget's theory are available. The flaws have been considered to be of such magnitude that it has been thought premature and misleading to apply Piaget's theory to education. Piaget's theory dominates contemporary developmental studies and, since 'new doctrines' have yet to emerge from his critics, this must provoke considerable caution in applications of his work.

Since it is in the nature of science to contest theories, this could lead to a complete embargo on the educational applications of much developmental theory. As a way of avoiding this conclusion, it has been suggested that educators are practical people who must deal with facts and that conflicting theories are rarely about facts, but about interpretations of facts.

So long as theoreticians agree on the facts, then the practitioner can work on the basis of secure knowledge. 'Whilst eventually the correct interpretation might make some difference, it often makes little difference at the present stage of technology.' Thus navigators do not suspend their calculations whilst they await the resolution of theoretical debates about the origins of the universe. Although the above example is an impeccable instance of Hilgard's view on the practical utility of contested theory, it might not be applicable to conflicts in contemporary social science. For one thing, educational prescriptions rarely arise from the notional facts of a body of knowledge. Rather, they arise from interpretations. The educational prescriptions emanating from Piaget's work do not arise from the largely uncontested facts that, at particular ages, most children fail specific archetypal tasks.

On the contrary, the prescriptions arise precisely from Piaget's contested interpretations of his observations. For example, Piaget's critics confirm his observations that children under the age of seven typically respond differently from adults on the whole range of tasks known in Piagetian terms as 'tests of conservation'. Piaget's interpretation is that these children lack the internalised operation of conservation and this is taken to be just one symptom of their being 'pre-operational'. From this it has been argued that for such children the curriculum should be dominated by direct sensory experience. However, Piaget's critics—whilst endorsing his observations—reject the interpretation.

Children's performance limitations on these tasks have been variously attributed to memory limitations, the level of experience with specific task content or inexperience in interpreting the social demands of the task. Some of these interpretations have been associated with educational prescriptions at odds with the Piagetian approach. These authors do not assume that young children lack logical operations and do not limit pedagogies to direct sensory experience as the essential educational medium for young children. Rather than searching for a solution to the problems of contested or condemned theory, as a basis for educational innovation, both psychologists and educationalists have tended to ignore the issues. For example, whilst Skinner's theory of language development was criticised by Chomsky and, whilst behaviourism generally has been criticised as naive in cognitive terms and untenable epistemologically, both find extensive use in contemporary educational practice and teacher education syllabuses.

Whatever the quality of particular theories, there remains the overriding and general problem of the nature of the link between schooling and developmental studies. Piaget asserted: 'That schooling should be adapted to the child is something that everyone has constantly urged.' This is simply not true. It is safer to say that no one has argued that schooling should be deliberately maladapted to the child.

The practicalities of avoiding such maladaption depend, in general terms, on what the nature of child development is taken to be. For those theorists who believe that development is merely the associative products of learning, there are no special assumptions in applying developmental psychology to schooling.

Special assumptions become necessary only when the claim is made that there is a natural course to human development or that there are natural limitations to human learning at certain stages. This claim is often advanced and, since it takes a variety of forms, it is necessary to examine its implications.Taken at its most general, the view of the superiority of natural propensities is well expressed by Smith who asserts that children know how to learn and that 'A fundamental problem for any instructor is to avoid interfering with natural processes of comprehension and learning.'

The educational implication of this is that 'There is only one reliable way to improve instruction, and that is to assist the instructor in understanding children...' A similar view is often deployed by popularisers of Piaget's work. Occasionally, a debilitating natural decline is posited. Bereiter and Scardamalia, for example, have taken the view that there is a natural decline in spontaneous curiosity. In establishing the educational relevance of such views, it is necessary to ask whether the postulated 'natural processes' are indeed natural or whether they are themselves the products of schooling, or the knock-on effects of schooling mediated by parents. Even if a natural order were established, its application to instruction depends on whether Nature were to be considered ideal, less than ideal, or simply immutable. It is interesting that Smith views children's natural ways of knowing as self-evident and good, whilst Bereiter and Scardamalia view children's natural decline in curiosity as simply an immutable fact. It is clear that divining educational implications from developmental studies involves value judgements on whether natural development should set the limits to which schooling might aspire.

There is a third stance on the form of development and its limitations which has its origins neither in an appeal to the superiority of Nature nor, initially at least, in the analysis of psychological processes. This is the stance initiated by Piaget. Arising from his rejection, on epistemological grounds, of empiricism and rationalism as accounts of the growth of understanding and his adoption of a constructivist stance, Piaget's view of the impact of experience on the processes of equilibration was that it necessarily yielded cognitive structures of particular and temporarily limiting forms. Piaget's view of development is thus not based on a naive view of the wisdom or otherwise of Nature. He observed '... let there be no misunderstanding.

Memory, passive obedience, imitation of the adult, and the receptive factors in general are all as natural to the child as spontaneous activity.' Piaget's theory has had enormous prominence in teacher education. This is not the place to describe or evaluate the work. The concern here is to raise, in principle, the kinds of problems peculiar to the application of Piaget's work to schooling, and hence to evaluate its place in teacher education. Instructional implications have been taken to arise from the functional aspect of the theory (that is the description of the dynamics of development) and from the formal aspect of the theory (that is the description of the sequential stages of underlying competence).

Piaget's view of the dynamics of development (most notably his conception of equilibration) arises out of his position as a constructivist. Before applying this notion to education, it would be necessary to be convinced on epistemological grounds of the necessity of adopting this model. Piaget's own view was that equilibration was an unnecessary concept when contemplating teaching school subjects '... whose contents have been invented or even developed by adults'. However, there are some school subjects 'whose contents depend more on a process of research and discovery during the course of which the human intelligence affirms its own existence'. In these latter subjects, and Piaget quoted physics and mathematics as examples, the operation of the learner's own processes of equilibration were considered crucial. In applying the stage model to education, different problems are met. The validity of the model would have to be established. This is extremely difficult since the theory is one of underlying competence.

Even if the theory were considered valid, there are massive technical problems in translating descriptions of competence into taxonomies for analysing children's available structures and related taxonomies for sequencing curriculum tasks. Considerable effort has been put into such work but the fundamental issues set out above seem to have been totally ignored. In the contemporary application of developmental psychology to teacher education, all the above fundamental issues seem to be largely ignored. Time constraints must account in good measure for the manner in which developmental studies are met by student teachers. Teacher education curriculums are very crowded. The most obvious impact of developmental psychology is in the form of textbooks. Typically students are required to purchase introductory texts in which are set out rendered down versions of psychological theories and their conjectured implications.

Frequently, texts introducing only developmental psychology are recommended or texts linking developmental psychology to the curriculum are offered.

Even at best, introductory texts written for teachers do little justice to the quality, complexity and subtlety of the psychologist's understanding of development and appear to do no justice whatsoever to the business of schooling. They appear to contain no model of the reader as learner-teacher; they are first and last guides to the psychological literature. Little effort is made to provide a serious rationale to the reader justifying either the content or organisation of the book.

In the popular work of Fontana, for example, he notes that the division of his book into two parts (developmental psychology followed by curriculum study) '... needs no lengthy justification. This provides a conceptual framework for prescriptions to be presented with coherence.' He leaves questions about relevance, significance and validity of the developmental theories unexamined. Other authors of texts on developmental psychology claim to provide perspectives within which teachers might interpret and understand children's behaviour.

The explicit claim is that the perspectives which psychologists so readily criticise within their own profession might prove useful as a heuristic with which to view classroom life. This approach passes on to the teacher the problems of translation discussed earlier. It avoids the question of whether the teacher's practical problems, goals and processes can be conceptualised within the terms offered, or whether they must be necessarily limited thereby.

It ignores the old adage that a perspective is not only a way of seeing—it is also a way of not seeing. Whilst no one would argue against the proposition that student teachers should learn to understand children, the techniques adopted by contemporary authors are educationally amorphous and question-begging. Whilst the above problems are not introduced to the reader of such texts, it seems inconceivable that the authors do not recognise them. However, by avoiding the issues, very strong claims may be made for the educational utility of developmental psychology.

It is claimed implicitly that developmentalists have generated descriptions of natural sequences and that these should be used to inform decisions about the aims of education and the means of schooling. Prescriptions are given for the design of learning environments, for techniques of diagnosis and assessment, and for the methods of teaching.

Whilst the textbook is the most evident mode of introducing student teachers to developmental psychology, it is not the only contact attempted. Students are sometimes required to undertake a child-study, with the objective of understanding the dynamics of a particular child. Alternatively, and increasingly, students meet bold statements of developmental theory (usually Piagetian) in the introductions to school schemes. Whether in child studies or in the rationalise to commercial schemes, the relevance of a development perspective is taken to be self-evident. Whilst not spelt out, it is implied that developmental psychology adds the gloss of objective, even scientific, knowledge to justify teaching procedures.

Impact of psychological studies on teaching

Many authorities in the field of educational psychology express considerable dismay and disappointment at the lack of impact of psychological studies on teaching behaviour. Ausubel and Robinson note, despite favourable responses on the part of teachers on psychology courses, that the behaviour of those same teachers observed later in the classroom, has typically shown distressingly little influence of the principles and theories which they had presumably learned. Some blame the quality of the psychology, others blame the quality of psychology teaching. None offers any evidence in support of the various conclusions. In stark contrast to the view of no effect, King has suggested that much of the ideology of teachers in the first school is propped up by their studies in developmental psychology.

Their ideology, according to King, revolves around the notion of 'child centred' education and involves attention to children's readiness to learn, their progress through stages, their inherent lack of malice and their subjective ways of know. All these, argues King, frame the designing of the early years' curriculum, including content and teaching methods. It has been suggested that this massive impact of developmental psychology is responsible for much of what is wrong with first school teaching. The view of crucial impact, like the view of nil impact, is based on no substantive evidence. King, for example, observed and interviewed only three teachers. His study, whilst provocative, provides little basis on which to discern the impact of developmental psychology and none whatsoever on which to damn it.

Relevant evidence seems to be unavailable. It would appear that those who wish to influence teaching processes must do so, at least in part, by influencing how teachers think and by endeavouring to understand teachers' existing theories and concepts as they relate to their classroom activities. However, research on teachers' thinking is largely undeveloped and it seems beset by methodological problems. The only research which would directly inform the issue of the impact of teachers' training would, as a minimum, have to link teachers' thinking to teachers' behaviour and thence to their children's learning.

The present use of developmental psychology in teacher education is characterised by ignorance. It has been argued above that we are ignorant of the problems of translation from descriptive science to prescriptive action and we are ignorant of the effects of current approaches to teaching developmental psychology to student teachers. More fundamentally, developmental psychology is, at best, vague about processes of development. In respect of the crucial educational task of managing learning, there are important gaps in our knowledge regarding

— the relationship between operational development and progress in curriculum subjects, and

— the processes of transition from task to task or cognitive stage to cognitive stage.

What we do not know here is precisely what a practitioner would need to know in order to optimise learning. We are also remarkably ignorant of the conditions and constraints under which teachers work. The practicalities of translating from theory to practice are largely ignored. Finally, we are generally ignorant of the effect of schooling as a factor in development.

In respect of cognitive growth, for example, the matter has received only the most general and trivial treatment. If developmental psychology is to be used with integrity in the education of teachers, each of these issues must become the subject of a great deal of work. There is a case for demanding that teachers address the problem of what it means to 'understand children'. Since this problem is broached in a wide variety of contexts (literature, common sense, philosophy, psychology, for example) there is some possibility that psychologists might be given a hearing, but no special voice. In this respect, psychological theory and findings should be presented—warts and all. If teachers learned nothing of immediate practical use in these lessons they might at least learn to pause and reflect on the complexity of the job.

But if this were the only claim for the utility of developmental psychology, it amounts to an impertinence, since it implies that teachers do not have enough to think about in respect of their profession and offers no assurance that reflection on complexity might lead to improved practice. To move towards making respectable claims for a hearing in teacher education, it seems important that more developmentalists address themselves directly to educationally relevant questions. Most generally, this would involve understanding schooling as a developmental factor and understanding it as a manipulable variable. Understanding schooling, as a preliminary to prescribing for schooling, would have enormous impact on the design of practicable applications work.

7

Directions for Counselling Programmes

The informal programmes have their place in an educational institution. But it needs hardly any emphasis that a programme, if it is to make its impact felt on the growth and development of students and enhance the quantity and improve the quality of the educational programme as a whole, there needs to be set up a well-organised structure covering the three major functions of the programme viz., adjustmental, orientational and developmental.

A structure never guarantees the success of an operation, but there is no doubt that a poor structure can be a major obstacle to success. It is desirable that the upcoming universities and colleges build this provision into their organisational structure at the planning stage itself and the old universities and colleges suitably add this provision into their educational programme and physical plan so that the students may avail of this service easily and profitably.

Great variety of institutions for higher education exist in our country at present. (a) Colleges constituent and affiliated, on the campus and at a distance. (b) Universities with under graduates on the campus along with the post-graduates or separate, large and complicated or small and uncomplicated, with or without strong traditions, with or without past experience in student guidance and counselling programme. It is not to be expected that any single pattern of organisation will fit all. Different structures will have to be planned to suit different set-ups.

1. *For constituent colleges on the campus:* If the number of students on rolls is 1000, a counselling officer assisted by the guidance committee can plan the programme according to their needs and implement the same with the co-operation of the deputy chief of UEIGB and academic adviser of SAB. If the number of students is less than 1,000, a liaison officer may be had. If the number of students exceeds 1000, an assistant counselling officer may be appointed to assist the counselling officer.

2. *For affiliated colleges at a distance:* If the number of students on rolls is 1000, a counselling officer assisted by the guidance committee can plan the programme and implement the same with the help of vocational guidance officer. If the number of students is less than 1000, a liaison officer may be had. If the number of students exceeds 1000, an assistant counselling officer may be appointed to assist the counselling officer for every 1000 students or part thereof.

3. *Universities:* Deans of Students, specially assisted by the heads of departments of psychology and education, and the guidance committee with the counselling officer can plan the programme and implement the same with the co-operation of the deputy chief of UEIGB and academic advisor of SAB. If the number of students exceeds 1000, assistant

counselling officers may be appointed. One assistant counselling officer may be had for every 1000 students. A part of these counselling officers may be taken from student leaders on some *ad hoc* remuneration or with special rights and facilities including representation of different groups, or sections of students. The counselling officer in the university should be in the Reader's grade while the assistant counselling officer may be in the lecturer's grade. Each university should have a specialist coordinator of guidance services to help the counselling officers or liaison officers in different colleges.

A guidance and counselling committee should be formed to serve in an advisory capacity or a policy making body for the programme. The committee can thrash out problems requiring group solution.

The committee should consist of the dean/principal, counselling officer, teachers representing different points of view, academic disciplines, interests and basic philosophies, student representatives, parents, deputy chief of UEIGB, vocational guidance officer, and so on. It is essential to determine the limits of responsibility of the guidance committee and identify the specific role to be assumed by each faculty and staff member. Clerical assistance needs to be provided to the counselling/liaison officer as a methodically organised guidance programme would require maintenance of a lot of record/information. Every university should have a counselling centre headed by a trained professional counselling officer who should be a Ph. D. or possess master's degree in psychology and counselling, with considerable counselling experience.

The centre should discharge the following functions:

i) give assistance to the university and constituent

colleges in developing, advising and counselling programmes and consultation on special psychological problems;

ii) give assistance to the university and constituent colleges in developing, advising and counselling programs and consultation on special psychological problems;

iii) provide psychological testing facilities for the university both for individuals and groups;

iv) carry on research on the development of testing procedures and experimental programmes in counselling; and

v) help in the training of post-graduate students in counselling and testing.

It would be ideal if the counselling centre includes special clinics and laboratories for speech and hearing problems, study skills and reading improvement. The centre should be situated at a convenient place so as to facilitate the provisions of counselling services for the whole university community, or at least the colleges in the immediate vicinity. If the counsellor creates a reputation for integrity and confidentiality, it will become an active centre; the faculty members will refer students to it and students too would like to visit it to get help in their problems and anxieties. Counsellors can develop confidence in the counselling Services by meeting new students at the time of orientation, visiting the hostel and giving talks to assemblies.

Counselling officer/liaison officer should be given a separate room which should afford him sufficient privacy. His office should be adequately furnished. It should have a small desk or table with a chair for the counselling/liaison officer and one or two extra chairs for the visitors. A few other small items of furnishing such as a small book-shelf, a filing cabinet, an almirah, curtains for the windows and doors, a flower vase or table lamp or even an attractive paper weight might improve the appearance of an otherwise unattractive room. The counselling/liaison officer should make the room as cheerful and pleasant, inviting, warm and attractive as possible so that the students like to visit it and feel welcome and at home.

It needs to be set up in every college and university. It should have adequate arrangements for the seating of the students who may visit it for consulting the occupational information material. It should also have sufficient space for conducting group discussions and other guidance activities. There should also be some provision for individual guidance.

Occupational information room should be distinct and prominently noticeable. However, if a separate room cannot be spared, a portion of a room or a verandah may be utilised for the purpose. Display of occupational information in an attractive manner is very important. Some suggestions are given below:

i) presentation of the information should be attractive and motivating.

ii) charts, posters and other visual aids should be at the eye level of the students.

iii) detailed information, if placed for reading, should be purposively arranged bearing close relationship with the materials displayed on the walls.

iv) materials should not be crowded in a particular place; it should be evenly distributed over places where students normally gather for receiving various services and need to stay for a reasonable time.

v) material displayed should be reviewed frequently with a view to updating the contents as also highlighting specific aspects of the information.

Evaluation of the programme will ensure its usefulness and make it respond to the needs of the student population.

An effective guidance and counselling programme presupposes information about the individual which is reliable, valid and comprehensive. This is possible when the work of collecting information is done on a systematic basis. Maintenance of cumulative Record Card is one of the most important activities of a good guidance programme. This record should contain:

a) student's identification, family history, personal history, health condition, and so on.

b) test results

c) problems inside and outside the college/university, emotional and social problems

d) specific assets and limitations

e) unusual talents

f) academic and co-curricular progress

g) placement

h) follow-up.

Counselling officer with the cooperation of other members of the faculty should maintain this record. If the records are to be of maximum value, they must be maintained regularly and kept upto date. Since some of the informations are of confidential nature, the records should be made available to only those persons who are likely to use the information for assisting the student in making adjustment and educational and vocational plans.

The desirable activities which could be taken up by a counselling/liaison officer in a university or a college are given below.

Educational talks: Talks on educational topics should be arranged by the counselling/liaison officer. He himself or the members of the guidance committee or some highly educated and experienced persons from the community or some neighbouring institution may be invited to deliver such talks. Some suggestive themes are adjustment with the institution, adjustment with peers, getting the best out of college/ university education, studying effectively, preparation of notes, preparing and taking examinations, utilisation of library services, participation in co-curricular activities, good work habits, entry and success in a job, taking an interview, living in hostels, choosing your career.

Orientation talks: Talks that are meant to give adequate information to the students regarding the courses of studies, the facilities available in the institution in the form of libraries, laboratories, workshops, playgrounds, hobbies, teaching personnel, freeships, fee concessions, stipends, scholar-ships, and so on. The students should also be made familiar with information about courses and careers open to graduates/ post-graduates, competitive examinations, correspondence courses, apprenticeship schemes, entry jobs which could be taken up fresh from the college/university without experience, courses and careers available abroad, changing occupational pattern, employment and occupational trends, guidance agencies at different levels, and so on.

Career talks: It means a talk about the details of a particular job. The talks may be delivered on themes such as avenues open to graduates and post-graduates, self-employment schemes, government service, scope of employment, methods of recruitment, discovering vocational interests and aptitudes, exploring vocations which interest you, planning your vocational programme, and so on.

Career conferences: It is a group activity organised for the purpose of providing occupational information of a preliminary or supplementary nature to a large number of students in a small or a big group. In a career conference, several speakers belonging to different professions come and deliver talks about their own fields to groups of students.

Plant tours: Visits to commercial establishments, industries, pro-fessional colleges, research institutions, and so on, should be arranged as these provide the students with direct and first hand experience of the work done and the physical and social environment in which it is done. To make the visit useful, the students should be prepared well in advance so that they know what to observe, which questions to ask and how to behave during the visit.

Personnel Counselling

Guidance is an all-inclusive programme, intended to help the students achieve their optimum potential. It is both a generalised and a specialised service. In such a programme, the total needs of the students need to be met by the total staff. One cannot assign the teaching-learning relationship to the teacher, the counselling relationship to the counselling officer and the smooth functioning relationship to the administrator. Everybody who comes into contact with the student, contributes in one way or the other in his growth and development. Hence the importance of making guidance a cooperative responsibility of all the members of the staff—professionally and technically qualified counselling officers and Deans, and the not well—qualified but very important administrators, teachers, advisors, wardens, physical education instructors, doctors, librarians, parents—in fact all those who come into contact with the student in some form or the other.

Administrator

The administrator occupies a key position in the guidance programme-whether it be the university or a college. In fact, the guidance programme can succeed only if it has the support and backing of the administrator. The administrator should assume proper leadership and be a source of inspiration to the personnel engaged in guidance work. He should give it the status of an important service. In consultation with the counselling/liaison officer and other members of the staff, he should prepare a yearly plan of guidance work, take general policy decisions regarding phasing of the programme, make provisions of time and allocate duties to the members of the staff. The administrator needs to play special attention to the following:

i) Provide suitable accommodation and facilities for the guidance service.

ii) If there is whole time counselling officer, arrange time schedule in such a manner that all students could benefit.

iii) If there is a part-time counselling/liaison officer, allow a relief of at least six periods in his teaching load so that at least the admission, orientation, student information and occupational information services are possible.

iv) Make adequate provision in the budget for carrying on the guidance programme; by considering it a fit charge on the students' amalgamated fund.

v) Establish and maintain a cumulative record system.

vi) Send teachers for inservice training.

vii) Give desirable publicity to the programme to improve relation of the institution with home, community and world of work.

viii) Offer special inducements and recognition to the members who make solid contribution to the programme.

ix) Evaluate the guidance programme in cooperation with the staff to determine and promote its effectiveness and evolve measures to strengthen it still further.

New programmes like guidance will succeed in proportion to the zeal and enthusiasm shown by the administrator—as is the administrator so will be the guidance programme in an institution.

Dean

Since guidance and counselling is one of the important student welfare services, the Dean has to ensure its effectiveness. He can contribute his share to this programme in a number of ways:

i) Establish rapport with students through personal contacts, public address system, group meetings, written communication, and so on.

ii) Organise and administer services such as orientation for new students, counselling services, financial aid to the needy, remedial services, and so on.

iii) Coordinate the various student activities so that every activity gets adequate time and finances.

iv) Act as an advocate of students in policy making bodies of the institution.

v) Initiate policy regarding behaviour of students during their spare time.

vi) Play the role of a liaison officer between students and faculty and students and management. Whenever there is a communication problem, students should be able to depend on the Dean.

vii) Keep a two-directional relationship with all student services and activities. The first is to encourage, support and coordinate, including representation of and to the vice-Chancellor and the Syndicate in the universities and to the Principals in colleges. Secondly, he must receive information from the directors of different services and counselling/liaison officer and so on, so that he is completely informed about everything taking place on the campus.

viii) Assist the university in understanding the needs and problems of students, guiding the youth in rational behaviour and in giving positive guidance to their future plans and aspirations. He should also create for students an atmosphere of rich opportunities, of friendly community living, an ambition for realising their true selves, for attaining excellence.

ix) Keep in touch with the various public organisations such as the rotary club, lions club and so on.

x) Keep adequate and uptodate records to increase the effectiveness.

xi) Create confidence in the students so that they confide in him. They should feel free to express their grievances and misunderstandings openly. They should have the confidence that the Dean could help them solve their problems, and The Dean should be able to come down from his ivory tower to the level of the student and consider him as an equal human being. He should listen to them, encourage their ideas, suggest new ideas.

xii) Ensure optimum utilisation of resources, human and material and create congenial atmosphere on the campus.

xiii) Keep his doors open to the parents also so that not only the educated but also uneducated parents may drop in his office for a word of comfort, encouragement and understanding.

The Dean should be advised on one hand by a committee consisting of the heads or personnel in charge of various services and, on the other, by the students' executive. This joint committee in turn should be advised by experts in various fields such as psychologists, doctors, counsellors, educators, social workers, who may be drawn from the faculties. The Dean should have high professional standing. He should have a pleasant personality, charming manners, fluent speech, good command over language, quick wit and humour. The Dean should be an academician and administrator, an educator and a counsellor, a diplomat and a public relations man, a coordinator and a guardian, a humanitarian and a sage—all rolled into one.

The Counselling officer should be a guidance-minded person with at least a year's full time course in guidance and counselling from a university. He is the nerve centre of the guidance programme. He should have a well- balanced personality, a broad outlook, an understanding attitude, a genuine interest in helping students. "The counsellor" in the words of

Williamson, "should be clearly more than a competent technician; he should be viewed as a broadly informed and cultivated educator". The counselling officer needs to discharge the following functions:

i) Arrange orientation programmes for the teachers to enlist their cooperation.

ii) Arrange orientation programmes for freshers and also for those passing through the transition period.

iii) Prepare an uptodate list of the resources—informational, referral and energy-available to him.

iv) Organise the guidance committee.

v) Set up an educational and occupational information centre.

vi) Display the information collected in an attractive way.

vii) Disseminate the information through educational and career talks, group discussions and film shows, and so on.

viii) Arrange talks by experts from different fields.

ix) Organise career days, career weeks, career conferences, parents' days, and so on.

x) Educate students regarding proper study habits and assist them in their development.

xi) Arrange individual discussions with students and their parents for giving them educational and occupational information.

xii) Arrange visits to places of work like industries, business establishments, offices, higher educational institutions and so on.

xiii) Maintain an active relationship with schools, colleges, university and other regional, national and social agencies.

xiv) Maintain an active liaison with clubs like lions club and rotary club.

xv) Refer the serious mental cases to clinical psychologists, psychiatrists or university health centres where the services of the clinicians are available, as his training and education does not equip him to deal with such cases

xvi) Maintain complete secrecy about the discussion between him and the client.

xvii) Administer psychological tests.

xviii) Provide counselling service to his students.

xix) Help in the placement of students.

xx) Take up research projects relating to the field of educational, vocational and personal-social guidance in the colleges and universities and convey the findings to important relevant agencies.

xxi) Prepare guidance leaflets, brochures and monographs and get them printed for distribution to the students.

The counselling officer should have six major qualities—belief in each individual; respect for individual human values; alertness to the world; open-mindedness; understanding of self; and professional commitment.

Liaison officer is a part time guidance worker, can be appointed from the rank of teachers. Liaison officer, in single or groups as convenient to respective colleges, can take charge of the guidance programme in a college. He should be a guidance-minded person with some specialised training in guidance at least for three months. The liaison officer should discharge the same duties as that of the counselling officer given above except the last five. The progress and efficiency of the guidance services in colleges will mainly depend on the ability, enthusiasm and dedication of liaison officers.

Teacher

An increased specialisation of labour is leading to an interdependence among agencies—social, political, economic and educational. The effective teacher in modern India, as elsewhere, cannot escape the influence of the rising complexities in the world of work and rapidly changing cultural values. He must contribute willingly and efficiently to the cause of guiding the youth in his classroom. Teacher and student relationship should be formal. Teachers and counsellors should join hands for an effective guidance programme. Teachers and counsellors need to combine their efforts to help young people to understand themselves, to see the subject-matter of each field in relation to their own strengths and limitations, and to appreciate the need for developing broad abilities and skills to meet the vocational demands of tomorrow as hundreds of new occupations are developing to meet the new needs, and hundreds of others are rendered obsolete or relegated to places of minor importance.

Teachers are the most useful allies of the counselling/liaison officers. It is they who have the closest, the most frequent and the most extended contacts with students in a natural situation. Without their co-operation, guidance service can never become an integral part of any educational programme. The teachers can help in the programme by:

i) playing a primary role in advising and orientation, in making known to the students the requirements and future job possibilities connected with their particular subjects;

ii) providing vocational motivation to the subjects taught by them;

iii) assessing the achievements of the students and thus enabling them to know better their strengths and weaknesses in certain subjects;

iv) enabling the students to explore and develop interest by integrating the curricular and co-curricular activities and thus orienting them towards worthy goals;

v) detecting early symptoms of any abnormality in the students' make up and drawing the counselling or liaison officer's attention; and

vi) rendering "mental hygiene first-aid" and helping students remain on the right track.

To be of solid help, the teacher should:

i) study the needs, interests, abilities and problems of each student in his class.

ii) win the confidence of the students and help them in every possible way to evaluate their own growth.

iii) get acquainted with the parents and take an active part in parent teacher association.

iv) instruct the students in appropriate methods of applying for posts.

v) co-operate with placement organisations in their task of making specific suggestions and finding suitable openings.

vi) follow-up those students they advise by obtaining progress reports on their satisfaction.

Teachers have an important role in assisting the students conserve their native capacities and invest and use the same so as to bring greatest satisfaction to themselves and benefit to society.

Tutor

The first line of reference on guidance matters is the tutor in collages. He is usually a teacher who does not actually teach the members of his tutorial group. This is a deliberate policy to remove guidance from the academic setting and to make it possible for a tutor to help with personal guidance without being hampered by any specific teaching relationship or overtones from the classroom situation. This places an extra responsibility on the tutor, namely that of developing a 'guidance' relationship with students he does not teach in a limited weekly tutorial period.

Tutoring means different things in different colleges and universities. In some tutoring refers to an academic relation between one teacher and one student concerned primarily with academic subject matter, not personal problems or extracurricular matters. The tutor-guardianship scheme is close to a student advisory system; tutor here is a synonym for a teacher, and 'guardianship' implies a caring or helping relation to a ward. The tutor can contribute to the guidance programme by:

i) orienting the members of his group regarding the curricular, co-curricular facilities and ancillary services available in the institution.

ii) collecting different types of information about the

student and assisting in the compiling of this information in the cumulative record.

iii) informing the members of his group regarding the occupational openings.

iv) arranging discussions on educational problems.

v) orienting the members of his group regarding the facility of scholarships, grants, loans, freeships and concessions available, their eligibility and how to apply for them.

vi) recommending the genuine cases for help.

vii) acquainting the members with proper study habits and assisting them in their development.

viii) meeting the parents for solving the problems of the students.

ix) arranging visits to places of work like industries, business establishments, offices, higher educational institutions, and so on.

x) detecting symptoms of abnormality in the students.

xi) rendering "mental hygiene first-aid" and helping the students remain on the right track.

Tutorial meetings can provide much needed close faculty student contacts.

Some colleges and universities have the scheme of assigning some guidance duties to the teachers who are specifically called advisers. In some institutions, all members of the faculty are assigned advisory duties; in others selected members of the faculty work as advisers to groups of students. Whatever pattern is adopted, there is no doubt about this fact that advisers support and supplement the guidance and counselling programme in a college or university. The boys and girls who have just come from the high school atmosphere of security to the free atmosphere of college/university do need some security, a place where they can belong, someone they can go to and talk their heart out with. The adviser can:

i) show personal friendship to the new students.

ii) explain the general programme of curricular and extracurricular activities to the advisers;

iii) help the student in the selection of subjects;

iv) serve as a "faculty friend" by being a personal friend to the student, by reacting sympathetically and in an understanding manner;

v) serve as a liaison between the student and the departmental heads, the administration and the Dean of students and the counselling/liaison officer.

vi) assist in the work of selecting students for admission through interviews;

vii) arrange pre-registration conferences with students living in the vicinity of the college;

viii) help in the general orientation programme;

ix) encourage cultural interests which will help students integrate their studies and new vocational, cultural and recreational interests and activities;

x) help by listening, by suggesting certain ideas and by working individually with students or if need be, in groups;

xi) be ready for reasonable requests for information from students and be helped to meet these demands by adequate briefing in the group meetings;

xii) refer students with more difficult problems to the counselling centre or to other officers on the campus.

xiii) arrange follow-up conferences to ensure that advisers are not meeting undue difficulty in adjusting to their academic programmes.

Students need to be assured of adviser's readiness to talk with them whenever they are feeling worried or uncertain as to future plans or available resources in emergencies, large or small. Some students need little assistance; others may need strong support and may also need to be referred to psychological counselling service. The adviser should be able to help each according to his need.

Warden

Warden is an important link in the process of guidance and counselling. He/she can ensure that hostel is not just a place for passing the night, but is also a place of education. A hostel should develop a reputation for promoting scholarship as well as a place for making good leaders and good citizens. Students coming to college from the rural areas, where they were recognised as individual members of the community, experience in college, particularly on university campuses, a vast impersonalism.

With an increasing number of students knocking at the doors of higher education, the sense of the impersonal threatens the very existence of the student. It is here that the hostel warden can play a crucial role. He/she can give recognition and love to the inmate, help him/her build up self-confidence and self-reliance. He/she can establish rapport through directness of approach, friendliness in manner, voice and sympathy and thus, create in the residents a much-needed sense of belongingness to an institution. The warden can contribute to the guidance and counselling programme in many ways:

i) orient the students regarding the customs and expectations of the hostel and help them anticipate some of the problems of group living and indicating the availability of help in the hostel so as to enable them to reach a satisfactory solution.

ii) provide help to those students who are handicapped by the lack of emotional stability or psychological resources which are needed in order to function well as students.

iii) collect all types of information regarding the resident in cumulative record and coordinate and use the information for the benefit of the student.

iv) take care of natural therapies which include day to day relations of residents in their rooms, in the mess and in co-curricular involvements.

v) establish a good communication system, so that the students could express freely, participate in the activities without any reservation.

vi) create a sense of belongingness among the residents through cultural programmes, informal evenings, dinner nights, celebration of days in the hostel.

vii) offer the student opportunity to achieve the kind of freedom, responsibility and skills which promise maturity and make the hostel a place par excellence for achieving the adult role.

viii) protect the weak, temper the strong, encourage the shy, bring out latent talents of the residents, stimulate self-discipline and serve as an interpreter of administrative policies of the institution.

ix) give sound advice recognising the needs of the students—security, recognition and love.

The warden is in a very good position of knowing the aptitudes and interests of the wards in co-curricular activities, emotional maturity, financial adequacy and ability to handle finances, ability to take individual responsibility, family background, social development and social maturity, vocational development, special talents like singing, dancing, sports and so on. No wonder, warden is a very important person in the entire superstructure of guidance and counselling.

Physical Efficiency

Physical efficiency is one of the basic requirements. Even for tough courses of studies as Medicine, Engineering and so on. Good physical health is essential. Thus physical education teacher is also an important link in the chain of guidance personnel. He can contribute to the guidance programme by:

i) giving the necessary data regarding the physical efficiency of the student, his performance in the physical efficiency tests, games and sports for the cumulative record.

ii) discovering the potentiality of the student in a particular game and arranging special training facilities for developing the same.

iii) bringing to the notice of the doctor the students with physical problems and handicaps for treatment.

iv) arranging coaching classes and demonstrations for the promising players.

Librarian

Librarian too has an important role in the overall guidance programme. He can contribute his share by:

i) circulating the latest information material among the teachers and students;

ii) providing right type of books on educational, vocational and personal guidance to both teachers and students;

iii) helping the counselling and the liaison officers in the classification, and filing of the occupational information material;

iv) displaying the material received from time to time in an attractive manner.

Medical Staff

Physical well-being or sound health is, in fact, a distinct asset in the general learning process. The conditions that hinder academic progress may not be serious illness but just mild generalised conditions as septic tonsils or adenoids, malnutrition or catarrh, or dyspepsia. Neither the teacher nor the counselling or liaison officer is a fit person to deal with all these problems.

Only a health specialist can handle all such problems. For the smooth progress of the student, medical assistance need to be provided. That the medical staff can contribute to the guidance programme in an institution by:

i) providing entrance and periodic medical examination for all students;

ii) reporting physical limitations to teachers and parents.

iii) developing a programme of helping students in physical hygiene.

iv) ensuring that information supplied about the health of students is utilised in the guidance programme.

Parents

Parents are the principal counsellors of the students. The favourable upbringing, plus the special help in the form of praise, admonition, reproof, and advice in difficult situations—all contribute to the guidance process.

The influence of parents on a student's life decisions is formidable. Parents can play a very important role in the guidance programme by:

i) getting maximum information regarding the educational and vocational possibilities for their children in the decades ahead.

ii) utilising good principles of mental hygiene and right living in their families.

iii) helping the children in developing effective study habits, plan their activities and budget their time for maximum achievement.

iv) showing the children how to postpone immediate pleasure in favour of later gratification.

v) getting all sorts of information regarding the facilities available and helping their children in utilising the same.

vi) help their children in discovering, developing and directing all of the inherent potentialities.

The Effectice Counsellor

A counsellor's personality is a crucial ingredient in determining the effectiveness of counselling. A few entry-level students decide to pursue careers in counselling because of the potential for advancement and recognition or because they need self-therapy, dysfunctional motivators for becoming a counsellor include the following:

— *Emotional distress:* Individuals may have unresolved personal traumas.
— *Vicarious coping:* They may live their lives through others rather than have meaningful lives of their own.
— *Loneliness and isolation:* Individuals who do not have friends may seek them through counselling experiences.
— *A desire for power:* They may feel frightened and impotent in their lives and seek to control others.
— *A need for love:* They may be narcissistic and grandiose and believe that all problems are resolved through the expression of love and tenderness.
— *Vicarious rebellion:* They may have unresolved anger and act out their thoughts and feelings through their client's defiant behaviours.

Certain functional factors motivate individuals to pursue careers in counselling and make them well suited for the profession. According to Guy, they often realise that they have most or all of the following skills:

— *Curiosity and inquisitiveness:* They possess a natural interest in people
— *Ability to listen:* They find listening stimulating.
— *Comfort with conversation:* They enjoy verbal exchanges.

— *Empathy and understanding:* They can put themselves in another person's place, even if that person is a different gender or from a different culture.

— *Emotional insightfulness:* They are comfortable dealing with a wide range of feelings, from anger to joy.

— *Introspection:* They have the ability to see or feel from within.

— *Capacity for self-denial:* They can set 'aside personal needs to listen to others or take care of others' needs first.

— *Tolerance of intimacy:* They can sustain emotional closeness.

— *Comfort with power:* They can accept power with a certain degree of detachment.

— *Ability to laugh:* They can see the bittersweet quality of life events and the humour in them.

There are also a number of personal characteristics associated with effective counsellors. They include stability, harmony, constancy, and purposefulness. The potency of counselling is related to counsellor's personal togetherness thinks that the personhood of counsellors is more important than their techniques. Also stresses the importance of personality in counselling. He cites research that indicates that effective counselling is more dependent on the personality of counsellors than on their knowledge or skills. His point is that, while knowledge and skills are important, education cannot change a person's basic characteristics.

Effective counsellors, on a personal level, have a vision of where they are going in life. They are growing as persons and are helping others do the same both personally and globally. In other words, effective counsellors are culturally sensitive: that is, they monitor their own biases, listen, ask for clarification, and explore racial and cultural differences. Related to this sensitive and growth—enhancing quality of helpers is their appropriate use of themselves—their use of self as instrument. People helpers must be able to use themselves in spontaneous, creative, empathetic, and altruistic ways.

It is helpful if their personalities have been tempered by multiple life experiences that have enabled them to realise some of what their clients are going through. The ability to work from a perspective of resolved emotional experience is what Rollo May characterises as being a wounded healer. Such individuals have gained insight into themselves and the world. They are able to be with their clients in ways not otherwise possible. Effective counsellors are also people who have successfully integrated scientific knowledge and skills into their personhood. That is, they have "achieved a balance of interpersonal and technical competence". Qualities of effective counsellors include the following:

— *Intellectual competence:* Counsellors must have a thorough knowledge of many helping theories as well as the desire and ability to learn. They must be able to think fast on their feet.

— *Energy:* Counselling is emotionally draining and physically demanding. Counsellors must have the ability to be active in their sessions and sustain that activity when they see a number of clients in a row.

— *Flexibility:* Effective counsellors are not tied to one specific set of responses. Rather, they adapt what they do to meet the needs of their clients.

— *Support:* Counsellors support clients in making their

own decisions. They also help engender hope and power and avoid trying to be rescuers.

— *Goodwill*: Counsellors must desire to work on behalf of clients in a constructive way that ethically promotes independence.

— *Self awareness:* This quality consists of a knowledge of self, including attitudes, values, and feelings and the ability to recognise how and what factors affect them.

— *Awareness of cultural experiences:* This skill is the ability to be comfortable with and relate well to people in populations who differ culturally from the counsellor.

The environment in which counsellors work is primarily social and problem-oriented. It calls for skill in interpersonal relationships and creativity. The more aligned counsellor's personalities are to their environments, the more effective and satisfied they will be. Wiggins and Weslander found empirical support for Holland's hypothesis. They studied the personality traits and rated the job performance of 320 counsellors in four states. Counsellors who were rated "ineffective" generally scored highest on the realistic and conventional scales. Other factors, such as sex, age, and level of education, were not found to be statistically significant in predicting effectiveness.

The results of this research affirm that the personality of counsellors is related to their effectiveness in the profession. Individuals who become counsellors experience the same difficulties as everyone else. They must deal with aging, illness, death, marriage, parenting, job changes, divorce, and a host of other common problems. Some of these life events, such as marrying late in life or experiencing the death of a child, are considered developmentally "off time," or out of sequence, Other events: consist of unintended but fortuitous chance encounters, such as meeting a person with whom one develops a lifelong friendship.

All such experiences are problematic because of the stress they naturally create. A critical issue is how counsellors handle these life events. Besides finding meaning in potentially problematic areas, other strategies counsellors use for coping with crisis situations include remaining objective, accepting and confronting situations, and asserting their own wishes.

Counsellors who have healthy personal lives and learn from both their mistakes and their successes are more likely than others to grow therapeutically and be able to concentrate fully and sensitively on client's problems. Therefore, counsellors and those who wish to enter the profession need to remain relatively free from triangling patterns with parents in their families of origin and be able to foster and maintain intimate yet autonomous relationships in the present as desired. To maintain a healthy approach, successful counsellors use preventive measures to avoid problematic behaviours particular to professional helpers, such as burnout. *Burnout* is becoming emotionally or physically drained to the point that one cannot perform functions meaningfully People cannot function adequately if they never step out of their professional roles. Counsellors must develop interests outside of counselling and avoid taking their work home, either mentally or physically. A number of researchers suggest ways in which counsellors can avoid or treat burnout: Among the suggestions are the following:

- Associate with healthy individuals.
- Work with committed colleagues and organisations that have a sense of mission. Be reasonably committed to a theory of counselling.

— Use stress-reduction exercises.
— Modify environmental stressors.
— Engage in self-assessment.
— Periodically examine and clarify counselling roles, expectations, and beliefs.
— Obtain personal therapy.
— Set aside free and private time.
— Maintain an attitude of detached concern when working with clients.
— Retain an attitude of hope.

No person possesses all the qualities of the perfect counsellor. Nevertheless, because of temperament, background, and experience, some are better suited to become counsellors than others. Those individuals whose personal attributes match the demands of the profession are more likely to be personally and professionally satisfied with the roles of counsellors.

Educationally, effective counsellor have gone through an a credited counselling programme or its equivalent on either a doctoral or master's level. Many have also achieved the skills of an experience necessary to work in counselling speciality areas. Furthermore, they have obtained licensure, certification, or both. Effective counsellor, regardless of speciality, keep their knowledge up to date by participating in continuing education programmes and supervisory activities.

Few, if any, people have the ability to work effectively as counsellors without formal education in human development and counselling. The level of education needed is directly related to the level of work. There are three levels of helping relationships: nonprofessional, paraprofessional, and professional. Each level of this hierarchy assumes that helpers have acquired the helping skills necessary for the task.

Nonprofessional helpers may be friends, colleagues, untrained volunteers, or supervisors who try to be helpful to those in need and possess varying degrees of wisdom and skill.

Paraprofessional helpers are usually human-service workers who have received some formal training in human-relations skills but work as part of a team rather than as individuals. People on this level often work as mental health technicians, child-care workers, probation personnel, and youth counsellors. When properly trained and supervised, paraprofessionals such as residence-hall assistants can have a major impact on facilitating positive relationships that promote mental health throughout a social environment.

Professional helpers are specifically educated to provide assistance on both a preventive and a remedial level. People in this group include counsellors, psychologists, psychiatrists, social workers, psychiatric nurses, and marriage and family counsellors/ therapists.In regard to the education of novice counsellors, Robinson and Kinnier find that self-instructional and traditional classroom training are equally effective at teaching skills. The results of their studies are important for counsellors on all levels because they imply that more time can be devoted to learning how to apply skills if self-instructional methods are used to obtain facts. In essence, better-educated counsellors can be efficiently self-trained up to a point.

Each professional speciality has its own educational and practice requirements. Counsellors need to know the educational backgrounds of other professions in order to use their services, if needed, and communicate with them in an informed manner. Psychiatrists earn a medical degree and complete a residency in psychiatry. They must pass both national and state examinations in order to practice. Psychologists may earn a doctor of philosophy degree (Ph.D.), a doctor of education degree (Ed.D.), or a doctor of psychology degree (Psy.D.). Their coursework and internships may be concentrated in clinical, counselling, or school-related areas. All states license psychologists, but the requirements for licensure differ from state to state.

Most clinically oriented psychologists are listed in the *National Register of Health Service Providers,* which has uniform standards for inclusion. Social workers earn a master's of social work degree that includes internships in social agency settings. The National Association of Social Workers offers credentials for members who demonstrate advanced clinical and educational competencies.

Professional counsellors obtain either a master's or a doctorate in counselling from a counsellor education or related program and complete internships in speciality areas such as rehabilitation counselling, school counselling, community/agency counselling, career counselling, gerontological counselling, addiction counselling, or marriage and family counselling. They are usually certified by the National Board of Certified Counsellors or are licensed to practice by individual states, or both.

The words licensure and certification have specific meanings. Fretz and Mills define licensure as "the statutory process by which an agency of government, usually a state, grants permission to a person meeting predetermined qualifications to engage in a given occupation and/or use a particular title and to perform specified functions." Certification, on the other hand, is either a professional, statutory, or nonstatutory process "by which an agency or association grants recognition to an individual for having met certain predetermined professional qualifications. Stated succinctly, certification ... is a 'limited license—that is, the protection of title only". Neither licensure nor certification ensures in and of itself that professional helpers will be effective, but these processes are first steps in promoting quality by assuring that practitioners who define themselves by a title actually meet the qualifications implied by that designation.

There are two areas of emphasis within the profession of counselling: counselling psychology and counsellor education. These two specialities share many common roots, concerns, and significant persons in their histories. Compared to counselling psychology, counsellor education is more of an emerging profession, partly due to the history, identity, and development of each speciality. The accreditation criteria for both counselling psychology and counsellor education in regard to graduate education have been summarised by Hollis and Wantz, although these criteria are constantly being modified or changed.

An accredited counselling psychology program is one that has met the standards drawn up by the APA in cooperation with the Division of Counselling Psychology. These programs are valued because they assure both students and prospective employers that at least minimum skills necessary to practice psychology as a profession have been achieved.

Graduates of accredited programs, therefore, have an advantage in obtaining employment and licensure. Not every program that applies for accreditation obtains this recognition, but those that do have met the following standards.

> Professional psychology programs generally are located in universities or schools of professional

> psychology that offer doctoral training and are approved by one of six regional accreditation bodies.
>
> The program must be clearly identified and labelled as a psychology program and must be a recognisable, coherent organisational entity.
>
> Faculty must be well qualified and must have clear authority and primary responsibility for all aspects of the program. The plan of study must be integrated and organised with assurance of breadth of exposure to the field of psychology including a curriculum with equivalency of at least 3 academic years of full-time resident graduate study. The course work must include scientific and professional ethics and standards, research design and methodology, statistics and psychological measurement, biological bases of behaviour, cognitive-affective bases of behaviour, social bases of behaviour, individual behaviour, and courses in speciality areas.
>
> Supervised practicum, internship, and field or laboratory training must be included. The minimum practicum experience is 300 hours, of which at least 200 hours are in direct service experience and 50 hours of formally scheduled supervision. Internship must be fulltime for 1 year or the equivalent with an experience of at least 1500 hours.

An accredited counsellor education program is one recognised at either the master's or doctoral level. The accrediting body for these programs is the Council for Accreditation of Counselling and Related Educational Programs (CACREP). This independent body evolved from the efforts of the Association for Counsellor Education and Supervision (ACES) and the American Counselling Association (ACA) to establish standards and guidelines for counselling independent of the National Council for Accreditation of Teacher Education (NCATE).

On the master's level, CACREP accredits programs in community counselling, mental health counselling, school counselling, marriage and family counselling/ therapy, and student-affairs practice in higher education with emphases in counselling, development, and administra-tion. Graduates from accredited master's programs have an advantage over graduates from nonaccredited programs in (1) obtaining admittance to accredited counsellor edu-cation doctoral programs, (2) meeting the educational requirements for counsellor licensure and certification, and (3) obtaining employment as a counsellor. The following broad standards must be met in an accredited counsellor education master's degree program.

— The entry-level program must be a minimum of two full Academic years in length with a minimum of 48 semester hours required of all students. The entry-level program in mental health counselling must be 60 semester hours long; and the entrylevel program in marriage and family counselling must also be 60 semester hours.

— Curricular experiences and demonstrated knowledge and skill competence is required of all students in each of eight common core areas: (1) human growth and development, (2) social and cultural foundations, (3) helping relationships, (4) groups, (5) lifestyles and career development, (6) appraisal, (7) research and evaluation, and (8) professional orientation.

— Clinical experiences are required under the direction of supervisors with specific qualifications. The student must complete 100 clock hours of a supervised practicum with 1 hour per week of individual supervision and 1½ hours per week of group supervision with other students in similar practice.

— The program must require that each student complete 600 clock hours of a supervised internship, which is to begin only after successful completion of the student's practicurn.

— Three full-time faculty members must be assigned to the academic unit in counsellor education. Qualifications of academic unit leaders, program leaders, and faculty are listed.

CACREP also accredits programs on the doctoral level (Ed.D. and Ph.D.). Standards at this level assume that an individual has completed an entry-level master's degree in counselling. Doctoral-level programs require more in-depth research, supervised field experiences, and specialisation and are similar in their overall scope to doctoral programs in counselling psychology. A growing number of graduate schools are applying for either APA or CACREP accreditation because of the benefits and recognition such accreditation brings to themselves and to their students. Rehabilitation counselling is accredited by the Council on Rehabilitation Education, Inc. (CORE), while marriage and family counselling/therapy is accredited by both the Commission on Accreditation for Marriage and Family Therapy Education (CAMFTE) and CACREP.

Details on the standards of these accrediting bodies may be obtained by writing to them at the addresses listed at the back of this book. Within the field of counselling, new specialities are emerging, such as gerontology and substance abuse. Professionals who wish to concentrate in new or nontraditional areas of service have a variety of guidelines to choose from, including those written by CACREP or NBCC. Regardless of the exact guidelines, all counsellors need a core base of knowledge in addition to a focused interest.

There is a need for continuing education of all counsellors, even after graduation from a well-planned program. The reason is that new ideas in the treatment and practice of clients are always evolving and must be evaluated, incorporated, and, it necessary, mastered. Counsellors who stop reading professional publications or stop attending in-service workshops and conventions quickly become dated in the delivery of skills.

Therefore, it is becoming increasingly common for boards of examiners of counsellors to require already licensed practitioners to obtain a certain number of continuing education units (CEUs), which are offered by approved professional organisations such as ACA, APA, or AAMFT, in order to retain their credentials. Engaging in such continuous efforts is sometimes expensive in terms of time and money, but the cost of not keeping up professionally is much higher.

Supervision is an interactive and evaluative process in which someone with more proficiency oversees the work of someone with less knowledge and skill in order to enhance the professional functioning of the junior member. At its best, supervision is a facilitative experience that combines didactic and experiential learning in the context of a developmental relationship. It allows both counselling students and counsellor educators to acquire expertise in theory and practice that is not possible to gain in any other way.

Supervision is a required area of instruction in all CACREP accredited doctoral programs. In addition, associations such as AAMFT and AMHCA mandate that practitioners who wish to enhance their qualifications in marriage and family therapy or mental health counselling undergo supervision from members of the profession who have received advanced training and have obtained approved supervisor status.

Standards for counselling supervisors have been developed for all counsellors affiliated with ACA. Often, supervised experiences can be counted toward CEUs by those already licensed as counsellors. To be effective, supervision must be given on a counsellor's developmental level. For beginning graduate students who have a noticeable gap between their knowledge of theory and practice, supervisors are most potent if they assume a highly structured teaching role. For example, supervisors may be more authoritarian, didactic, and supportive than they would be with advanced graduate students or experienced counsellors. In the latter cases, supervisors might be more confrontive and consultive.

While supervision, like counselling, may increase one's self-awareness, this process is focused on professional rather than personal growth. In setting up supervisory situations, one must address several myths and many realities. Myths are made up of extreme views: for example, "one supervisor can perform all supervisory roles," "individual supervision is best," or "individuals do not need training to supervise". Realities include the following facts:

— There is not just one theoretical model of supervision but several.
— Before a productive supervisory relationship can be established, the developmental level of the supervisee must be verified and a written plan of realistic goals must be completed.
— There is a significant relationship between a supervisor's credibility, such as trustworthiness, and a supervisee's performance.

The literature and the sophistication of supervisory techniques in counselling are growing. For example, the reflective team model is a recent innovative way of providing group supervision, especially in working with couples and families. In this model graduate students are asked to collaborate, brainstorm, and take their client's perspectives as they advance hypotheses about client behaviours, view situations from the client's framework, and work cooperatively.

There are instruments and training modules to guide supervisors and supervisees through the process of becoming skilled and responsible counsellors. Counsellors who take advantage of supervisory opportunities, especially opportunities for *peer supervision* can both gain and give information about themselves and their clinical abilities. This increased awareness is the bedrock on which other positive professional experiences can be built.

Theoretical Approaches

When professional counselling began to emerge in the late 1940s and early 1950s, there were only two major theoretical orientations: Williamson's clinical-counselling (directive) approach and Rogers's client-centered (nondirective) approach. Psychoanalysis was accepted as a general background for all counsellors. Such a limited choice of theoretical models made the process of becoming a counsellor less complicated but no less intense. Today, as then, effective counsellors decide which theory or theories and methods to use on the basis of their educational background, philosophy, and the needs of clients.

Most counselling theories have been developed by exceptional practitioners who have formulated theories on the basis of experience and observation. Yet most theorists are somewhat tentative about their positions, realising that no one theory fits all situations. Indeed, one theory may not be adequate for the same client over an extended period. Counsellors must choose their theoretical positions carefully and regularly reassess them. Some theoretical models are more comprehensive than others, and effective counsellors are aware of which theories are most comprehensive and for what reasons. Five requirements of good theory:

— *Clear, easily understood, and communicable:* It is coherent and not contradictory.

— *Comprehensive:* It encompasses explanations for a wide variety of phenomena.

— *Explicit and heuristic:* It generates research because of its design.

— *Specific in relating means to desired outcomes:* It contains a way of achieving a desired end product.

— *Useful to its intended practitioners:* It provides guidelines for research and practice.

In addition to those five qualities, a good theory for counsellors is one that matches their personal philosophies of helping. Counselling theory must fit counsellors like a suit of clothes. Some theories, like some suits of clothes, need tailoring. Therefore, effective counsellors realise the importance of alterations. Counsellors who wish to be versatile and effective should learn a wide variety of counselling theories and know how to apply each without violating its internal consistency. If counsellors depart from a theory they have subscribed to, they should have good reasons for doing so. One of the primary reasons for such a shift in style elates to the client's developmental level. To be effective, counsellors must consider how far their clients have progressed in their structural development, as described by Piaget.

Theory is the foundation of good counselling. It challenges counsellors to be caring and creative within the confines of a highly personal relationship that is structured for growth and insight. Theory has an impact on how client communication is conceptualised, how interpersonal relationships develop, how professional ethics are implemented, and how counsellors view themselves as professionals.

For instance, counsellors who base their theoretical approach on the writings of Lawrence Kohlberg conceptualise counselling as a developmental process of social interaction, but counsellors who conceptualise counselling as a learning process are more concerned with the way in which the environment is set up. Without theoretical backing, counsellors operate haphazardly in a trial-and-error manner and risk being both ineffective and harmful. Brammer and Shostrom stress the pragmatic value of a solidly formulated theory for counsellors:

> Theory helps to explain what happens in a counselling relationship and assists the counsellor in predicting, evaluating, and improving results. Theory provides a framework for making scientific observations about counselling. Theorising encourages the coherence of ideas about counselling and the production of new ideas. Hence, counselling theory can be very practical by helping to make sense out counsellor's observations.

Boy and pine elaborate on the practical value of theory by suggesting that theory is the why behind the how of counsellors' roles, providing a framework within which counsellors can operate. Counsellors guided by theory can meet the demands of their roles because they have reasons for what they do. Boy and Pine point out six functions of theory that help counsellors in a practical way:

— Theory helps counsellors find unity and relatedness within the diversity of existence.

— Theory compels counsellors to examine relationships they would otherwise overlook,

— Theory gives counsellors operational guidelines by which to work and helps them evaluate their development as professionals.

— Theory helps counsellors focus on relevant data and tells them what to look for.

— Theory helps counsellors assist clients in the effective modification of their behaviour.

— Theory helps counsellors evaluate both old and new approaches to the process of counselling. It is the base from which new counselling approaches are constructed.

The ultimate criterion for all counselling theories is how well they provide explanations of what occurs in counselling. Their value as ways of organising information hinges on the degree to which they are grounded in the reality of people's lives.

In its infancy, counselling was a profession where theoretical purity was expected and actually necessary for counsellors seeking employment. It was important that counsellors be able to identify their practices as stemming from one of fewer than half a dozen available choices (psychoanalysis, directive trait-factor, client-centered, and so on). But with the flood of new theories—cognitive, behavioural, and affective—that were formulated during the 1960s, allegiance to a specific theory began to wane in popularity and importance. The development of microskills *training* hastened the demise of theoretical positions stemming from one specific source.

Eclectic counselling

An eclectic approach can be hazardous to the counselling process if the counsellor is not thoroughly familiar with all the processes involved. But such a way of working can be helpful if done properly. The hazardous approach of undereducated counsellors is sometimes sarcastically referred to as "electric": they try any and all methods that "turn them on." The problem with an electric orientation (that is, an unsystematic eclectic approach) is that counsellors often do more harm than good if they have little or no understanding about what is helping the client.

To combat this problem, McBride and Martin advocate a hierarchy of eclectic practices and discuss the importance of having a sound theoretical base as a guide. The lowest or first level of *eclecticism* is really syncretism—a sloppy, unsystemic process of putting unrelated clinical concepts together. It is encouraged when graduate students are urged to formulate their own theories of counselling without first having experienced how tested models work.

The second level of eclecticism is *traditional.* It incorporates "an orderly combination of compatible features from diverse sources [into a] harmonious whole". It is more thought out than syncretism, and theories are examined in greater depth. On a third level, eclecticism is described as professional or theoretical or as *theoretical integrationism.* This type requires that counsellors master at least two theories before trying to make any combinations. The trouble with this approach is that it assumes a degree of equality between theories (which may not be true) and the existence of criteria "to determine what portions or pieces of each theory to preserve or expunge". It differs from the traditional model in that no mastery of theory is expected in the traditional approach.

A final level of eclecticism is called *technical eclecticism* and is exemplified in the work of Arnold Lazarus. In this approach, procedures from different theories are selected and used in treatment "without necessarily subscribing to the theories that spawned them". The idea is that techniques, not theories, are actually used in treating clients. Therefore, after properly assessing clients, counsellors may use behavioural methods (such as assertiveness training) with existential techniques (such as confronting persons about the meaning in their lives) if the situations warrant. This final approach is in line with what Cavanagh proposes as a healthy eclectic approach to counselling, one that requires counsellors to have:

1) a sound knowledge and understanding of the counselling theories used;
2) a basic integrative philosophy of human behaviour that brings disparate parts of differing theories into a meaningful college; and
3) a flexible means of fitting the approach to the client, not vice versa.

Counsellors who follow this model may operate pragmatically and effectively within an eclectic framework. The critical variables in being a healthy eclectic counsellor are a mastery of theory and an acute sensitivity to knowing what approach to use when, where, and how.

A review of effective counselling would not be complete without examining the systems to which counsellors adhere. A system is a unified and organised set of ideas, principles, and behaviours. Systems associated with counselling are concerned with diagnosis, theory, ethics, and law. Counsellors have both borrowed and created systems that fit the profession. Indeed, the strength of counselling ultimately depends on a continuation of that process. This section briefly explores problems associated with systems, especially in the most important area of counselling: treatment. Counselling started like a person who mounted a horse and rode off in all directions; that is, the person had no focus or planned direction.

In many respects, the history of counselling parallels psychology's, which evolved from various disciplines sixty years earlier than counselling when the American Psychological Association was established. Like psychology, counselling has passed through a number of stages, some of which have regenerated themselves, such as the emphasis on humanistic education in the 1930s and 1970s and the emphasis on authoritarian and vertical counselling relationships in the 1940s and 1980s. As far back as the late 1940s, professionals noticed the lack of a system for counselling. Robert Mathewson observed that counselling was in "a search for a system . . . to win free from inadequate frames borrowed from traditional philosophy and education, from psychology from political formulations underlying democratic government, from the concepts of physical science, etc."

Until the late 1940s, counselling used a variety of systems. Because the profession was without an organisational base, different factions defined what they did according to the system that suited them best. Competition between points of view, especially those connected with theories, was often spirited. Some counsellors recognised the need for a unifying systematic approach to their discipline, but the unplanned growth of the profession proved an obstacle. Leo Goldman promoted the first major search for a unifying system of counselling. Before Goldman, pioneers such as Ralph Berdie proposed that counselling should cast off its "borrowed procedures, theories, and methods from a variety of disciplines" and define itself more fully. Berdie suggested that counsellors become applied behavioural scientists, but it was Goldman who devoted an entire issue of his journal to the innovative Cube concept. The *Cube,* a systematic way of organising counselling services, was a radical idea and the cause of much discussion.

In a thought provoking article, Clyde Parker noted "For too long we have allowed the profession to be directed by what is new and different rather than by any systematic exploration of the alternative modes available. Using the Cube as a guide, we can see how our efforts might range from individual, direct, therapeutic interventions to attempts at creating a more humane institutional environment by effective use of the media."The Cube model describes three dimensions of counsellor intervention: the target, the purpose, and the method. The *target is* the population to be served, such as a group.

The *purpose is* the rationale for offering services, such as increasing awareness or changing behaviour. The *method is* the means by which counsellors accomplish this purpose. Although the Cube model generated a tremendous amount of research in its presentation of 36 potential areas of counselling, its overall impact on counselling was not as great as expected. The main reason that its impact was diminished was its timing: during the 1970s, it had to compete with a number of other ideas about counselling. Moreover, the Cube did not address theory directly.

There are not many current attempts to develop systems unique to counsellors. Ivey's integration of develop-mental growth with counselling strategies stands out as one of the most unique. Basically, this approach applies Piagetian concepts of cognitive levels to clinical interviews with adults and children. Therefore, if clients do not initially recognise their feelings, counsellors will work from a sensorimotor level to bring out emotions. In a similar way, clients who are interested in planning strategies for change will be helped using a formal pattern of thought. *Developmental counselling and therapy* (DCT) "specifically addresses the sequence and process of development as it occurs in the natural language of the interview". Another attempt, not nearly as elaborate as Ivey's, is the continuum system of Celotta and Telasi-Golubcow. In this approach, client's problems are classified along a continuum from behavioural-specific to general systems. The initial orientation of counsellors is toward behaviour problems.

Relationship

Clients and counsellors sometimes have different perceptions about the purpose and nature of counselling. Clients often do not know what to expect from the process or how to act. Seeing a counsellor is a last resort for many individuals. They are likely to have already sought help from more familiar sources, such as friends, family members, ministers, or teachers. Therefore, many clients enter counselling reluctantly and hesitantly This uncertainty can inhibit the counselling process unless some structure is provided. "Structure in counselling is defined as a joint understanding between the counsellor and client regarding the characteristics, conditions, procedures, and parameters of counselling". Structure helps clarify the counsellor-client relationship and give it direction; protect the rights, roles, and obligations of both counsellors and clients; and ensure the success of counselling.

Practical guidelines are part of building structure. They include time limits, action limits (for the prevention of destructive behaviour), role limits, and procedural limits. Guidelines also provide information on fee schedules and other important concerns of clients. In general, structure promotes the development of counselling by providing a framework in which the process can take place, "it is therapeutic in and of itself". Structure is provided throughout all stages of counselling but is especially important at the beginning. Dorn states that "clients usually seek counselling because they are in a static behaviour state". That is, the client feels stuck and out of control to change behaviour.

To help clients gain new directions in their lives, counsellors provide constructive guidelines. Their decisions on how to establish this structure are based on their theoretical orientation to counselling, the personalities of their clients, and the major problem areas with which they will deal. Too much structure can be just as detrimental as not enough. Therefore, counsellors need to stay flexible and continually negotiate the nature of the structure with their clients. The importance of structure is most obvious when a client arrives for counselling with unrealistic expectations. A counsellor needs to move quickly to establish structure at such times.

One way is for counsellors to provide information about the counselling process and themselves with professional disclosure statements like the counsellor-client contract that follows. These statements often define a counsellor's philosophy of human nature as well as the purposes, expectations, responsibilities, methods, and ethics of counselling. Initiative can be thought of as the motivation to change. Most counsellors and counselling theories assume that clients will be cooperative. Indeed, many clients come to counselling on a voluntary or self-referred basis. They experience tension and concern about themselves or others, but they are willing to work hard in counselling sessions. Other clients, how ever, are more reserved about participating in counselling. Vriend and Dyer estimate that the majority of clients who visit counsellors are reluctant to some degree.

When counsellors meet clients who seem to lack initiative, they often do no know what to do with them, much less how to go about doing it. Therefore, some counsellors are impatient, irritated and insensitive and may ultimately give up trying to work with such persons. The result is not only termination of the relationship but also scapegoating—blaming a person when the problem was not entirely his or her fault. Many counsellors end up blaming themselves or their clients if counselling is not successful. Such recriminations need not occur if counsellors understand the dynamics involved in working with difficult clients. Part of this understanding involves assuming the role of an involuntary client and imagining how it would feel to come for counselling. A role-reversal exercise call promote counsellor empathy in dealing with reluctant and resistant clients.

A reluctant client is one who has been referred by a third party and is frequently "unmotivated to seek help". Many school children and court referred clients are good examples. They do not wish to be in counselling, let alone talk about themselves. Many reluctant clients terminate counselling prematurely and report dissatisfaction with the process. A resistant client is a person in counselling who is unwilling or opposed to change. Such an individual may actively seek counselling, but does not wish to go through the pain that change demands. Instead, the client clings to the certainty of present behaviour, even when such action is counterproductive and dysfunctional. Some resistant clients refuse to make decisions, are superficial in dealing with problems, and take any action to resolve a problem.

According to Sack, the most common form of resistance is the simple statement 'I don't know.... Such a response makes the counsellor's next move difficult. Otani has proposed four broad categories of resistance: "amount of verbalisation; content of message; style of communication; and attitude toward counsellors and counselling sessions." There are several ways in which counsellors can help clients win the battle for initiative and achieve success in counselling. One way is to anticipate the anger, frustration, and defensiveness that some clients display. Counsellors who realise that a percentage of their clients are reluctant or resistant can work with these individuals because they are not surprised by them or their behaviours.

A second way to deal with a lack of initiative is to show acceptance, patience, and understanding as well as a general nonjudgmental attitude. This stance promotes trust. Nonjudgmental behaviour also helps clients better understand their thoughts and feelings about counselling. It opens them up to themselves and the counselling process. A third way to win the battle for initiative is for counsellors to use persuasion.

All counsellors have some influence on clients, and vice versa. How a counsellor responds to the client, directly or indirectly, can make a significant difference in whether the client takes the initiative in working to produce change. Roloff and Miller mention two direct persuasion techniques employed in counselling: the "foot in the door" and the "door in the face." In the first technique, the counsellor asks the client to comply with a minor request and then later follows with a larger request. In the second technique, the counsellor asks the client to do a seemingly impossible task and then follows by requesting the client to do a more reasonable task.A fourth way a counsellor can assist clients in gaining initiative is through confrontation. In this procedure the counsellor simply points out to the client exactly what the client is doing, such as being inconsistent. The client then takes responsibility for responding to the confrontation.

The three primary ways of responding are denial, accepting all or part of the confrontation as true, or developing a middle position that synthesises the first two. Doing something differently or gaining a new perception on a problem can be a beneficial result of confrontation, especially if what has previously been tried has not worked. Finally, Sack recommends the use of pragmatic techniques, such as silence (or pause), reflection (or empathy), questioning, describing, assessing, pretending, and sharing the counsellor's perspective, as ways to overcome client resistance. These techniques are especially helpful with individuals who respond to counsellor initiatives with "I don't know."

Counselling can occur almost anywhere, but some physical settings promote the process better than others. Benjamin and Shertzer and Stone address external conditions involved in counselling. Among the most important factors that help or hurt the process is the place where the counselling occurs. Most counselling occurs in a room, although Benjamin tells of counselling in a tent. He says that there is no universal quality that a room should have "except that it should not be overwhelming, noisy, or distracting". Shertzer and Stone implicitly agree: "The room should be comfortable and attractive". There are certain features of a counselling office that will improve its general appearance and probably facilitate counselling by not distracting the client.

The distance between counsellor and client can also affect the relationship. Individuals differ about the level of comfort experienced in interactions with others. Among other things, comfort level is influenced by cultural background, gender, and the nature of the relationship. A distance of 30 to 39 inches has been found to be the average range of comfort between counsellors and clients of both genders. This optimum distance may vary because of room size and furniture arrangement.

How the furniture is arranged depends on the counsellor. Some counsellors prefer to sit behind a desk during sessions, but most do not. Pietrofesa, Hoffman, and Splete note that a desk can be a physical and symbolic barrier against the development of a close relationship. Benjamin suggests that counsellors include two chairs and a nearby table in the setting.

The chairs should be set at a 90 degree angle from one another so that clients can look either at their counsellor's or straight ahead. The table can be used for many purposes, such as a place for a box of tissues. Benjamin's ideas are strictly his own; each counsellor must find a physical arrangement that is comfortable for him or her. Benjamin and Shertzer and Stone agree that, regardless of the arrangement within the room, counsellors should not be interrupted when conducting sessions. All phone calls should be held. If necessary, counsellors should put do-not-disturb signs on the door to keep others from entering. Auditory and visual privacy are mandated by professional codes of ethics and assure maximum client self-disclosure.

The way that counsellor and client perceive one another is vital to the establishment of a productive relationship. Warnath points out that "clients come in all shapes and sizes, personality characteristics, and degrees of attractiveness. Some clients are more likely to be successful in counselling than others. The most successful candidates for traditional approaches tend to be YAVIS: young, attractive, verbal, intelligent, and successful. Less successful candidates are seen as HOUNDs or DUDs (dumb, unintelligent, and disadvantaged). These acronyms are cruel, but counsellors are influenced by the appearance and sophistication of the people with whom they work. A number of stereotypes have been built around the physical attractiveness of individuals. The physically attractive are perceived as healthiest. The way in which counsellors interact with clients may be influenced by physical factors.

Clients who were seen by their counsellors as most attractive talked more and were more spontaneous when compared to other clients. Therefore, aging clients and those with physical handicaps may face invisible but powerful barriers in certain counselling situations. Counsellors become aware of the importance of physical attractiveness in their own lives and monitor their behavioural reactions when working with attractive clients. Otherwise, stereotypes and unfounded assumptions may "lead to self-fulfilling prophecies".The nonverbal behaviours of clients are also very important. Clients constantly send counsellors unspoken messages about how they think or feel. Mehrabian and his associates found that expressed like and dislike between individuals could be explained as follows:

> Total liking equals 7 per cent verbal liking plus 38 per cent vocal liking plus 55 per cent facial liking. The impact of facial expression is greatest, then the impact of the tone of voice (or vocal expression , and finally that of the words. If the facial expression is inconsistent with the words, the degree of liking

conveyed by the facial expression will dominate and determine the impact of the total message.

Thus, a client who reports that all is going well but who looks down at the ground and frowns while doing so is probably indicating just the opposite. A counsellor must consider a client's body gestures, eye contact, facial expression, and vocal quality to be as important as verbal communication in a counselling relationship. It is also crucial to consider the cultural background of the person whose body language is being evaluated and interpret nonverbal messages cautiously.

The personal and professional qualities of counsellors are very important in facilitating any helping relationship. Okun notes that "it is hard to separate the helper's personality characteristics from his or her levels and styles of functioning, as both are interrelated". Okun lists five important characteristics that helpers should possess: self-awareness, honesty, congruence, ability to communicate, and knowledge. Counsellors who continually develop their self- awareness skills are in touch with their values, thoughts, and feelings. They are likely to have a clear perception of their own and their clients' needs and accurately assess both. Such awareness can help them be honest with themselves and others. They are able to be more congruent and build trust simultaneously.

Counsellors who possess this type of knowledge are most likely to communicate clearly and accurately. Three other characteristics that make counsellors initially more influential are perceived expertness, attractiveness, and trustworthiness. Expertness is the degree to which a counsellor is perceived as knowledgeable and informed about his or her speciality. Counsellors who display certificates and diplomas in their offices are usually perceived as more credible than those who do not and, as a result, are likely to be effective. Clients want to work with counsellors who appear to know the profession well. Attractiveness is a function of perceived similarity between a client and counsellor, Counsellors can make themselves attractive by speaking in clear, simple, jargon-free sentences and offering appropriate self-disclosure.

Counsellors who use nonverbal cues in responding to clients, such as head nodding and eye contact, are seen as more attractive than those who do not. The attire of the counsellor also makes a difference. Clothes should be clean, neat, and professional looking but not call attention to themselves. Trustworthiness is related to the sincerity and consistency of the counsellor. The counsellor is genuinely concerned about the client and shows it over time by establishing a close relationship with the client. "There is and can be no such thing as instant intimacy" or trustworthiness. Rather, both are generated through patterns of behaviour that demonstrate care and concern.

Most clients are neither completely distrusting nor given to blind trust. But, as Fong and Cox note, many clients test the trustworthiness of the counsellor by requesting information, telling a secret, asking a favour, inconveniencing the counsellor, deprecating themselves, or questioning the motives and dedication of the counsellor. It is essential, therefore, that the counsellor respond to the question of trust rather than the verbal content of the client in order to facilitate the counselling relationship.

Many beginning counsellors make the mistake of dealing with surface issues instead of real concerns. For example, if a client asks a counsellor, "Can I tell you anything?" a novice counsellor might respond, "What do you mean by anything?" An experienced counsellor might say, "It sounds as if you are uncertain about whether you can really trust me and this relationship. The goals of counselling change over time and change according to the intimacy and effectiveness of the counselling relationship. How much change happens or whether there is a second session is usually determined by the results of the first session. In the first session, both counsellors and clients work to decide if they want to or can continue the relationship.

Counsellors should quickly assess whether they are capable of handling and managing client's problems through being honest, open, and appropriately confrontive. On the other hand, clients must ask themselves if they feel comfortable with and trust the counsellor before they can enter the relationship wholeheartedly. Benjamin distinguishes between two types of first interviews: those initiated by clients and those initiated by counsellors. When the initial interview is requested by a client, the counsellor is often unsure of the client's purpose. This uncertainty may create anxiety in the counsellor, especially if background information is not gathered before the session.

Benjamin recommends that counsellors work to overcome these feelings by listening as hard as possible to what clients have to say. He cautions against using any type of formula to begin the session. The helping interview is as much an art as a science; every counsellor must work out a style based on experience, stimulation, and reflection. Benjamin also advises the counsellor not to inquire initially about any problem the client may have.

The client may not have a problem in the traditional sense of the word and may just be seeking information. When the first session is requested by the counsellor, Benjamin believes that the counsellor should immediately state his or her reason for wanting to see the client. In the case of a school counsellor, for instance, a session might be requested so that the counsellor can introduce himself or herself to the client. If the counsellor does not immediately give a reason for requesting the session, the client is kept guessing and tension is created.

Patterson and Eisenberg think that all clients enter counselling with some anxiety and resistance regardless of prior preparation. Benjamin hypothesises that most counsellors are also a bit frightened and uncertain when conducting a first interview. Uncertain feelings in both clients and counsellors may result in behaviours such as seduction or aggression. Counsellors can prevent such occurrences by exchanging information with clients. Manthei advocates that counsellor's presentations about themselves and their functioning be *multimodel*: visual, auditory, written, spoken, and descriptive. While such presentations may be difficult, they pay off by creating good counsellor-client relationships. Overall, early exchanges of information increase the likelihood that clients and counsellors will make meaningful choices and participate more fully in the counselling process.

The initial counselling interview can fulfill two functions: (1) it can be an intake interview to collect needed infor-mation about the client, or (2) it can signal the beginning of a relationship. Either type of interview is appropriate, and there are certain tasks common to both, though the skills emphasised in each differ. If the purpose of the first interview is to gather information, the structure of the session will be counsellor-focused: the counsellor wants the client to talk about certain subject matters. The counsellor will respond to the client predominantly through the use of probes, accents, closed questions, and requests for clarification. These responses are aimed at eliciting facts. The probe is a question that usually begins with who, what, where, or how. It requires more than a one or two word response: for example, "What do you plan to do about getting a job?" Few probes ever begin with the word why, which usually connotes disapproval and places a client on the defensive.

Interviews that focus on feelings or relationship dynamics differ markedly from information-oriented first sessions. They concentrate more on the client's attitudes and emotions. Common counsellor responses include restate-ment, reflection of feeling, summarising feelings, request for clarification, and acknowledgment of nonverbal behaviour. A restatement is a simple mirror response to a client that lets the client know the counsellor is actively listening. Reflection of feeling is similar to a restatement, but it deals with verbal and nonverbal expression. Reflections may be on several levels; some convey more empathy than others. An example is this counsellor response to a client who is silently sobbing over the loss of a parent: "You're still really feeling the pain."

Summarising feelings is the act of paraphrasing a number of feelings that the client has conveyed. For example, a counsellor might say to a client: "John, if I understand you correctly, you are feeling depressed over the death of your father and discouraged that your friends have not helped you work through your grief. In addition, you feel your work is boring and that your wife is emotionally distant from you."

Acknowledgment of nonverbal behaviour differs from the previous examples. For instance, acknowledgment comes when the counsellor says to a client: "I notice that your arms are folded across your chest and you're looking at the floor." This type of response does not interpret the meaning of the behaviour.

There is no one place to begin an initial interview, but many experts recommend that counsellors start by trying to make their clients feel comfortable. Counsellors should set aside their own agendas and focus on the person of the client. Shertzer and Stone call this type of behaviour rapport. Rapport is established and maintained by counsellors who are genuinely interested in and accepting of their clients. Ivey states that the two most important microskills for rapport building are basic attending behaviour and client-observation skills.

A counsellor needs to tune in to what the client is thinking and feeling and how he or she is behaving. Establishing and maintaining rapport is vital for the disclosure of information and the ultimate success of counselling. One way in which counsellors initiate rapport is by inviting clients to focus on reasons for seeking help. Such noncoercive invitations to talk are called door openers and contrast with judgmental or evaluative responses known as door closers.

Appropriate door openers include inquiries and observations such as "What brings you to see me?" "What would you like to talk about?" and "You look like you are in a lot of pain. Tell me about it." These unstructured, open-ended invitations allow clients to take the initiative. In such situations, clients are most likely to talk about priority topics. The amount of talking that clients engage in and the insight and benefits derived from the initial interview can be enhanced by the counsellor who appropriately conveys empathy, encouragement, support, caring, attentiveness, acceptance, and genuineness.

Empathy

Empathy involves two specific skills: perception and

communication. An effective counsellor perceives the cultural frame of reference from which his or her client operates, including the client's perceptual and cognitive process. Nevertheless, a counsellor who can accurately perceive what it is like to be the client but cannot communicate that experience is a limited helper. Such a counsellor may be aware of client dynamics; but no one, including the client, knows of the counsellor's awareness. The ability to communicate clearly plays a vital role in any counselling relationship.In the initial interview, counsellors must be able to convey primary empathy.

Primary empathy is the ability to respond in such a way that it is apparent to both client and counsellor that the counsellor has understood the client's major themes. Primary empathy is conveyed through nonverbal communication and various verbal responses. For example, the counsellor, leaning forward and speaking in a soft, understanding voice, may say to the client: I hear that your life has been defined by a series of serious losses. Advanced empathy "is a process of helping a client explore themes, issues, and emotions new to his or her awareness". This second level of empathy is usually inappropriate for an initial interview because it examines too much material too quickly.

Empathy may be fostered by attentiveness-the amount of verbal and nonverbal behaviour shown to the client. Verbal behaviours include communications that show a desire to comprehend or discuss what is important to the client. These behaviours indicate that the counsellor is focusing on the person of the client. Equally important are the counsellor's nonverbal behaviours. According to Mehrabian, physically attending behaviours such as smiling, leaning forward, making eye contact, gesturing, and nodding one's head are effective nonverbal ways of conveying to clients that the counsellor is interested in and open to them. Egan summarises five nonverbal skills involved in initial attending. They are best remembered in the acronym SOLER.

The S is a reminder to face the client squarely, which can be understood literally or metaphorically depending on the situation. The important thing is that the counsellor shows involvement and interest in the client. The O is a reminder to adopt an open posture, free from crossed arms and legs and showing nondefensiveness. The L reminds the counsellor to lean toward the client. Leaning too far forward and being too close may be frightening, but leaning too far away indicates disinterest. The counsellor needs to find a middle distance that is comfortable for both parties. The E represents eye contact. Good eye contact with most clients is a sign that the counsellor is attuned to the client. For other clients, less eye contact is appropriate. The R is a reminder to the counsellor to relax.

A counsellor needs to be comfortable.Okun lists supportive verbal and nonverbal behavioural aids that counsellors often display throughout counselling. The last nonverbal behaviour on Okun's list, occasional touching, is politically sensitive and somewhat controversial. Although Willison and Masson point out that human touch may be therapeutic in counșelling, Alyu emphasises that the wide range of individual motivations for, interpretations of, and responses to touch make it, an extremely unclear and possibly a dangerous means of communication in therapy.

Young suggests that touch should be appropriately employed, applied briefly and sparingly, and used to communicate concern. Counsellors who use touch in their work should do so cautiously and with the understanding that what they are doing can have adverse effects. This same critical scrutiny is suggested when using any verbal or nonverbal technique.

When building a relationship, counsellors must also realise what they should not do. Otherwise, nonhelpful behaviours may be included in their counselling repertoire. Patterson and Eisenberg list four major actions that usually block counsellor- client communication and should be generally avoided: advice giving, lecturing, excessive questioning, and storytelling by the counsellor. Advice giving is the most controversial of these four behaviours. Knowles found that 70-90 percent of all responses from volunteer helpers on a crisis line consisted of giving advice.

When a counsellor gives advice, especially in the first session, it may in effect deny a client the chance to work through personal thoughts and feelings about a subject and ultimately curtail his or her ability to make difficult decisions. A response meant to be helpful ends up being hurtful by disempowering the client. For example, if a client is advised to break off a relationship he or she is ambivalent about, the client is denied the opportunity to become aware and work through the thoughts and feelings that initially led to the ambivalence.

Sack suggests that advice giving need not always be destructive. He notes that there are emergency situations when, for the immediate welfare and safety of the client, some direct action must be taken, which includes giving advice. He cautions counsellors, however, to listen carefully to make sure the client is really asking for advice or simply being reflective through self-questions. There is a big difference between "What should I do?" and "I wonder what I should do?" in addition, Sack advocates the responses developed by Carkhuff as ways in which counsellors can answer direct requests for advice. In this model, counsellors respond using one of seven approaches: respect, empathy, genuineness, concreteness, self-disclosure, confrontation, and immediacy. Sack concludes that counsellors must examine their roles in counselling to "free themselves of the limitations and pitfalls of giving advice and move toward employing a variety of responses that can more appropriately address their clients' needs".

Lecturing, or preaching, is "really a disguised form of advice giving". It sets up a power struggle between the counsellor and client that neither individual can win. For example, if a sexually active girl is told "don't get involved with boys anymore," she may do just the opposite to assert her independence. In such a case, both the counsellor and client fail in their desire to change behaviours. Patterson and Eisenberg suggest that counsellors are probably lecturing when they say more than three consecutive sentences in a row to their clients. Instead of lecturing, counsellors can be effective by following the client's lead. Excessive questioning is a common mistake of many counsellors. Verbal interaction with clients needs to include statements, observations, and encouragers as well as questions. When excessive questioning is used, the client feels as though he or she is being interrogated rather than counselled.

The client has little chance to take the initiative and may become guarded. Counselling relationships are more productive when counsellors avoid asking more than two questions in a row and keep their questions open rather than closed. Storytelling by the counsellor is the final nonhelpful behaviour. Its use has been explored by Patterson and Eisenberg. There are a few prominent professionals who can use stories to benefit clients.

Milton Erickson, a legendary pioneer in family counselling, was one. His stories were always metaphorically tailored to his clients' situations. They were beneficial because they directed clients to think about their own situations in light of the stories he told. Most counsellors, however, should stay away from storytelling because the story usually focuses attention on the counsellor instead of the client and distracts from problem solving.

The counsellor helps the client explore specific areas and begin to identify goals that the client wants to achieve. Hill emphasises that establishing goals is crucial in providing direction. Egan observes that exploration and ultimately the identification of goals often occurs when, client is given the opportunity to talk about situations to tell personal stories. The counsellor reinforces the client's focus on self by providing structure, actively, and helping identify and clarify goals.Rule states that goals "are the energising fabric of daily living" but at often elusive. He describes some goals as unfocused, unrealistic, and uncoordinated.

Unfocused goals are not identified, or not prioritised. Some times counsellors and clients may leave unfocused goals alone because the time an expense of chasing them is not as productive as changing unwanted behaviours. If most cases, however, it is helpful to identify a client's goals, put them into a work able form, and decide which goals to pursue first. Unrealistic goals, include happiness, perfection, progress, being number one, and self-actualisation. They have merit but an not easily obtained or sustained. For example, the client who has worked hard and happy about being promoted will soon have to settle into the duties of the new job and the reality of future job progress. Unrealistic goals may best be dealt with by putting them into the context of broader life goals. Then the counsellor may encourage the client to devise exploratory and homework strategies for dealing with them.

Uncoordinated goals are generally divided into two groups: those probably really uncoordinated and those seemingly uncoordinated. In the first group are goals that may be incompatible with one another or with the personality of the client. A person who seeks counselling but really does not wish to work on changing is an example of an individual with incompatible goals. These clients are often labelled resistant. Into the second group, Rule places the goals of clients who appear to have uncoordinated goals but really do not.

Dyer and Vriend emphasise seven specific criteria for judging effective goals in counselling:

1) Goals are mutually agreed on by client and counsellor.
2) Goals are specific.
3) Goals are relevant to self-defeating behaviour.
4) Goals are achievement and success-oriented.
5) Goals are quantifiable and measurable.
6) Goals are behavioural and observable.
7) Goals are understandable and can be restated clearly.

In the exploratory and goal-setting stage of counselling, several problems may inhibit the building of a solid client-counsellor relationship. The most notable include moving too fast, moving too slow, fear of intensity, client rambling, and excessive time and energy devoted to probing the past. Counsellors who are forewarned about such potential problems are in a much better position to address them effectively. It is vital that counsellors work with clients to build a mutually satisfying relationship from the start. When this process occurs, a more active working stage of counselling begins.

Termination of counselling may be the least researched aspect of counselling. Termination refers to the decision, one sided mutual, to stop counselling. Termination will occur naturally and leave both the clients and counsellors pleased and satisfied with results. It is almost as through we operate from a myth that termination is a process from which the counsellor remains aloof and to which the client alone is responsive.

Addressing the process of termination directly has been avoided for several reasons. Ward has suggested two of the most prominent. First, termination is associated with loss-a traditionally taboo subject in all parts of society. Even though Hayes points out that loss may be associated with recreation, transcendence, greater self-understanding, and new discoveries, counselling is generally viewed as emphasising growth and development unrelated to endings. Second, termination is not directly related to the microskills that facilitate counselling relationships. Termination is not a process usually highlighted in counsellor education. There are several important functions of termination.

1) Termination signals that something is finished. Life is a series of hellos and good-byes. Hellos begin at birth, and good-byes end at death. Between birth and death, individuals enter into and leave a succession of experiences, including jobs, relation-ships, and life stages. Growth and adjustment depend on an ability to make the most of these experiences and learn from them. To begin something new, a former experience must be completed and resolved. Termination is the opportunity to end a learning experience properly, whether on a personal or professional level. In counselling, termination is more than an act signifying the end of therapy; it is also a motivator. Both client and counsellor are motivated by the

knowledge that the counselling experience is limited in time. This awareness is similar to that of a young person who realises that he or she cannot remain a promising youth forever. Such realisations may spur one on to hard work while there is still time to do something significant. Some counsellors, such as those associated with strategic, systemic, and solution-focused family therapy, purposely limit the number of counselling sessions so that clients and counsellors are more aware of time constraints and make the most of sessions.

2) Termination is a means of maintaining changes already achieved and generalising problem- solving skills acquired in counselling. Successful counselling results in significant changes in the way the client thinks, feels, or acts. These changes are rehearsed in counselling, but they must be practised in the real world. Termination provides an opportunity for such practice. The client can always go back to the counsellor for any needed follow-up, but termination is the natural point for the practice of independence to begin. It is a potentially empowe-ring experience for the client and enables him or her to address the present in an entirely new or modified way. At termination, the opportunity to put "insights into actions" is created.

3) Termination serves as a reminder that the client has matured. Besides offering the client new skills or different ways of thinking about him or herself, effective counselling that ends with an appropriate termination marks a time in the client's life when he or she is less absorbed by and preoccupied with personal problems and more able to deal with outside people and events. This ability to handle external situations may result in more interdependent

relationships that are mutually supportive and consequently lead toward a "more independent and satisfying life".

There is not a specified time to terminate a relationship. If the relationship is ended too soon, clients may lose the ground they gained in counselling and regress to earlier behaviours. On the other hand, if termination is never addressed, clients can become dependent on the counsellor and fail to resolve difficulties and grow as persons. There are, however, several pragmatic considerations in the timing of termination:

— Have clients achieved behavioural, cognitive, or affective contract goals? When both clients and counsellors have a clear idea about whether or not particular goals have been reached, the timing of termination is easier to figure out. The key to this consideration is setting up a mutually agreed-upon contract before counselling begins.

— Can clients concretely show where they have made progress in what they wanted to accomplish? In this situation, specific progress may be the basis for making a decision about termination. Is the counselling relationship helpful? If either the client or the counsellor senses that what is occurring in the counselling sessions is not helpful, termination is appropriate.

— Has the context of the initial counselling arrangement changed? In cases where there is a move or a prolonged illness, termination should be considered.

There is no one right time to terminate a counselling relationship. The "when" of termination must be figured out in accordance with the uniqueness of the situation and overall ethical and professional guidelines.

Termination is an issue during individual counselling sessions. Initial sessions should have clearly defined time limits. A range of 45-50 minutes is generally considered adequate for an individual counselling session. It usually takes a counsellor 5-10 minutes to adjust to the client and the client's concerns. Counselling sessions that terminate too quickly may be as unproductive is ones that last too long. Benjamin proposes two important factors in closing an interview. First, both client and counsellor should have be aware that the session is ending. Second, no new material should be introduced or discussed during this ending. If the client introduces new material, the counsellor needs to work to make it the anticipated focus of the next session.

A counsellor can close an interview effectively in several ways. One is simply to make a brief statement indicating that time is up. For example, he or she might say, "It looks like our time is up for today." The simpler the statement, the better. If a client is discussing a number of subjects in an open-ended manner near the end of a session, the counsellor should remind the client that there are only 5 or 10 minutes left. The client can then focus attention on important matters.

As an alternative or in addition to the direct statement, the counsellor can use nonverbal gestures to indicate that the session is ending. These include looking at his or her watch or standing up. Nonverbal gestures are probably best used with verbal indicators. Each reinforces the other. Toward the end of the interview it is usually helpful to summarise what has happened in the session. This summation may be initiated either by the counsellor or the client. A good summary ties together the main points of the session and "should be brief, to the point, and without interpretation". If done mutually, a summary allows counsellor and client to realise what each has gotten out of the session and provides a means of clearing up any misunderstandings.

An important part of terminating any individual session is setting up the next appointment. Most problems are resolved over time, Clients and counsellors need to know when they will meet again to continue the work in progress. It is easier and more efficient to set up a next appointment at the end of a session than to do it later by phone. It is vital to the health and well being of everyone that the subject of termination be brought up early so that counsellor and client can make the most of their time together. Individuals need time to prepare for the end of a meaningful relationship. There may be some sadness, even if the relationship ends in a positive way.

Thus, termination should not necessarily be presented as the zenith of the counselling experience. Hackney and Cormier stress that it is better to play down the importance of termination rather than play it up. The counsellor and client must agree on when termination of the relationship is appropriate and helpful. Generally, they give each other verbal messages about a readiness to terminate. For example, a client may say, "I really think I've made a lot of progress over the past few months." Or a counsellor may state, "You appear to be well on your way to no longer needing my services." Such statements suggest the beginning of the end of the counselling relationship. They usually imply a recognition of growth or resolution.

A number of other behaviours may also signal the end of counselling. These include a decrease in the intensity of work; more humour; and less denial, withdrawal, anger, mourning, or dependence. Hackney and Cormier believe that, in a relationship that has lasted more than three months, the final three or four weeks should be spent discussing the impact of termination.

For instance, counsellors may inquire how their clients will cope without the support of the relationship. Counsellors may also ask clients to talk about the meaning of the counselling relationship and how they will use what they have learned in the future. Shulman suggests that, as a general rule of thumb, one-sixth of the time spent in a counselling relationship should be devoted to focusing on termination. Maholick and Turner discuss specific areas of concern when deciding whether to terminate counselling. They include the following:

— An examination of whether the client's initial problem or symptoms have been reduced or eliminated

— A determination of whether the stress-producing feelings that led to counselling have been eliminated

— An assessment of the client's coping ability and degree of understanding of self and others

— A determination of whether the client can relate better to others and is able to love and be loved

— An examination of whether the client has acquired abilities to plan and work productivity

— An evaluation of whether the client can better play and enjoy life

These areas are not equally important for all clients, but it is essential that, before termination of counselling, clients feel confident to live effectively without the relationship. There are at least two other ways to facilitate the ending of a counsellor-client relationship. One involves the use of fading. Dixon and Glover define fading as a gradual decrease in the unnatural structures developed to create desired changes. In other words, clients gradually stop receiving reinforcement for behaving in certain ways. A desired goal of all counselling is to help clients become less dependent on the counsellor and the counselling sessions and more dependent on themselves and interdependent with others.

From counselling, clients should also learn the positive reinforcement of natural contingencies. To promote fading, counselling sessions can be spaced further apart or simply shortened. Another way to promote termination is to help clients develop successful problem-solving skills. Clients, like everyone else, are constantly faced with problems. If counsellors can help their clients learn more effective ways to cope with these difficulties, clients will no longer need the counselling relationship. This is a process of generalisation from counselling experience to life. At its best, this process includes an emphasis on education and prevention as well as decision-making skills for everyday life and crisis situations.

Resistance to termination may come from either the counsellor or client. Patterson and Eisenberg note that resistance is especially likely when the counselling relationship has lasted for a long time or has involved a high level of intimacy. Other factors that may promote resistance include the pain of earlier losses, loneliness, unresolved grief, need gratification, fear of rejection, and fear of having to be self-reliant. Some of these factors are more prevalent with clients, while others are more likely to characterise counsellors.

Clients resist termination in many ways. Two easily recognised expressions of resistance are (1) asking for more time at the end of a session and (2) asking for more appointments once a goal has been reached. Another more troublesome form of client resistance is the development of new problems that were not part of his or her original concerns, such as depression or anxiety.

The manifestation of these symptoms makes termination more difficult; and in such situations, a client may convince the counsellor that only he or she can help. Thus, the counsellor may feel obligated to continue working with the person for either personal or ethical reasons. Regardless of the strategy employed, the termination process is best carried out gradually and slowly. Sessions can become less frequent over time; and client skills, abilities, and resources can be highlighted simultaneously.

Sometimes when clients are especially hesitant to terminate, the counsellor can "prescribe" a limited number of future sessions or concentrate with clients on how they will set themselves up for relapse. These procedures make the covert more overt and help counsellors and clients identify more clearly what issues are involved in leaving a helping relationship.

Client resistance often results from a fear of change. If clients come to value a counselling relationship, they may fear that they cannot function well without it. For example, people who have grown up in unstable or chaotic environments involving alcoholism or divorce may be especially prone to hold on to the stability of counselling and the relationship with the counsellor. It is vital that the counsellor recognise the special needs of these individuals and the difficulties they have in coping with loneliness and intimacy. It is even more critical that the counsellor take steps to help such clients help themselves by exploring with them the advantages of working in other therapeutic settings, such as support groups.

For such clients, counselling is potentially addictive. If they are to function in healthy ways, they must find alternative sources of support. Some counsellors are reluctant to say good-bye at the appropriate time. Clients who have special or unusual needs or those who are very productive may be especially attractive to counsellors. Goodyear lists eight conditions in which termination may be especially difficult for counsellors:

— When termination signals the end of a significant relationship.
— When termination arouses the counsellor's anxieties about the client's ability to function independently.
— When termination arouses guilt in the counsellor about not having been more effective with the client.
— When the counsellor's professional self-concept is threatened by the client who leaves abruptly and angrily.
— When termination signals the end of a learning experience for the counsellor (for example, the counsellor may have been relying on the client to learn more about the dynamics of a disorder or a particular subculture).
— When termination signals the end of a particularly exciting experience of living vicariously through the adventures of the client.
— When termination becomes a symbolic recapi-tulation of other farewells in the counsellor's life.
— When termination arouses in the counsellor conflicts about his or her own individuation.

Counsellors recognise any difficulties they have in letting go of certain clients. A counsellor may seek consultation with colleagues in dealing with this problem or undergo counselling to resolve the problem. Premature termination has to do with how well the client has achieved the personal goals established in the beginning and how well he or she is functioning generally.

Baruth and Huber note that there are some clients who show little, if any, commitment or motivation to change their present circumstances and request that counselling be terminated after the first session. Other clients express this desire after realising the work necessary for change. Still others make this wish known more indirectly by missing or being late for appointments. Regardless of how clients express a wish for premature termination, it is likely to trigger thoughts and feelings within the counsellor that must be dealt with. The topic of premature termination be discussed openly between a counsellor and client if the client expresses a desire to terminate before specified goals have been met or if the counsellor suspects that premature termination may occur. With discussion, thoughts and feelings of both the client and counsellor can be examined and a premature ending prevented. Sometimes a client fails to keep an appointment and does not call to reschedule.

In such cases, the counsellor should attempt to reach the client by phone or mail. If the counsellor finds that the client wishes to quit, an exit interview should be set up. Ward reports four possible benefits from such an interview:

— An exit interview may help the client resolve any negative feelings resulting from the counselling experience.

— It serves as a way to invite the client to continue in counselling if he or she so wishes.

— Another form of treatment or a different counsellor can be considered if the client so desires.

— An exit interview increases the chances that the next time the client needs help, he or she will seek counselling.

In premature termination, counsellors often make one of two mistakes. One is to blame either the counsellor or the client for what is happening. A second mistake on the part of the counsellor is to act in a cavalier manner about the situation. An example is the counsellor who says, "It's too bad this client has chosen not to continue counselling, but I've got others." To avoid making either mistake, Cavanagh recommends that counsellors find out why a client terminated prematurely. Possible reasons include the following:

— To see if the counsellor really cares.

— To try to elicit positive feelings from the counsellor.

— To punish or try to hurt the counsellor.

— To eliminate anxiety.

— To show the counsellor that the client has found a cure elsewhere.

— To express to the counsellor that the client does not feel understood.

Counsellors need to understand that, regardless of what they do, some clients terminate counselling prematurely. Such a realisation allows counsellors to feel that they do not have to be perfect and frees them to be more authentic in the therapeutic relationship. Ideally, counsellors are aware of the anatomy of termination. With such knowledge, they become empowered to deal realistically with situations concerning client termination. Not all people who seek counselling are equally ready to work in such a relationship, and the readiness level may vary as the relationship continues. Some clients need to terminate prematurely for good reasons, and their action does not necessarily reflect on the counsellor's competence. Counsellors can control only a limited number of variables in a counselling relationship. The following list includes several of the variables most likely to be effective in preventing premature termination:

— *Appointments*: The less time between them and the more regular they are the better.

— *Orientation to counselling*: The more clients know about the process of counselling, the more likely they are to stay with it.

— *Consistency of counsellor*: Clients do not like to be processed from counsellor to counsellor. Therefore, the counsellor who does the initial intake should continue counselling the client if at all possible.

— *Reminders to motivate client attendance*. Postcards, telephone calls, or e-mail can be effective reminders. Because of the sensitivity of counselling, however, a counsellor should always have the client's permission to send an appointment reminder.

A counsellor sometimes needs to end relationships with some or all clients. Reasons include illness, working through counter-transference, relocation to another area, an extended trip, or the realisation that client needs could be better served by someone else. There are also poor reasons for counsellor-initiated termination. They include a counsellor's feelings of anger, boredom, or anxiety. If a counsellor ends a relationship because of such feelings, the client may feel rejected and even worse than he or she did in the beginning. It is one thing for a person to handle rejection from peers; it is another for that same person to handle rejection from a counsellor. Although a counsellor may have some negative feelings about a client, it is possible to acknowledge and work through those feelings without behaving in an extreme or detrimental way. Both London and Seligman present models for helping clients deal with the temporary absence of the counsellor. These researchers stress that clients and counsellors should prepare as far in advance as possible for temporary termination by openly discussing the impending event and working through any strong feelings about the issue of separation.

A client may actually experience benefits from counsellor-initiated termination by realising that the counsellor is human and replaceable, understanding that a person has choices about how to deal with interpersonal relationships, exploring previous feelings and major life decisions, and learning more clearly that new behaviours carry over into other life experiences. There may also be a refocusing during the termination process that helps clients see issues on which to work more clearly. Seligman recommends a more structured way of preparing clients for counsellor-initiated termi-nation than London does, but both models can be effective.

It is important in any situation like this to make sure a client has the names and numbers of a few other counsellors to contact in case of an emergency. The process of termination, like counselling itself, involves a series of check points that counsellors and clients can consult to evaluate the progress they are making and determine their readiness to move to another stage. Patterson and Eisenberg present eight guidelines a counsellor can use to end an intense counselling relationship in a positive way;

1) "Be clearly aware of the client's needs and wants." At the end of a counselling relationship, the client may need time to talk to the counsellor about the impending termination. This may require a few sessions to complete.

2) "Be clearly aware of your own needs and wants." Counselling is not a one way street, and counsellors who take care of others without taking care of themselves will most likely experience difficulty in terminating relationships. It is vital that a counsellor acknowledge personal feelings and needs about a counselling relationship before it ends.

3) "Be aware of your previous experiences with separation and your inner reaction to these experiences." The feelings generated from one intense relationship may be similar to those that occur in another. A counsellor should be emotionally self-aware to avoid counter-transference and be genuine in relationships.

4) "Invite the client to share how he or she feels about ending the experience." This guideline is similar to the first, but it focuses on the emotions, not the thoughts, of the client. Clients need to express themselves as completely as possible if closure is to be of maximum benefit.

5) "Share honestly with the client how you feel about the counselling experience." This is another aspect of the counsellor's being real in the relationship. Part of this sharing includes revealing to the client what you, as a counsellor, have learned from this particular experience.

6) "Review the major events of the counselling experience and bring the review into the present." The focus of this process is to help a client see where he or she is now as compared to the beginning of counselling and realise more fully the growth that has been accomplished. The procedure includes a review of significant past moments and turning points in the relationship with a focus on personalising the summary.

7) "Supportively acknowledge the changes the client has made." At this point the counsellor lets the client know that he or she recognises the progress that has been achieved and actively encourages the client to maintain it.

8) "Invite the client to keep up to date on what is happening in his or her life, Counselling relationships eventually end, but the caring and concern the counsellor has for the client are not automatically terminated at the final session. Clients need to know that the counsellor continues to be interested in what is happening in their lives.

Follow-up

"Follow-up entails checking to see how the helpee is doing, with respect to whatever the problem was, sometime after termination has occurred". In essence, it is a positive monitoring process that encourages client growth. Follow-up is a step that some counsellors neglect. It is important because it reinforces the gains clients have made in counselling and helps both counsellor and client re-evaluate the experience. It also emphasises the counsellor's genuine care and concern for the client. Follow-up can be conducted on either a short- or long-term basis. Short-term follow-up is usually conducted three to six months after a counselling relationship terminates. Long-term follow-up is conducted at least six months after termination.

Follow-up may take many forms, but there are four main ways in which it is usually conducted. The first is to invite the client in for a session to discuss any progress he or she has continued to make in achieving desired goals. A second way is through a telephone call to the client. A call allows the client to report to the counsellor, although there is only verbal interaction. A third way is for the counsellor to send the client a letter asking about the client's current status. A fourth and more impersonal way is for the counsellor to mail the client a questionnaire dealing with current levels of functioning.

Many public agencies use this type of follow-up as a way of showing accountability. Such procedures do not preclude the use of more personal follow-up procedures by individual counsellors. Although time consuming, a personal follow-up is probably the most effective way of evaluating past counselling experiences. It helps assure clients that they are cared about as individuals and more than just statistics. Sometimes, regardless of the type of follow-up used, it is helpful if the client monitors his or her own progress through the use of graphs or charts. Then, when relating information to the counsellor, the client can do so in a more concrete and objective way. If counsellor and client agree at the end of the last session on a follow-up time, this type of self-monitoring may be especially meaningful and give the client concrete proof of progress and clearer insight into current needs.

Counsellors are not able to help everyone who seeks assistance. When a counsellor realises that a situation is unproductive, it is important to know whether to terminate the relationship or make a referral. A referral involves arranging other assistance for a client when the initial arrangement is not or cannot be helpful. There are many reasons for referring, including the following:

— The client has a problem the counsellor does not know how to handle.

— The counsellor is inexperienced in a particular area and does not have the necessary skill to help the client.

— The counsellor knows of a nearby expert who would be more helpful to the client.

— The counsellor and client have incompatible personalities.

— The relationship between counsellor and client is stuck in an initial phase of counselling.

Index